UNVEILED

WHAT A PIRATE, A POT FARMER, AND A GAGGLE OF PROSTITUTES
TAUGHT ME ABOUT BEING THE CHURCH

JON PETERSEN

Published by CityForce Media, Inc.
P.O. Box 1059
Castle Rock, Colorado 80104
For more information, visit: www.CityForce.org

Manuscript prepared by Rick Killian, Killian Creative, Boulder, Colorado.
www.killiancreative.com

Design by Peter Gloege, LOOK Design Studio.

ISBN: 978-0-9997491-2-8 (paperback)
ISBN: 978-0-9997491-3-5 (eBook)

Printed in the United States of America
25 24 23 22 21 20 19 (KDP) 3 4 5 6

To

Floyd and Sally McClung

Thank you for the years,
the friendship, and the love of the Father
that heals the broken heart!

CONTENTS

Introduction ix

Prologue xvii

PART ONE: Hungry for God

1 A Towhead Grows Up in Post-World War II Japan 1

2 Chased Down 15

3 A Gaijin Goes to America 25

4 The Church I Encountered in the 1970s 37

5 A Battle for Hearts *and* Minds 47

PART TWO: Becoming Jesus-centric

6 The Holy Spirit Underground 67

7 Meeting the Pirate 81

8 "No Measurable Spiritual Gifts" 93

9 Destiny Confirmed in Freakdom 105

10 The End of a Good Thing, the Beginning of Another 119

PART THREE: Jesus Across Cultures

11 The Dreaded "Missionary Thing" 135

12 Amsterdam 147

13 Prayer as "the Air We Breathe" 159
14 Red-Light Jesus 171
15 Walls Come Tumbling Down 185

PART FOUR: Becoming the Family...

16 And Then Everything Changed...Again 199
17 Into and Out of the Wilderness 217
18 What Unity Can Look Like 233
19 City Transformation 245
20 Church Transformation 257

PART FIVE: ...of *the* Loving Father

21 Meeting *the* Father 269
22 The Call to "Father" Like Him 279
23 Being the Family of God 291

PART SIX: Pulling It All Together

24 The Unveiling 305

Notes 313
About the Author 314

INTRODUCTION

Throughout history, God, the Weaver of our stories and that of the Church, searched for those who would receive and propagate His plan and His presence. From Noah to Abraham, then from Abraham's son and on through the generations, the Weaver made covenants to move ever closer to reveal His intentions to these deliverers. In time, we see the sons and daughters of Abraham, Isaac, and Jacob in captivity, outside of the covenant land. God approaches His young, hand-chosen deliverer, Moses, and gives him these instructions for weaving Israel back into a people and to bring them "home":

> *"I have indeed seen the misery of my people in Egypt. I have heard them crying out because of their slave drivers, and I am concerned about their suffering. So I have come down to rescue them from the hand of the Egyptians and to bring them up out of that land into a good and spacious land, a land flowing with milk and honey . . . the home of the Canaanites, Hittites, Amorites, Perizzites, Hivites and Jebusites. And now the cry of the Israelites has reached me, and I have seen the way the Egyptians are oppressing them. So now, go. I am* sending you in *to Pharaoh* to bring my people out *of Egypt."*
>
> **—EXODUS 3:7–10 (emphasis added)**

The Weaver's strategy here was painfully obvious: He was longing to "send His ambassadors in" to "bring His people out" of captivity and into His eternal presence, as was Creation's original purpose.

> *"I will walk among you and be your God, and you will be my people. I am the* Lord *your God, who brought you out of Egypt so that you would no longer be slaves. . . I broke the bars of your yoke and enabled you to walk with heads held high."*
>
> —**LEVITICUS 26:12–13**

God and His ways are the vertical (warp) threads of the tapestry on the loom holding this design: the firm, immovable truths of His character that tie heaven and earth together. He was inviting Moses to *"go in"* to the horizontal (woof) realm of a captive earth and *"bring out"* His inheritance—the people of God's choosing and promises. (We have our part in the weaving as well.) Everything about His plan shouted "redemption," the buying back and restoring of what had been destroyed around Eden's two trees. But the horizontal (woof) cross threads of humanity's imperfection—unlike heaven's perfect, immovable, vertical threads—were conditional and demand our participation. Would Moses accept the invitation to partner with God to weave the Father's dream tapestry? Would he stay true to the pattern of heaven, or fumble implementing the design?

After a feisty negotiation with God, Moses accepted the invitation. By doing so, Moses aligned himself with the Father's heart and stood in the vortex of His Kingdom purposes. Imperfect as Moses and our understanding of His Law were to God's eternal dream, they housed a reflection of His image, but not the "exact representation" itself. They looked forward to the "perfect image" of the Father's design and foretold of the coming of a perfect sacrifice, a new law written on men's and women's hearts and the redeeming of all that was poisoned at the Fall. Jesus was that "exact representation" of the Father's character, the perfect image, and ultimate pattern embedded in the Weaver's tapestry.

Nothing but Jesus—the centerpiece of all creation.

Much like Moses, Jesus was "sent in" to our world to "bring us out," while intersecting with the Father's desire to "come down" to bring His creation back "up" into His created purposes. On the day of His death, the curtain separating those in the outer courts from the Holy of Holies tore from top to bottom to unveil the new plan: We would all now be welcomed into His presence again. God was inviting us home.

> *"No longer will they teach their neighbor,*
> *or say to one another, 'Know the* LORD,*'*
> *because they will all know me,*
> *from the least of them to the greatest,"*
> *declares the* LORD.
> *"For I will forgive their wickedness*
> *and will remember their sins no more."*
>
> **—JEREMIAH 31:34**

Jesus came down to bring us up to the Father's purposes and sent us in—to *"Go into all the world"* (Mark 16:15)—and bring His creation out of captivity and into the fullness of Father's plan. We, the reconciled, are now invited to become reconcilers. We have been redeemed to receive the Creator's invitation to partner with Him until *"The kingdom of the world has become the kingdom of our Lord and of his Messiah"* (Revelation 11:15). This is our present and future hope!

God, the Weaver, will not be done with the tapestry until it reveals the image of His Son in the present and in the future age to come. He has laid the warp (vertical) threads of the Kingdom on His loom through Jesus. Now we, the woof (cross threads) in His plan, work day in and day out to ensure that the image is unveiled in all we are and do.

But the same question arises: How do we stay faithful to the heavenly pattern and design?

THE UNVEILING

The future of God's people lies in bringing forward the redemptive lineage of Christ through the generations. In this book, I will look back at the past six decades (over the span of my life and times) and see how the Father-King has set the immovable threads of the warp on the loom, the nonnegotiables of His Kingdom, that they may remain unbroken from one generation to the next. I believe that the past sixty years have revealed how God's heavenly purposes are affecting life on earth:

» Thread 1—The reemphasis of the Holy Spirit that culminated in the 1960s.

» Thread 2—The re-centering of Jesus in His Church in the 1970s.

» Thread 3—The new missionary fervor and reemphasis of taking the Gospel to all nations in the 1980s.

» Thread 4—The reframing of the Church as the Kingdom Family and not just an institution in the 1990s.

» Thread 5—The resurgence of God as the Father of that Kingdom Family—and His people as son and daughter servants in the Family of the Servant King in the 2000s.

Now, in the 2010s, we are being summoned to pull the threads through from history, intersecting them with His unshakeable, immovable Kingdom threads to reveal His pattern: *"Christ in you* [plural], *the hope of glory"* (Colossians 1:27).

This is not to say God was not actively working in these five arenas throughout history, but those of my generation seem to be witnesses to an intensification and systematic emphasis on each of these during each decade of the past half century. Each warp (vertical, foundational) thread is rooted in the millennia of ebb and flow in Church history and has stood the test of time. They now stand out in relief again in the most recent decades. It begs the question, "Father, what are You up to?"

We have seen these five components ripening in our hands in one generation, leaving us with a legacy to pass on to a new generation of Christ's disciples in the Church. We, like Moses, are to go into earth's fabric, bear witness of the Father's longing heart for His creation and bring the errant threads into alignment with the Master Weaver's pattern.

THREE PARALLEL STORIES

While my own redemptive story was unfolding, I found myself riding the wave of the various cultural and spiritual movements that paralleled God's redemptive process for each decade. Pure grace! The Church's story is so dramatic that my grandfather's generation would recognize neither the new cultural realities nor the new face of the global Church in this rising generation. Most importantly, God's story of redemption was surrounding us, romancing us to return to creation's purpose while coursing with redemptive intent through the chaotic yet thrilling years of my time on earth. The whole creation seems to be in childbirth again, groaning, looking for the unveiling of Christ's image in His sons and daughters.

So, in this book, I want to weave God's story and the Church's story together through the course of my own. Like a little brook, my personal journey flows into the creek that is the Church's story, which pours into the mighty river that is the Kingdom of God, flowing from creation to the present and into the "summation of all things" in Christ. I've had some marvelous opportunities to be a "fly on the wall" to different moves of God in His Body on earth. Because I am dedicated to God, my story tells part of His.

Throughout each decade of my own journey, I have included a summary of "lessons learned" and key growth ingredients embedded by the Father, via six developmental phases of a person's life (as outlined by Robert Clinton's book *The Making of a Leader*):

1. Sovereign Foundations,
2. Inner-Life Growth,
3. Ministry Maturing,
4. Life Maturing,
5. Convergence, then
6. Afterglow.

It's a common pattern I've seen in those whom God prunes as they answer His call on their lives.

From our foundation years, conversion season, to early and later ministry experiences, God is busy moving each of us toward convergence, the weaving of His Son's image through all the seasons, belief systems, assignments, and relationships. We will celebrate the Father's redemption of "all things" and how we can anticipate some of the seasonal lessons that lie before us, designed not to make us "successful Christians," but effective Kingdom emissaries.

I'm writing to "sons and daughters" to say,

> God has set the table for you. Know and receive the inheritance that others have fought to lay at your feet. Do this in honor of those who have run before you, to receive and honor them. Resist the temptation to reinvent the wheel through ignorance, arrogance, and independence. Rather, pick up the threads of the Kingdom from the trustworthy predecessors God has provided.

God's Church is a multigenerational family that has been chosen to reflect heaven's master plan to earth's "lost tribes"—to unveil Christ's image to the peoples of the earth. Our Father is waiting to lead us as a "new community people" into His superior purposes.

Many of these "sons and daughters" are not being intentionally mentored, fathered, encouraged, or championed. Some are even being used as pawns to further the vision of those they serve. Many leaders are unaware of the family legacy that has been cultivated for them over the years. Some feel orphaned and disconnected from a father's love, while others are chasing an anemic and shallow vision that hasn't been rooted in God's multigenerational foundational legacy. Many carry intense pain from childhood and early ministry involvement and urgently need to be encouraged to embrace their broken stories as candidates for their Father's great redemption. The Father's redemption story in our lives releases His innate dreams in each of us and provides the requisite character that deposits a legacy into Christ's younger disciples. This process is shepherded by the Holy Spirit to ensure that we are forged into a dangerous ambassadorial corps of this exquisite Kingdom.

My heart's desire is not to propose formulas, "how-tos," or to render brittle theological suppositions. I would rather brag on God's amazing faithfulness to me and all of His children. I want to testify to His wisdom dispensed to the "household of faith" throughout the past decades. I want you to marvel at the beauty of the tapestry and the pattern that God is unveiling through His Church. I want us to stand on the precipice of the future with joy and contemplate how He wants us to continue the tapestry's pattern into the coming generations—one that won't be fully finished until He returns to establish His Kingdom on earth.

So, we pass the baton, or in this case the weaver's shuttle, from generation to generation. Our only response for being included in His Master Plan should be to worship Him by echoing Paul's declaration,

> **Now to the King eternal, immortal, invisible, the only God, be honor and glory for ever and ever. Amen.**
>
> **—1 TIMOTHY 1:17**

PROLOGUE

A World War II soldier—a medic—stood guard one night outside of his camp in Papua New Guinea. The Allies were still locked in battle with the Japanese. As he stood, fighting to stay alert in the stillness of the night, a white light encircled him. He didn't hear the sound of a helicopter or anything mechanical that could have been the source, and he could see nothing around him for the brightness.

Then, as quickly as it came, it was gone. The medic had no sense of how long it had lasted.

On finishing his watch, he reported the incident to his superiors, but no one else had seen any light. He later learned, however, that a guard near his station had been killed about the same time, and his body was not found until his relief came at dawn.

A sense of divine protection rolled over him.

The next night, the same thing happened. This time, like Samuel, the medic fell to his knees and asked the Lord what He wanted. There was no audible voice. Nothing appeared to him. But when the light disappeared, he had a strong sense he was to go to Japan after the war and preach the Gospel to the Japanese.

The medic's name was Lyle Petersen—my father.

As he'd done faithfully throughout his three years stationed in the Pacific, Lyle wrote home to his childhood sweetheart.

He wrote about what had happened and about his new conviction. "Dimples," as they had called her when she was young, was unfazed by the news, accepting it just as he'd stated it. At the ripe age of eight, Lyle had informed his buddy Albert that he would one day marry Dimples, Albert's sister. Upon returning from the war in 1946, he did just that.

After they wed, Lyle and Alice Petersen attended Bob Jones University and honed their pastoral skills by interning in several Appalachian mountain churches. Then, deemed ready for the mission field, they sailed for Japan in May 1951.

Just eight months after their arrival, on January 15, 1952, Lyle and Alice became my mom and dad. That was the day my story began.

My parents were never supposed to have children. Soon after they married (and before they headed overseas), doctors told them that it was an unlikely proposition. Thus I wasn't just a surprise, but also a bit of a miracle. I think it made my parents wonder about what I was supposed to become.

The story of who I was to become didn't really get interesting until God took hold of me when I was seventeen. As Michelangelo did with his *David*, God started chipping away from me everything He'd never intended to be Jon Petersen. It would be a process that would go on for more than fifty years. It's still happening today.

This is how it happened.

PART ONE:

HUNGRY FOR GOD

A TOWHEAD GROWS UP IN POST–WORLD WAR II JAPAN

Japan had long held an animosity toward Christianity. From the expelling of Portuguese Jesuit missionaries and the torture of their converts in the 1600s to its declaration of war on the Western interlopers of the United States and the British Empire in 1941, Japan was simply not open to outside ideas or influences. By right of centuries of imperial succession, Japan saw itself as the master of its destiny—responsible for spreading its wisdom to greater Asia, by invasion and conquest if necessary.

All that ended with the bombing of Hiroshima and Nagasaki. Japan not only surrendered to end World War II in the Pacific, but it gave up its imperial imperative to "ensure the stability of East Asia" and "cultivate friendship among nations and to enjoy prosperity in common with all nations"[1] under its rule.

Cowed into submission and forced to redefine itself as a democracy separate from its imperial history, Japan could no longer remain isolated and self-defining. That didn't mean it would embrace change willingly, however.

World War II left Japan in shambles. With entire cities devastated by Allied bombs, it would take the island nation decades to recover. It was a conquered land with a defeated sense of identity.

Tokyo was rebuilt but marked by the hands of those who had beaten it into submission: All of the streets were laid out in a grid by the American Army—English letters one way and numbers the other. It was impossible to go anywhere in the city and be untouched by the stigma of conquest.

Soon after they arrived, Lyle and Alice were assigned to a small church plant in the fishing village of Tateyama in Chiba Prefecture on Sagami Bay. Tateyama was a long way from not much!

Recovery came slowest to the towns and villages at the edges of the new Japan. Tateyama was a place where rats enjoyed the open sewers and squatty-potty toilets were the norm. Disease was rampant. The postwar missionaries were inoculated against all manner of seen and unseen biological terrorists, but often still fell ill. Staying on assignment took a spirit of resilience and tenacity that I still marvel at today.

Newcomers like Lyle and Alice were immediately the center of attention wherever they went. Invaders in a conquered land proclaiming a foreign God, they were not met with open arms, especially by the local Shinto and Buddhist priests. My dad, being tall and thin, usually stood head and shoulders above everyone, everywhere he went. (He quickly earned the Japanese nickname of *denshinbashira*, which means "telephone pole.") As you can imagine, he and my wee mother were a constant spectacle as they stood in the neighborhood streets, telling the story of Jesus with their flannel-graph board figures and whimsical little "Gospel puppets."

Then came me.

As blond as my Scandinavian roots foretold I should be, I was a spectacle from the first time I ventured into the village on my father's shoulders. (I must have been like a placard proclaiming, "Here come the foreigners.") On one hand I was a celebrity whose hair everyone wanted to touch. On the other, I would never fit in. It was a double-edged sword: I was an anomaly, but I was *their* anomaly. I was isolated, but also looked after by all of our neighbors. For the most part, I could wander freely around the village, like Huckleberry Finn, with my trusty dog, Brownie. I could always find someone to feed me, watch over me, or help me get home. There was even a pond in our front yard, teeming with bullfrogs, put there, I was convinced, solely for stuffing into my pockets. In many ways it was an idyllic childhood.

But socially and spiritually, I was an outsider with a confused cultural identity. An American by birth and a Baptist by default, I would join our neighbors as they made *omochi* one day (a sticky rice concoction one pounds into submission with large wooden mallets. It poofs when you cook it; so yummy!) and then next I'd be saying grace over squid or octopus tentacles as if that's what every Midwestern family in the United States did every night of the week. (I loved going to the beach with my parents and picking our dinners fresh out of the fishermen's nets!) One day we'd be standing in the streets with the rest of the village, watching the *oshogatsu* (Shinto New Year's) parade. The next day, we'd be fellowshipping with other missionaries in Tokyo in a service replete with its own hymnals and three-point sermon in a service that would be hard to distinguish from any in the Bible Belt.

But counter to the faith of my parents and our Baptist missionary community came the uninvited spiritualism of Japan. As it would turn out, Japan was not just the land of my childhood adventures; it was also the land of my nightmares. The scientific, Western evangelicalism of our missionary community had no grid for the actual forces behind Japan's ancestor worship and other mystic traditions. The local Shinto and Buddhist priests had no affection for people coming into their jurisdiction and preaching their foreign God. As a defeated nation, they had no power to force us out, but they did what they could to resist. As a result, we experienced intense spiritual oppression.

One of the local traditions involved a purification ritual called *harae,* which was performed before a family moved into a home. A village Shinto priest would be summoned to purify the home from any "evil" that might linger from previous occupants. In performing this ritual, the priest would don what looked like a "devil mask" and, with a *shide* (a wand used to "to move energy") he would "sweep away" contending spirits to make room for protective ones. Despite my parents' protest, *harae* was performed on our new home before we were permitted to move in. I was four at the time, but I can remember the masked priest waving his *shide.* (It still sends a chill through me.) Looking back, I believe the ritual marked our home as enemy territory, making it a target for spiritual malice.

It's hard to pinpoint the effects of such practices, but a few nights after the "cleansing," I experienced the first of the nightmares that would plague me into my teens. I can remember only the last part of these horrid dreams.

> *I fall, in sheer darkness. I tumble and spin, down, down, down into a dark pit. Then, out of the black void above me, dives a dragon with the same fiery, half-mad eyes I had seen through the priest's mask. As I fall, the dragon slowly gains on me, snapping its smoking jaws in an effort to devour me. As I twist, trying to get away, I see a pool of fire dancing at the bottom of the pit. The flames seem to be reaching for me.*

That was when I'd scream.

My parents always came running. My father would scoop me into his arms and cradle me, my mother cooing and caressing my hair.

"It's only a dream, Jonny," he'd say.

I never quite believed him.

One *oshogatsu* parade deepened my anxiety. The major festival during that season—called *Obon-dori*—was a big event in our little town. There was always a huge parade, and the streets were lined with spectators. Because of the novelty and the community nature of the event, my parents usually attended.

Perched on my dad's shoulders, I was able to see everything, including the approach of the large rolling "ark" of the temple high priest lumbering down the street toward us. It was the center of the festivities. A band of men "clothed" in the traditional minimalistic attire—which amounted to little less than a sumo wrestler's loin-cloth—pulled the ark with long hemp ropes. *Saké* flowed freely at these celebrations, leaving virtually everyone seriously inebriated. The throngs cheered louder when they saw the ark approaching.

When it rumbled by us, I looked up to see yet another dragon-faced devil mask staring at me, with piercing eyes. I was transfixed in horror. Those were the eyes from my nightmares.

Then, with no warning, the dragon priest reached over the edge of the railing and plucked me from my father's shoulders. This was not some strange tradition, but the random, impulsive act of a drunken man. Without a word, he lifted me into the lumbering mobile shrine and dropped me in a heap beside him. He began dancing around me, chanting in Japanese. Looking back, I suspect they were some kind of incantations he meant to curse and silence our family.

The sides of the ark were too high for me to jump down from, and I could see no other way of escape. Terrified, I cried for my father. I caught glimpses of him pushing his way through the throngs, struggling to keep me in sight. The attending priests on the ark mocked my fear, pointing and laughing derisively.

Eventually, my father caught up. He demanded my return, a demand echoed by the crowd. The dragon priest reluctantly returned me to my place on his shoulders. Though I wept hysterically, terrified, the priests acted as if it had all been an innocent prank.

I think my parents chalked it up to being one of those things that happen to foreigners in a strange land, but for me the consequences were severe. Having come face-to-face with my nightmare in real life, *again*, the frequency and the clarity with which I saw the dragon in my dreams intensified. It was as if he were inching closer and closer to catching me every time I shut my eyes. At the bottom of my young heart, I felt incredibly vulnerable, alone, oppressed, and dejected. Aside from our home, there was no place I belonged, and even in our home I didn't feel safe. That fear and the deep sense of foreboding would intensify as I got older.

By day, I was playful little "Jonny-chan"; by night I dreaded the darkness and sleep because of the dragon. Then, about a year after the parade abduction, I was playing in my backyard, trusty Brownie by my side, when a man in a sailor suit asked me if I wanted to see his big ship in the bay. Being five and greatly taken with ships of all kinds, I followed him out the back gate and down to the harbor.

For the rest of that frantic day, my parents canvassed the neighborhood to see if anyone had seen "Jonny-chan." No one had. My parents were beside themselves.

Then, late that night, a man came running to our home, shouting that he had seen Jonny-chan coming down the road with a young man. When the "nice sailor" and I came around the corner to our street, it was lined with neighbors shouting profanities and hitting the sailor with all manner of instruments. Terrified and relieved, I ran into the arms of my weeping parents.

I have almost no other memories of that day. Maybe it was all innocent, but that seems unlikely. That episode further solidified the messages plaguing my young heart: I was alone, and no one could protect me from outside evil.

When I turned six, my parents were offered a position as house parents at the dormitory for the Christian Academy of Japan (CAJ). It meant we would trade the backwardness and disease of Tateyama for the bustle and modernity of Tokyo. I was initially excited about the change, until my parents showed me my room—a bunk and a cubby with twelve other missionary kids, whose parents worked in various parts of the country. Though I'm sure my parents meant nothing of the kind, it felt like rejection. I was once again unfit and isolated.

A few months after the move to Tokyo, a doctor determined that my young, developing reproductive system was in trouble and in need of surgery. I was terrified by the worried looks on my parents' and doctors' faces as I drifted into darkness on the operating table. I still remember the stench of ether in the cloth pressed against my face. And I vaguely remember being instructed to "Count backward from ten."

In the after-fog of the anesthesia, I overheard the doctor telling my father that the surgery was only partially successful. I would need a follow-up surgery in two years. With a sober heart, my father told me that the doctors were not sure I would ever be able to have children. At the vulnerable age of six, I was simply not able to comprehend the magnitude of that revelation. But that pronouncement slithered into my tender spirit, convincing me further that I was flawed, alone, and would stay alone. I was broken, unnatural. I would never find a place where I felt safe. I remember no prayer in that room that day, no hope, nor any comfort of the Holy Spirit. The "fog of whispers" seemed to be increasing in intensity, and the "coffin nails" of oppression were sealing me into a dark, hopeless future.

I entered preadolescence with all the usual confusions, and then some. It wasn't long before other temptations entered my life. A year or so after my surgery, I was standing on a pile of glass refuse with Hans Rudy, a Swiss friend and fellow missionary kid. We loved to comb our "mountain" of multicolored bits of glass pieces. (They weren't sharp, but had rounded edges as if they had all been pulled from years in the sea.) We collected pieces of various sizes and hues, but I don't recall what we ever did with them.

In the midst of scavenging for our little treasures, we looked up to find a man standing directly in front of us, a malevolent grin on his face. He extended his hand, revealing a photograph held between two filthy fingers. The photo showed a man and a woman in a sexual position. I was repulsed and transfixed at the same time.

I looked up into his dark eyes. He said, "This is what life is about." Then he smirked and walked away. I studied Hans's shocked face.

The next instant, we looked all around, but there was no sign of the man.

After this incident, my soul was in turmoil. That photo became a seed, planted in my mind and spirit. Ultimately, it germinated into an attraction to pornography that would last into my twenties.

This battle for my heart escalated as I hit my teen years. I embarked on a full double life. In the classroom I was outgoing, well-liked, active, and a decent student. I traded the isolation of my younger years in Tateyama for the stranger, cloudier isolation of popularity. I had "friends," but no one to really talk to. Maybe calling them partners in crime would be more accurate.

We were stuck in a world we didn't choose or fit into. Frustrated and angry, we acted out. It was something we could control, even if it created self-destructive problems. We'd sneak off to downtown Tokyo when we got a chance and come back with all the pornography, records, and alcohol we could get our hands on. We'd attend movies we knew our parents would prohibit. We sought music that resonated with our angst. It was the 1960s, so you can imagine what we were into: the Beatles, Led Zeppelin, Bob Dylan—along with some homegrown Japanese rock and roll. Such music seems harmless by today's standards, but it was considered the fruit of an "evil" African beat to many in the church of the day. (Our missionary community was very conservative.) It was the type of music that "gives kids the wrong urges." And it seemed to stand for everything our parents were against.

Perfect.

We hid our illicit treasures in our tiny dorm cubicles. We clowned around in class, defied our dorm parents (for me, my *actual* parents) when we could get away with it, and thrashed about trying to figure out who we were. We were fighting to feel loved by others, but we didn't even know how to love ourselves.

The years of anxiety and spiritual confusion manifested into an odd handicap. When I took high school speech class, I found myself mysteriously tongue-tied when asked to speak publicly. My teacher was discerning enough to see this strange reaction to public speaking and quickly shifted me into the drama class. Being someone else was easy. I became active in drama and won a blue ribbon at the Far East Speech Tournament in Tokyo for a solo dramatic interpretation. (I did a monologue as an insane child locked in a basement by his father. Why did I identify with that kid so closely?)

I was fine being someone else; I just couldn't stand up and *be me*. When I tried, nothing would come out of my mouth but gagging sounds. Small blotches would break out all over my body. Looking back, I've often wondered how much of my childhood abductions and nightmares had to do with that.

I know I risk leaving the wrong impression by listing all of these dark incidents while leaving out the larger adventures of growing up in a place I now regard with great affection. (I visit Japan often, and treasure each chance to go "home" whenever I can.) I'm sure that, if you'd met me at the time, you would have thought I was a typical confused adolescent, caught in a tug-of-war between the land of my nationality and the very different place I acculturated. Of course, spiritual darkness is harder to detect, and it rarely manifests in public. But I had serious self-worth issues. I battled with pornography, and I battled deep depression. I felt unworthy: unworthy of attention, unworthy of respect, and unworthy of truly being loved. Try as they might, my parents couldn't break through that wall, and I resisted them when they tried.

I am not, nor have I ever been, a victim. My birth into a caring missionary family in postwar Japan was the design of my loving heavenly Father. The nightmares, abductions, evil, and fear I experienced were not caused by God. Instead, they were opportunities for Him to later reveal His overwhelming redemptive power in the areas that wanted to crush my young heart. Experiencing loneliness and fear through my journey provided the vacuum for God's love and healing power to assail the lies that had become rooted deep inside of me.

It all had to come to a head. As I finished my junior year and got ready for my senior year at CAJ (and the "escape" from Japan), I was raring for a fight. To inaugurate that summer, our parents decided to ship us all off to Hi-BA camp ("High School Born Again-ers"—

go figure) on the coast, hoping it might provide a chance for God to work on our hearts.

The day before we left, I had unloaded my empty whiskey bottle collection on my mom in a fit of anger. Angry and tired of being just another dorm kid, I told my parents I'd do anything that would get them forced off the mission field if they didn't make us a family again. I was tired of sleeping in the dorms and having to share my parents with all the other kids. I insisted they give me the guest bedroom in their little residential apartment on the first floor of the boarding unit. I'll never forget the pain in my mother's eyes as I boarded the train and we departed for camp. She was certainly at the end of her rope with me.

I know she must have been praying, but what happened at camp turned out being abundantly above anything she could ask or hope for.

God was about to step into my mess.

UNVEILING YOUR FUTURE

No one grows up without facing some level of temptation, trauma, and angst. My story is no exception. I know that many of you reading this book have experienced far worse than I have. At the same time, many of the things that make us who we become are rooted in those years when we experience so many negative events. When we are in God's hands, the good is honed as part of the unique gift each of us is to the world, and the bad is redeemed—often in a way that becomes foundational to our lives and purposes on earth.

We all want to know what our future holds. God keeps much of it a mystery, but He deposits a sense of destiny that is the golden thread we hold on to as life unfolds. God addresses certain issues in each phase of our lives. Understanding these phases of growth is paramount for a leader's life. It's also a fabulous tool for discipling others.

In 1989 and 1990, I had the privilege of being a student of J. Robert Clinton—known to us as Bobby. His class was titled "Leadership Emergence Patterns" and was designed to help us see the full scope of what God was doing in each stage of our lives, and to recognize the special challenges we face as we move from stage to stage. This allowed us to see that we are not really alone in most of the core trials and challenges we experience as we grow toward greater influence. Clinton also helped us realize the incongruities we needed to resolve (and often heal) and the obstacles we needed to overcome to reach the next plateau. We delved into the phases of leadership development that occur over the course of a lifetime. (This course formed the basis of Clinton's excellent book *The Making of a Leader.*)

The Making of a Leader outlines six stages of personal and leadership development:

1. Sovereign Foundations (birth to late teens)*
2. Inner-life Growth (twenties)
3. Ministry Maturing (late twenties to early forties)
4. Life Maturing (late forties to early fifties)
5. Convergence (mid-fifties and through your sixties)
6. Afterglow (which I'll forego in this book, since I've yet to experience it. "Last embers" is not yet indicative of my journey. I'm busier than ever!)

---

* These time spans are different for every person, and there is a great deal of overlap. As a rule, Sovereign Foundations end at our conversion experience—when we are born again—and we then launch into our Inner-Life Growth phase. These will be different for those who come to Christ later in their lives, so these age ranges are for general reference. The ranges stated here, however, mirror my journey.

Although I have simplified Bobby's terms and the detail found in his book, it's easy to look back and see where I walked the paths of each of these stages throughout my life—and how each was vital to what I'm doing now. Looking at each in context, I see the trajectory of God's purposes in my life, and I think the stages will give you insight into your own as well.

Our stories are unique, but God's goal for all of us is to be formed into a distinctive expression of His Son—to have our mourning turned into dancing; to find our place in God's family; and to recognize, realize, and fulfill our one-of-a-kind destinies—to discover our special part in the overall puzzle. It is a common narrative for all of us "pilgrims."

This first part of *Unveiled* focuses on my foundation years (Phase 1: Sovereign Foundations and Phase 2: Inner-Life Growth), formed from my hunger for more significance and a greater connection to true love. These two stages, which often encompass our childhood, adolescence, and at least part of our twenties, tend to reveal five main components that God is working to build in our lives:

1. He's preparing our *destiny*: All of the events—good and bad, orchestrated by Him and not—that make up our early lives are meant to highlight the line between the seen and unseen—between our inner and outer worlds. They reveal there is "something more" to us: the eternal nature of our unique purpose on the earth.

2. He determines our *context*: Our cultural, social, and religious contexts are critical to God's plan for us as His earthly ambassadors.

3. He sets us in a *family*: For better or for worse, our families shape us and form the soil of God's great redemption

during our lifetime. We are not formed in a vacuum. God places us in context with others to live and work together to help us grow up and bring out our best. (God has not led me by mission in my life. He has always led me into relationship. Mission came out of that.)

4. He gives us *basic skills and talents*: The seeds of our skills and talents manifest early in life. They are like God's tool-chest, given to be honed for a lifetime of usefulness.

5. He calls us to *lead others*: Potential leadership abilities (gifts) are often latent but begin to emerge in these formative years, even though they seldom take full shape until much later. For some, this call to influence is welcome from the start. For others, it is reluctantly embraced.

Everything God does is redemptive! No depth of rejection, abuse, failure, or pain trumps the power of His Gospel and the unrelenting, redeeming love He longs to unleash on us. Through these we find the solid ground of who we are and why we're here. We find identity, purpose, and mission. We find the family we will walk through life with, influencing and being influenced. This is not a journey for the faint of heart, nor are we fully ready for it upon graduation from college. It takes a lifetime to walk into.

Welcome to the journey.

CHASED DOWN

We marched off to Hi-BA summer camp that June of 1969, ready for mischief.

The ten of us going to "futon" together were the same ones who participated in the Tokyo runs and were involved in whatever "unapproved" activities were happening at CAJ. We supplied the booze, circulated the magazines, or bobbed our heads to the beat of the rock-and-roll drums.

To set the tone for what we planned to be a raucous senior year, we planned to (literally!) start things off with a bang.

Concealed in our bags and distributed carefully between all of us to avoid detection, we had a stash of hundreds of Chinese-made firecrackers.

Our plan was to play it cool for the week and then, on the last night of camp (when there was no real time left to punish us), we would sneak under each of the girls' cabins, plant the fireworks, and then (at a predetermined cue) set off the pyrotechnics.

It would be as brilliant as it was devious.

So much for the plans of mice and boys.

The week limped along, and, for the most part, we participated in the fun and games our adult leaders had planned. We tolerated the hymn singing and evening speakers with silent disdain. We'd heard it all before. We knew what they were going to say.

We weren't going to let them tug our heartstrings. We knew they were all hypocrites. We weren't going to fall for any of it.

On the last night, we showed up for the campfire, all but rubbing our hands together in anticipation of what we were going to do after one more boring sermon. To make it all the more laughable, the speaker that night was our shop teacher.

Of all of our teachers at CAJ, Mr. Graybill was probably the most unlikely choice to tap as a preacher. He was well-liked, and taught us how to do woodworking, build cabinetry, and the like. But he was also the least dynamic person I could think of. We had fun in his class—he was a nice guy—but he was quiet and unassuming. He was just a salt-of-the-earth missionary man with a diminutive wife.

And he was not a great example to the rest of the missionary parents either. His son, Michael, was among our crew of miscreants.

As Mr. Graybill was introduced to speak, I remember thinking, *Oh my gosh, this guy? What on earth will he have to say?*

As it would turn out, quite a lot.

He spoke for about twenty minutes. As he started, all I could think about was our firecrackers and the mayhem we would unleash in the middle of the night. It was all I could do not to chuckle to myself and elbow my coconspirators.

As Mr. Graybill finished, however, all I could think about was something he'd said. The words kept ringing in my head:

"You know, you can't run from the love of God. He *will* chase you down."

The ten of us shuffled back to our cabin a little more subdued than you would think, given our plans. As we got about halfway back to our cabin, though—*Bam!*—God let off the fireworks, in more ways than one.

The sky erupted in a flash, and thunder rattled our simple pine cabins and shook the ground. In the same instant, it was as if God poured out a huge bucket on our camp. The skies opened up, and we were soaked to the skin before we made it to our door.

As the wind gusted, it felt like our cabin was going to fly apart at any second. As soon as we got through the door, we realized water was splattering everywhere through the porous roof and walls, which were designed to let in the gentle breeze, not keep out a monsoon torrent. The *tatami* (straw mats) that covered the floor emitted a mildewy odor as they got soaked.

For the next several minutes, we scrambled to protect our clothing and bedding. At first, we tried to protect the bundles of firecrackers, but that soon proved useless. There was no going out into that storm in the middle of the night anyway. Our plans were thoroughly doused.

I don't know how long it was before the rest of the guys in my cabin gave up on the idea, but once I'd protected my gear as best I could and settled onto a stool, wrapped in my blanket, I was out. Each cabin had a little space heater and a small kerosene stove in case anyone wanted to make tea or something. We had them both going full-blast, and we huddled as close to them as we could without setting ourselves on fire. I shivered and pulled my blanket tight around me—as much against my conscience, I think, as the cold.

Mr. Graybill's words kept turning over and over in my head.

"You can't run from the love of God. He *will* chase you down."

More than once, we thought the winds would pick up the whole cabin and send us spinning off toward Oz. It was hard not to come out of our skins each time the gales crashed against the cabin, again and again. We must've been a miserable sight—a bunch of wet puppies huddled together, unhappy and stewing in our own regrets. A strong conviction had come over each of us through the words spoken that night. I felt squeezed. It was like I was in a straitjacket. I knew I couldn't continue on the path I'd been blazing for the past several years.

I realized none of my actions or demands were making me happy. None of it brought any satisfaction, nor did any of it make me feel better about myself. That night, my thoughts lost in thunderclaps, I felt strongly that God was pursuing me—and I was getting tired of running away.

I don't know how long we sat like that, but I was so lost in thought that I didn't even notice when the storm ceased.

In the unexpected lull, one of the other guys said, "I felt something at the campfire last night."

Yeah, I thought. *Me too.*

I didn't want to be chased anymore. I didn't want to be who I was becoming. I didn't want my anger, my animosity toward my parents and toward the missionary community in general. I didn't want any more of the deep depression that gripped my soul because I didn't know who I was. I wanted to let it all go. It was too much.

I thought I had been inoculated against the effects of sermons by missionary speakers, but I began to realize I wasn't as immune as I thought. Although I had heard similar sermons myriad times, this was the first time I'd ever experienced the inescapable virgin sting of conviction and felt a sense of the inescapability of God's love. We'd been ambushed by a greater pyrotechnical display than anything we'd planned. My gig was up. My heavenly Father was trapping me in the arms of His irresistible, irrepressible affection. I was never going to be able to wriggle loose from Him again.

We talked for a short while about what each of us had felt at the campfire that night. It was the first time we had ever *really* talked to each other. God must've been there, because Mr. Graybill's words hit us all the same.

As the confessions rolled out about who we *didn't* want to be anymore, someone suggested we pray. It was also the first time I had legitimately prayed in my life (expect for maybe as a very young child). I told God what I was sorry for. I confessed what I didn't want in my life anymore, and I asked Him to guide me into the life He was calling me to, whatever that might be.

It wasn't as spectacular a spiritual experience as some I would have later, but I do remember the deep sense of peace that settled over me. I'd never experienced anything like it before. Though it didn't solve all of the afflictions, self-doubt, and depression that would continue to plague me over the next several years, it was a break in the storm. It weakened their hold on me. And I no longer had a desire for the things that had tempted me before, the things that were feeding my depression.

That night proved to have the same release for all of us.

As the tears abated and we started coming back to ourselves, someone asked an even bigger question: "What if we brought this back to the school?"

It was a notion that thrilled us.

By the time the sun rose the next morning, we had created a prayer strategy for the guys' and girls' dorms, as well as the rest of the student body. Then we agreed that, once we got back, we'd organize a bonfire for all of the magazines, books, records, and whatever else we'd been accumulating that we felt drew us away from God.

It was amazing. When we lit that fire, a whole pile of other kids followed along, and it all went up in smoke. The flames leapt high into the night sky, as did our spirits from the freedom we felt.

From there, our prayer meetings grew. Even the teachers started getting convicted. God started pulling them closer to Him, and during the following months, our assemblies started having a lot more depth and meaning. Some of our guys started leading the younger kids to turn their lives over to Jesus in the same way we had that night in our sodden cabin.

That little revival continued throughout my senior year.

At our 35th class reunion in 2005, our former headmaster and several former teachers joined us in Chicago to celebrate. All those years later, these faculty, who had become our friends, testified how this move of God impacted both the school and their own lives. One of our teachers declared that the 1969–1970 school year was the turning point of his spiritual journey. Missionaries in Japan still talk about it as an example of what can happen when we let God have His way.

When I came home from camp, I had truly changed. I was so different that my parents immediately noticed. That was the first time I was able to talk to them openly and honestly. Over the next year, I continued in the process of repentance and reconciliation with them. (But there was a good deal of damage to repair, and I still had my spells of angst and self-criticism.) I stopped living a double life. I got release from much of my anger, and I lost the desire to run off to who knows where to do who knows what, to act up in class, and to look at the wrong things. It was a true conversion.

I was so impacted by the experience that, in the months following, my friend Todd and I would sit in a rowboat and I'd play my guitar, singing and worshiping the Lord until my fingers were nearly bleeding. My life had been upended, and I was (unknowingly) moving into a phase of life when the Father would be setting a bull's-eye on the rest of my fragile and pummeled identity. He wasn't going to stop until He had it all.

Throughout this last year in Japan, many of the good things I'd done during my years in junior high and high school returned to the forefront. I continued being active in music and theater, as well as being an important part of our basketball team. Formerly, I participated to get attention; now I could enjoy these activities. In the years before, we'd ridden our motorcycles around Japan's villages like a biker gang, racing through farmers' fields and "tearing things up." Now we just had fun.

My fellow seniors voted me the "most talented" guy in our class (a big fish in a little pond, as the saying goes), because I excelled in sports, art, music, and drama. When I climbed on a plane in June of 1970, bound for a summer job and then for Biola College (formerly the Bible Institute of Los Angeles), I felt like God had big things planned for me, but I had no idea what awaited.

My adventure of life with God was just getting underway.

UNVEILING YOUR FUTURE

God's first (and ultimate) call is into relationship with Him. It is the foundation upon which all else is built. If that foundation is absent or compromised, things fall apart. (True, even if the relationship is there, sometimes things still fall apart, but that's a much different story. God is often in the deconstruction business, because He's planning a reconstruction or renovation to do something more vital to Him down the road—so sometimes things break so He can put them back together with us.)

In our early years, our temptations, traumas, and angst can pull us away from others. These challenges make us feel, "I'm worthless." "I'm ugly." "I'm all alone." "I'm unlovable." Though the work of redemption took years to overcome these strongholds in my mind, I was eventually reconciled to my parents through God's touch in that soggy cabin. It gave me the ability to look back with a deep sense of gratitude and joy for *all* I had experienced growing up (though it would take time to redeem some events fully).

The pressures and pain we encounter throughout our formative years are designed to reveal God's tenacious love and unbridled power to redeem us and bring us into alignment with His destiny for our lives. None of the enemy's pits can ultimately entrap us. A pit can be transformed into an artesian well, a conduit for the Father's overwhelming and lavish love. He turns our mourning into dancing and our anger into forgiveness.

I have met leaders well into their forties and fifties who have yet to reconcile painful childhood experiences. "It's all in the past," they say, yet they are unable to see that the unresolved past is very much alive in their present, squeezing the life out of their spirits while they "get on" with God's work. They've never redeemed their trauma. God is waiting for an invitation to reveal Himself as having been present during those painful years, despite His apparent absense.

Many years removed from the little towhead having nightmares in Tateyama, Japan, I look back on my redemptive journey without feeling a prick of pain or regret—just an overwhelming sense of gratitude that God used everything in those formative years to prepare me for my destiny. Growing up in another culture, the exposure to missionary thinking and practice in the '50s and '60s (along with being constantly surrounded by good, God-loving people), sowed the seeds for my future calling and purpose. Without these experiences and the subsequent redemptive journey, I would be without the deep well that I now draw from when I say to my young charges, "If He can get me, He can get you."

No one who wants to influence others for God can move into the fullness of his or her calling without journeying deep into the pain of their yet-unredeemed childhood relationships and experiences. We don't need to keep secrets. We need full exposure in the light of His love. (Winning this battle is also the prerequisite for the successful parenting of our biological and spiritual children down the road.)

In my teen years, the sprigs of my talents and gifts began to emerge, but they were not yet seated in the confidence of God's love. I was voted "most talented," but my motivation for engaging in so many activities was to battle the loneliness and sense of unworthiness I felt. I was fighting myself to prove I was worth something, that I was significant in the world.

My mother never praised me verbally until I was eighteen (when I was the lead in the spring play), one month before my graduation. Meanwhile, my father incessantly praised me to compensate for the lack of maternal praise. Neither seemed genuine to my fragile heart. In the years to come, I took responsibility for my own wrong responses, and I extended ruthless forgiveness toward my parents' imperfections. Who was I to judge, anyway? (A lesson I learned more fully after I had kids of my own!)

When God intervened at summer camp on the eve of my senior year, the tide began to turn. I experienced His unrelenting love for the first time. The dark arenas of my foundational years were about to move me into my conversion years. In "Clinton-speak," my conversion sealed the Sovereign Foundations stage of my life, and I launched into the phase of Inner-Life Growth. This transition from childhood through conversion begins the journey of casting a spotlight on the fractured cisterns of our hearts, the entanglements of our sin patterns, and the residual fears planted by our traumas that have taken root in our worldview. In the Inner-Life Growth stage, God is calling us to own these things and come to Him for their redemption, redesign, and renovation. This reconstruction then gives us the solid ground upon which to stand and then step into who God has called us to be.

A GAIJIN GOES TO AMERICA

On June 16, 1970, I jetted across the Pacific with thirteen bewildered classmates to live alone in the United States for the first time. We landed in San Francisco, where my friend Todd Halberg (later to become my brother-in-law) and I left our classmates and took the road south to Los Angeles. I was a missionary kid with a lot of baggage—both literal (suitcases and guitars and such) and spiritual. I was coming to my homeland for the first time, and massive culture shock was not the only thing on the agenda.

It was the beginning of summer and school wouldn't start until fall, so one of my first stops was to Verdugo Hills, a nursing home in Glendale, California, where one of my dad's friends had arranged a summer job. I would spend much of my time there wheeling the residents around and trimming rosebushes. (Officially, I was a gardener.)

So, for that first summer of life on my own, it was the geriatric community of Verdugo Hills, a tank-shaped fellow worker named Art, a wee Greek man named Mr. Calaveras, and me. Mr. Calaveras was an octogenarian and would sit in his wheelchair on the porch of the infirmary, sporting a straw hat, garden snips in hand. He proceeded to instruct me in the finer points of tending roses. My rose-trimming "ministry" noticeably improved under his watchful and kind tutelage.

It didn't take long for me to discover I was utterly unable to feel at home in the land of my citizenship. This was the first time I was truly on my own, and I felt the sting of being a third-culture kid—in limbo somewhere between being Japanese and American (not to mention the weight of my family's Nordic roots)—more than ever. The food was too rich, the desserts too sweet, and the transportation system sucked. Not only that, but they'd given me a room all by myself, so I was also spending more time alone than ever before.

I've always been a bit introverted, so it wasn't entirely uncomfortable. Some good came out of it. Being alone with so many strange "foreign" things going on around me made me hungrier for God in the way I'd met Him at summer camp. Television and the radio had little appeal to me, so I read—*a lot*. I remember devouring the Scriptures like crazy and getting even hungrier for the God I read about.

My dad's friend took me to church with him, but I had a hard time connecting with it. I was in a new place, but it was the same old religion I had soured on as a missionary kid. The services were all the same—three hymns from an old hymnal with words from the last century, a lofty prayer, a fifteen-minute sermon, a closing hymn, benediction, and we were done in just under an hour. (We had to beat the Lutherans and the Presbyterians to the lunch places, after all.) Worst of all, no one seemed hungry for more of God. Everyone seemed content with the complacent lives they lived. I grew anxious for school to start.

Then, just before summer ended, Mr. Calaveras touched my shoulder one day and said, "I will pray for you every day until the day I die." Despite my gratitude and amazement, I felt somewhat skeptical. *What kind of person says something like that?* I wondered. It seemed like a crazy promise, but I had no idea how much it would make a difference in the years to come. I truly felt the weight of the prayers.

Unfortunately, starting at Biola wasn't exactly the lift I had hoped. Though I was a music major, Biola required I take Bible classes as well. The classes covered the same dispensational theology I had grown up with. (This theology teaches, among other things, that Bible times had been a "dispensation" when miracles and signs and wonders were necessary to establish Jesus as the Messiah. Such things were no longer necessary today as we had the Bible to live by.) It wasn't that it was bad; it just presented little context for helping me grow. It felt like something was missing. It was dry, intellectual information that didn't seem to lead toward experiencing God more deeply.

I was finally interacting with others my age, but many of my peers seemed to have a very narrow worldview. They talked about themselves as though it was a well-honed art form (far from the deferential humility of the Japanese people). Steeped in the reserved, almost tribal and ordered "group society" of Japanese and mission field culture, I felt assailed by the brash individualism of American society. Why did people greet me with "How are you doing?" when they never intended to listen when I told them? I took offense at an American lifestyle that left me lonelier, more critical, and more in need of "heart" surgery than ever. I was growing bitter at my new surroundings.

By November of my freshman year, though, I had finally found some footing. As one does, I made some like-minded friends who empathized with me and the other third-culture kids. The first of these friends was my roommate, Dan Johnson. We soon learned we weren't the only ones who were dissatisfied with what we were getting in class. It wasn't the discontentment that connected us as much as the hunger for more. Like my friends back at CAJ, we wanted to conspire together for revival. But where would we find it?

The answer came the night when Dan burst into our room and announced, "Dude! You gotta come to Bible study with me!" (Wouldn't Mom be proud that I'd take time out of school to attend a Bible study?)

Why? I wondered, but what came out of my mouth was "Where?"

"Calvary Chapel in Costa Mesa," he answered. "There are all these hippies there!"

Hippies at church? This I've got to see.

What happened next only upped the intrigue. We snuck out of the building, jumped over the back campus wall under the cover of darkness, and piled into a waiting VW van that sped off before we could close the door. *What's with these guys?* I wondered. When I asked about all the clandestine measures, I was told Calvary Chapel had been blacklisted by the school administration due to its "aberrant theology." (Okay, maybe Mom wouldn't have been so excited after all.)

It was too late to turn back now. My hungry heart led the way.

As soon as I walked into the adobe-style building and sat down, I encountered my first introduction to the spirit of Calvary Chapel—and what would come to be known as the "Jesus people." A businessman in a three-piece pin-striped suit shuffled over to a row of beach hippies directly in front of me and plunked himself down. "I heard you guys were forming a Jesus 'rock-and-roll' band?" he inquired.

They nodded.

"Rock and roll" in church? I thought. *More aberrant theology?*

"Well," he went on, "God told me I'm supposed to buy you your first drum set."

There was an instant celebration.

I'd never seen or heard anything like this before. There was certainly something different about these guys. I was hooked before the service even began.

Calvary Chapel was like nothing I had ever experienced before, and everything I had ever wanted at the same time. First of all, there didn't seem to be anything "traditional" about it. The music and talk from the podium were all contemporary—no "high church-ese" here. No "thees" and "thous" and other King Jamesisms. While there were a lot of hippies, some whose attire would make my mother cringe, others wore suits and wouldn't have been out of place in any church I'd visited growing up. (Because of furloughs and fund-raising efforts, I had seen many different American churches in my life.)

Despite their differences, those in the service all seemed to have one thing in common—they were *all* hungry for God! It was my kind of place.

There were several hundred present. The audience seemed to have a core of older Foursquare Gospel members and a fresh influx of "freaks" who were coming off the streets and beaches. They'd all gathered to sit under the teaching of the Calvary Chapel pastor, Chuck Smith.*

The worship music was straight out of the Bible—Scripture put to folk or other music of the day. The hymnals lay in the seatbacks untouched. (The new music that emerged from these gatherings eventually birthed Maranatha Music and other contemporary Christian music labels.) Little attention was paid to the clock. There was no dress code, no order of service, no religious haze in the air. Just a tangible love for and sense of acceptance by God.

---

* Chuck Smith is credited as one of the founders of the "Jesus Movement."

People were hugging each other and freely talking about Jesus as if it were the most natural thing. Everyone was searching for a way to express love for Him. Upon perusing the small store in the lobby, I met artists who had found creative expressions of their faith through paint, leather, woodworking, and other crafts. The whole atmosphere, in the services and in their lifestyle, seemed to be rooted in stories of Jesus's life and "the power of the Holy Spirit"—a phrase that caused a strange tingling in my heart, which was both cautionary and tantalizing. It was the first time I'd ever seen God's boundless love in tangible form.

I started to sneak away regularly to attend Calvary Chapel whenever I could. (They had Bible studies and meetings every day of the week, so I had lots of opportunities.) One Tuesday night featured Lonnie Frisbee. He was a berobed, long-haired "freak" who had been recruited to the Calvary Chapel staff by Pastor Chuck. I had grown up on sermons that took one Scripture, made three points about it, and closed with some kind of historical illustration or story. Lonnie's preaching was more like a meandering conversation.

As Lonnie sat on a stool, he taught straight out of the Scriptures in a kind of stream of consciousness. He quoted huge chunks of Scripture verbatim, and he testified to things *he'd seen God do right in front of him!* Stories of physical healings were new to me—and somewhat troubling, given my dispensational roots. However, it was exciting to think of the God of the Bible still being as active as He was when Jesus walked the earth. I couldn't get enough of it.

As I returned to my Bible classes and dug into the Scriptures, I realized a war had begun for my soul. Without realizing it, I'd stepped right into the middle of a move of God that would have repercussions not just for my life, but for all Christians, and for the

Church itself, for decades to come. I immediately began experiencing a head and heart division. On one hand, there was what I had learned of Jesus growing up on the mission field and in my Bible classes at Biola: a standard, intellectual, conservative evangelical message. Much of it focused on what Jesus no longer did today. On the other hand, I was witnessing a radical, emotional, overpowering "presence" of God every time I walked into Calvary Chapel. And they kept talking about miracles like they were commonplace. Both sides couldn't be right.

I remember attending the church and seeing large circles of "Jesus freaks" sitting cross-legged with a Bible on each lap. It was not unusual to catch a whiff of marijuana or to see a lot more skin than I was used to in public. There was no sense of "change your behavior to conform to God's rules" with these people. It was, "Come, encounter Jesus, and He will change your life."

After one meeting, a guy came up behind me and tapped me on the shoulder. He had a patch over one eye.

"You know what? These guys just prayed for my eye," he told me.

"What's wrong with your eye?" I asked.

"I don't have one," he responded flatly.

"You don't have an eye?"

"Nope."

I had no idea how to respond. I thought about asking him how they could pray for an eye that wasn't there. Instead, I said, "Well, I hope God answers your prayer for—" then left the sentence dangling. *What was God going to do to an eye that wasn't there?* I had no idea what he was expecting.

A week later, the same guy saw me and came straight over. I didn't recognize him at first. "Look what God did for me!" he exclaimed.

I looked at him, puzzled. Then I realized why I hadn't recognized him. The patch was gone, and there was a blue eye in its place!

"I have a brand-new eye!" he cried, slapping me on the shoulder. (Now, looking back, I admit that I never looked under his patch to see whether or not his eye was missing, but that never occurred to me at the time. He might have been lying as part of some stunt to get attention or something, but he seemed genuine and I took it all as the real deal.)

There was no grid for this in the "Jesus doesn't do that anymore" theology of my upbringing. This was like something straight from the life of Jesus. I could hardly believe it, but there it was. I'd just experienced what I took for a miracle! What was I going to do with that?

Every time I visited Calvary Chapel, my perspective on church and spirituality was radically challenged. At the same time, I was learning more about the Bible than I ever had before.

In a lot of ways, the Church was at a crossroads in the early 1970s, and the epicenter of the conflict—at least for the United States—was Southern California. By attending Biola and sneaking off to Calvary Chapel whenever I could, I had accidentally stumbled into what was probably the greatest controversy of the twentieth-century church: the Holy Spirit's role in believers' lives.

I was standing in the middle of the intersection of that crossroads. It was a struggle for the heart and mind of the Church, hundreds of years in the making. And while theologians on both sides of the issue—Were the Holy Spirit's activities in the book of Acts for today or not? Did you have to "receive the Holy Spirit" as part of growing in Christ, or did you get all the Holy Spirit you would ever receive when you were born again?—continued to argue about it, I was going to have to decide for myself.

UNVEILING YOUR FUTURE

In California in 1970, it was cleanup time! Anger, pornography, resentment, and loneliness were being served notice—the voids they were trying to fill in my life were being filled with something else. The move to the United States and the repeated encounters with the Holy Spirit at Calvary Chapel were major components of my Inner-Life Growth. Isolation or a change of geography and context are often events God uses to get to the issues of our hearts. He got to my issues by challenging my presuppositions about Him, church, and destiny. Twentysomethings are typically high on energy and idealism, but low on experience, knowledge, and confident convictions about life. It is not unusual for young leaders to have broken relationships with their parents, or to have no relationship at all. They're a bit like ships at sea with no anchorage—they want to sound like they're firm in their beliefs, but when the seas around them get rough, they have a tendency to drift with the currents.

Into this surreal world of my own confused identity came the Holy Spirit. Encountering the Spirit sparked a sense of curiosity about my destiny, and about what was causing my depression. The Spirit got to the roots of my know-it-all aura and showed me conviction needed to come from a more stable knowledge base. There was still a lot I needed to learn and get perspective on.

This second phase of development, the Inner-Life Growth phase (often launched around one's conversion), is looking for that firmer ground to stand on, that certainty of identity that we can anchor to in a storm. As a result, it is marked by an increased hunger for God, the desire to please Him and obey His precepts, and an increased dedication to meditating in the Word, prayer, and fellowship. We are willing to do this outside work to establish the inner peace and conviction that will help us understand how to relate to and influence our world.

When I was being disagreeable with my parents growing up, my dad used to say, "If everyone was going right, you'd go left." In those days in California, I began to realize that my disagreeability with the "norms" of my upbringing and church context were the seeds of a yet-unsanctified gift. I was created by God to "go right when others go left," to be a change agent and a pioneer. It took time to hear my heavenly Father say that same phrase over the pain of my earthly father's voice. (Dad and I talked about this years later and found a way to laugh about it together.) It was the Father's voice that eventually healed me.

The Inner-Life Growth phase of a leader's development is orchestrated by God to uncover the seeds of destiny and begin reclaiming the past, via the work of Christ, the Word, and walking in total dependence on the Holy Spirit. (What the devil had meant for evil, God will turn to good.) Leaders who miss the full effects of this restoration process in their twenties and thirties often are seduced by "success" in ministry—they look to outward accomplishments to define their relationship with God rather than a genuine relationship with Him that is more concerned with developing character and maturing their faith. Letting success rather than relationship define them leaves the keel of their "ship" vulnerable, and when a "storm" comes, it's often unimpeded in its destruction. This often shipwrecks both their ministries and their lives.

This Inner-Life Growth stage usually takes up the bulk of our thought life and focus in our twenties (or at least whatever is left over after the usual concerns with finishing school, finding a spouse, starting a career, settling into being "an adult," and beginning a family). During my senior year at CAJ, the anger at my parents and Japan's missionary community weakened in the light of God's love. Although it would take another decade or more to rework and repair this broken pattern, I began to sense a flicker of gratitude for the uniqueness of my childhood. My early and adolescent years in Japan, my parents, my gifts, my new desire to influence people for good, and my growing sense of destiny were all foundational to who I am and how I relate to others. My conversion also began to reveal some leadership gifts. It allowed me to experience how my changed life affected those around me. Leadership wasn't something I aspired to, unlike some of my friends. I started out reluctant toward any exposure to the limelight of responsibility and opportunity. But as I felt God guiding me into influence and being a pioneer, I grew more comfortable with organizing those around me to make things happen.

There was going to be a lot of honing of my ego and ambitions before I came to learn what use I would be to God's Kingdom on earth. I had "head knowledge," but I needed depth, perspective, and wisdom. And I needed more grace in my heart. Although my healing journey had begun, my initial spiritual formation would take another twenty years or so. As I approached the age of forty, I finally sensed freedom from many of the lies that had imprisoned me. Through the compression of the hardships and valuable lessons I learned, I concluded that Jesus had been there all along, waiting for my understanding and my obedience to heal the fractured foundations of my formative years. I'd felt so alone, but I never had been.

In the five decades following that night at summer camp, God wove the image of His Son and the design for His Church into my mind and soul. He showed me how the threads of my days were interwoven with His heavenly tenets to reveal Jesus's image in everything He and I did together. His plan was slowly unveiled through the experiences and people that have crossed my path. It didn't come easily, but I wouldn't trade one agonizing day of the process. It was the adventure that has led to everything I am doing now, and hope to do in the decades to come.

Looking back, I clearly see that God was up to something in my life. I know He's up to something in yours as well. I don't want to present my life as a pattern for you to follow, but as an example of what God can redeem and accomplish if we let Him. There's little to no joy in the journey without Him, and we can't afford to let what the enemy meant for harm get in the way of God bringing good through us. We need to stay open to and actively engage in His redemptive process.

THE CHURCH I ENCOUNTERED IN THE 1970s

As I would first experience in the conflict between my classes at Biola and my time at Calvary Chapel, my story has often found me at intersections of major developments in the Church's journey. My personal life and understanding of God have paralleled what the Church was learning and embracing as God directed its path. As a result, I've had the opportunity to be "a fly on the wall" more than once as God moved to correct His Church, pushed her in a new direction, or repositioned her so He could fulfill His promises to her.

As I look back, I sense that the mid-twentieth century found the Western church struggling with a curious mix of contradictions. Many of the foundational strands of God's tapestry were tangled or left dangling in confusion. In the United States, the rising crescendo of a social gospel from the 1800s (think abolition, the Salvation Army, women's suffrage, etc.) flew too close to the sun, believing, for example, that Prohibition would solve more problems than it would create. Zealous evangelists and other devoted believers hoped to spur a more perfect nation under God by outlawing alcohol, which they saw as the cause of so many social ills.* That Prohibition was

* It's worth noting that the hard drinking of the pre-Prohibition years did significantly lessen in the wake of Prohibition's being repealed. Beer and wine became more prevalent than hard alcohol. This did impact domestic violence, which was the issue Prohibition sought to resolve (the appeal of "for the sake of our children" was an influential part of the battle cry against alcohol). But we also learned it's hard to legislate people into having better hearts.

ever passed in the first place—as a grassroots movement that led to a constitutional amendment, no less—was a tribute to the power of pulpits all across America in the first half of the twentieth century.

When Prohibition was repealed in 1933, however, in some of the worst days of the Great Depression, it was a severe blow to American evangelical moxy. Christians felt their impact on society waning. Feeling like their cultural influence had been rejected, they began to withdraw within the "safe" walls of local churches. Christianity slowly became a subculture, and churches seemed to draw the lines of their influence at their thresholds. It was as if they were saying, "If you need help, enter here, but it's too dangerous for us to wander out there." With their outward thrusts into society blunted, many in the Church sought to be moral anchors. The responsibility to be "right" slowly replaced the call to "do good." The Gospel became the decision to follow Christ, what doctrines you believed, and was used to persuade others to the goodness and righteousness of God—which it did. However, the active, outreach role in society began to atrophy. Influencing society was placed on the backburner for many.

In an effort to maintain the "good works" of the Gospel, other church denominations held fiercely to the notion that they were the primary manifestation of a godly life, and of the Gospel message itself. These churches, often termed "mainline" denominations, began to drift away from a clear Gospel of salvation. This, in turn, widened the chasm between them and the evangelicals, who emphasized "the decision" to follow Christ as the foundation of all that was good and holy. These soon became two distinct streams of the American church.

This particular division in Church history is imperative for us to understand today, as the Lord is graciously weaving the various "legs" of the Gospel back into the tapestry of our thinking and practice. As George Santayana once said, "Those who cannot remember the past are condemned to repeat it." It's important to know where we came from, and what we did right (and wrong) so that we can move forward effectively.

At the same time, the early twentieth century saw the fresh breath of God spreading throughout His people, via the Pentecostal revival. In 1906, Acts chapter 2 fell anew on a racially diverse congregation meeting in a "tumble-down shack" on Azusa Street in Los Angeles. This raised new questions about the proper demonstration and functions of God's works on earth. While many embraced it, others—like the missionaries in Japan I grew up with—all but called it heresy. Rather than reviving the Church as a whole, Pentecostalism created a flurry of new denominations that proclaimed the importance of being "baptized in the Spirit" in addition to being born again.

The more established, traditional denominations pushed such things aside as excesses. "You get everything you need from God when you proclaim Jesus Lord and Savior," they said. "This includes the Holy Spirit, who does the work of making us born again." Anything beyond that was excess emotionalism—flakiness rather than solid biblical scholarship. However, few who experienced the baptism of the Holy Spirit could deny it was God at work in His people—and many wanted the "more of Him" that it promised.

While I was bumping along with my missionary-kid buddies in Japan, Episcopalian Vicar Dennis Bennett was having an encounter with the Holy Spirit at Saint Mark's Church in Van Nuys, California. He declared to his congregation on Easter Sunday, April 3, 1960, that he had spoken in tongues. His church was stunned and unsure of the direction Bennett was leading, which created growing tensions among his large congregation: "One man stood on a chair shouting, 'Throw out the damn tongue speakers.'" The curate tore off his vestments, threw them on the altar, and stalked out of the church, crying, "I can no longer work with this man."[2]

The news was not well-received by many Episcopalian "higher-ups," local church leaders, and congregation members. Eventually, Bennett resigned.

Both *Time* and *Newsweek* ran articles on Bennett and the church that year. Other stories appeared on local and national television. The fact that this *charisma* ("gift")—speaking in tongues—historically identified with the Pentecostal traditions was entering a mainline church was big news. This began the mainstreaming of practices like speaking in tongues and praying for healing, which previously were found almost exclusively in Pentecostal churches.

As others like Bennett began embracing the gifts of 1 Corinthians 12 in the more traditional denominations, the "Charismatic Renewal" was born.* The healing evangelists of the 1940s and '50s (John G. Lake, Aimee Semple McPherson, Oral Roberts, Kathryn Kuhlman, among others) prompted traditional believers to question how much of the Holy Spirit they really had. They began to attend services and revivals, open to what God was doing. Many of these believers brought the "Pentecostal baptism" with them when they returned to their home churches. You can imagine how that went over.

After Bennett was forced to resign, the Episcopal bishop in Seattle assigned him to the floundering St. Luke's Episcopal Church (where they probably hoped he'd quietly "go away"). Much to the

---

* The term "charismatic" was coined by American Lutheran minister Harald Bredesen in 1962 to describe the "renewal" of these 1 Corinthians 12 "grace gifts" in mainline Protestant denominations. Incidentally, my wife Mindy's movie-star grandmother, Dale Evans (wife of Roy Rogers), was led into an encounter with the Holy Spirit by Bredesen in Seattle's Space Needle Coffee Shop in 1965. Grandma Dale often told us how that experience gave her the grace to endure the heat of a Hollywood career and the pain of losing three children.

Anglican higher-ups' chagrin, the church soon became a center of growth and national influence—a charismatic training ground of sorts. The blossoming controversy and press coverage created an awareness of the emerging charismatic renewal, resulting in its spread to other mainline churches, where leaders were receiving and publicly announcing this new spiritual experience.

Soon after the Episcopalians jumped into the fray, the Catholic Charismatic Renewal was ignited (in 1967) at Duquesne University in Pittsburgh, Pennsylvania. Many church leaders began holding meetings for seekers, as well as healing services where the sick were anointed with oil and prayed for according to James 5:14–15.

Resisting God's Spirit is not recommended. It is like painting a bull's-eye on one's chest, inviting God to, "Come and get me!" (Ask Jonah.) Can you imagine a more insane way to deal with God than to resist something that He is, loves, or originates? Dennis Bennett's encounter with the Holy Spirit might have been the birth of the Charismatic Renewal, but it was the result of a long succession of men and women seeking a deeper relationship with God's Spirit.

With the Pentecostals having to fight for legitimacy in the first half of the twentieth century, you would think they would have been glad when more mainline denominations started embracing the same "baptism in the Holy Spirit" they'd made the center of their distinction. This was not the case. The now "older brother" Pentecostals were not exactly enamored with this new form of Holy Spirit theology or practice coming from the bowels of churches that had, up to that point, told the Pentecostals they were completely wrong about the Holy Spirit. Relationships between Pentecostal churches and these charismatic "upstarts" remained frosty throughout much of the 1960s. Thanks to leaders like David du Plessis ("Mr. Pentecost"), Jack Hayford, and others, however, the atmosphere began to thaw as the '70s began. An increasingly united front was established at the national and global level as the renewal of the Spirit went mainstream. Then with the coming of the Jesus Movement and the revival it wrought, it became impossible to ignore the fact that God was in these things that were turning so many away from sex, drugs, and rock and roll to become "freaks" for Jesus instead.

The questions I faced as a budding twentysomething in California were the same ones faced by the Church in the decades before: "What do we do with the gifts and manifestations of the Holy Spirit? Are they for today, or are they excesses?"

Our Japanese missionary leaders—like many U.S. evangelical denominations—taught that the gifts of the Spirit had passed away with the last apostle who'd walked with Jesus. They based this on Scriptures like 1 Corinthians 13:8–10:

> **Love never fails. But where there are prophecies, they will cease; where there are tongues, they will be stilled; where there is knowledge, it will pass away. For we know in part and we prophesy in part, but when completeness comes, what is in part disappears.**

For them, the "completeness" mentioned in this passage was when the Bible was compiled into one book. Therefore, the gifts of the Spirit (speaking in and interpreting tongues, words of knowledge and wisdom, prophecy, miracles, etc.) were no longer needed, because we now had God's Word from which to judge truth. We no longer needed special prophetic communication directly from God. They contended that, through the Bible alone, we could come to know God's love, which superseded all of the gifts (which 1 Corinthians 13 does clearly teach). Therefore, the Church no longer needed any other manifestations of the Spirit but the faith, hope, and love that could be found through the Scriptures. Evangelical Christianity went on to teach that Christians received all of the Holy Spirit they would ever get when they accepted Jesus as Lord and Savior. There was no subsequent "second blessing" or "baptism of the Holy Spirit."

For Pentecostals, however, this second blessing/baptism of the Holy Spirit was the entryway to all the gifts of the Spirit. Without it, we were missing out on the miracles and the full power of God. Traditional denominations taught that this was a distraction and even a deception. Newer denominations taught that you'd never find more of God without a fuller understanding and interaction with the Holy Spirit, and that the second blessing was essential to continuing the work of the book of Acts. Throughout the twentieth century, these two rivers of faith divided and converged and divided and converged again, creating a good deal of confusion. And while the Church was at odds with itself, secularism rose to unparalleled popularity throughout the United States.

The debate between the Pentecostal expansion and the charismatic renewal is critical for us to understand today. Although the sound of battle is more muted, the seduction of trying to be the Church without total dependence on God or to interpret Scriptures to fit our own presuppositions is always with us. God has repetitively warned His Church over the centuries not to "despise the Holy Spirit." It is imperative that we hold the ground the last generation gained for us in our love of and interactions with the Holy Spirit.

What was happening at Calvary Chapel in 1970 was one of the convergence points of these two streams, and its effects were amazing. Still, coming from a "the Bible is all you need" tradition, I was both confused and exuberant. I was hungry for more of God, but I had a difficult time letting go of what I'd been taught about the Holy Spirit. I struggled with this for the rest of my freshman year at Biola and into the next.

When I witnessed God's love in action as I never had before, I experienced a whole new set of questions about what it meant to walk in the fullness of God and His will for my life. I was in for quite a ride as I "surfed" into the currents of my generation's dysfunctions *and* its unique callings and giftings as the wave of the Spirit washed over America and the world.

I didn't know it at the time, but I was in the middle of this fight. It wouldn't be long before I had to choose a side.

UNVEILING YOUR FUTURE

Then in 1967 in San Francisco, something new was birthed from this hedonistic hippie culture: Young people were turning away from drugs and the sexual revolution to claim they had found "love, peace, and joy" in Jesus instead. They looked like hippies, but they had cast off the hippie value system and hooked into life in the Holy Spirit, replete with many Pentecostal and charismatic manifestations. They traded "ushering in a new Aquarian age of utopia" for "Pentecostal's premillennial utopia and the soon appearing kingdom of Jesus Christ."[3]

That year, street ministries such as Clayton House, the "Living Room," the Soul Inn, and the Veg Hut all contributed to making San Francisco's Haight-Ashbury district the birthplace of the Jesus—or Jesus People—Movement. Street youth were "done" with cultural American Christianity, but they seemed freshly receptive to Jesus, the Bible, prayer, and the Holy Spirit.

This movement spread across the country in a viral, unintentional manner as groups like the Jesus People Army, Gospel Outreach, the Children of God, Calvary Chapel, and many others emerged. "This collection of movements that was loosely drawn together and classified under one broad umbrella known as the JPM [Jesus People Movement], cross-pollinated with nearly every denomination of Christianity in America."[4]

During my introduction to the JPM, I was mesmerized by the presence of God at Calvary Chapel and the teaching of Chuck Smith. Chuck had received a prophetic word that the Lord was changing his name to "Shepherd,"* because the Lord was going to make him the shepherd of many flocks and the church would not be large enough to hold all of the people who would be flocking to hear the Word of God.[5] I was one of thousands who were shepherded by Chuck's expository teaching, which sparked a global movement of hundreds of churches in the decades that followed.

I observed a collective desire in the movement to return to the life of the early Church, a direct dismissal of the traditions of "our fathers' churches" for a truer "Father's Church." Radically counterculture in nature, the JPM trended toward asceticism. It focused on neo-monastic community more than the individual. There was a boisterous commitment to miracles, signs, and wonders; healing; prayer; evangelism; and God's Word. It was an echo of "Celtic monasticism," emphasizing forest gardening, intentional community, self-sufficiency, subsistence agriculture, sustainable living, and ecological sensitivities—all new to modern Church thinking.

When I later pastored a church, I knew several converted hippies in Grants Pass, Oregon, who lived in the forest while dedicating themselves to reforestation and living off the land. In the late 1970s, I drove up remote fire roads to hold Bible studies and take Communion with these forest "seed planters." Many lived in vans,

---

* This was not the "shepherding movement" that later distorted the roles of pastors and "shepherds" to overemphasize the authority of "fathers" in the faith.

tree houses, and teepees. They made clothes for their children from products they had grown. In those days, we were worried about an impending glacial age. (They feared "global cooling" at that time, rather than "global warming.")

The Church in most of the West was caught off guard by this new cultural U-turn and began to brace itself against the growing onslaught of moral and religious decline. The Church began to lose its position in culture. It also lost an alarming number of members. Historian Hugh McLeod contended that the '60s represented a "rupture as profound as that brought about by the Reformation."[6] Much of the Church, seeking to protect its children from the trappings of liberal hippie culture, began denouncing such weighty matters as long hair on men, sandals in church, and those "abominable clothes" (or lack thereof). The Church was shoring up its walls again, and rich opportunities to reach a new generation were being ignored.

I share this bit of JPM history to illustrate how our future is rooted in our past. This was the soil, the DNA that shaped the destiny I was to discover. Too often we try to separate ourselves from the greenhouse that is our generational garden. Embrace it! Despite its frailties and imperfections, it will shape you and be the ecosystem that births you into God's purposes for your life.

Too many times we get hung up on the forms and miss what is really going on. If you are unsure about your destiny, the first thing to do is not change your outward appearance but hang out with God. Having a sense of destiny is commensurate with getting His perspective and responding to His tests of integrity, obedience to the Word, and what I refer to as "blessing backward"—the systematic and tenacious commitment to forgive those from our past whom we have not loved by our words and actions. Be brutal with yourself on this front! The other things will follow.

A BATTLE FOR HEARTS *AND* MINDS

As forays to Calvary Chapel became more frequent in the spring of my freshman year, life got gradually more complicated. I was soon leading a "double life" between my classes at Biola and trying to slake my thirst with the Jesus People.

Calvary held Bible studies that went systematically through the Scriptures every night of the week, Saturday nights were concerts, and Sunday hosted a full slate of services. The Saturday concerts were incredible, featuring many of the names that would rise to the top of contemporary Christian music in the next decade: Keith Green, Love Song, Barry McGuire, The 2nd Chapter of Acts, Servant, Phil Keaggy, Larry Norman, among others. Every concert also featured a short Gospel invitation, and people were coming to Jesus left and right.

The sense of the Holy Spirit at the meetings and concerts was still troubling to my Baptist soul, however, because it was all deeply mixed with that crazy, uncomfortable-to-my-intellectual-Christianity charismatic stuff. At the same time, I was instinctually driven to know why I was on the earth and what I was supposed to do with my life, things I was told could be received as a prophetic "word" from the Lord. (More charis-mania!)

As I approached my nineteenth birthday, I was straddling two different cultures, two different subcultures between Bible school and the Jesus Movement, and two different theologies. And I was trying to figure out who I was and why I was here. You can see how many balls I was juggling. Both my brain and my spirit were getting a workout. The gulf between what I was witnessing and what I had experienced in my formative years revealed a deep deficit in my heart. I was hungry for more of Jesus and getting more and more willing to cross established lines to know, love, trust, and experience Him better.

Our "sneaking out" to Calvary Chapel became well known on campus. A couple hundred of us were making the trek regularly by then. Thus, a new battle began. Professors began questioning some of us about the incursions into the charismatics' camp—a group they saw as enemies of biblical orthodoxy. Some considered this movement "of the devil." While I understood most of their arguments intellectually, my heart was shouting louder that they had things wrong, and that God was more at work on the beaches with the hippies than He was among the better-behaved in our classrooms. What I'd been indoctrinated with was losing ground to the hunger and thirst that was warming my spirit every day. God was birthing a new "normal" in my arid heart, though I was still in the chrysalis of my transformation. This struggle would go on in me for roughly a year.

Then, to make matters even more complex, I fell in love.

✦ ✦ ✦ ✦ ✦

Near the end of my freshman year (May 1971), I was sitting in a practice session for the Biola Chorale with about seventy other music majors. It was a spectacular choir. We competed with most of the big schools in Southern California, including USC, UCLA, Chapman College, and Westmont, and we held our ground with them. It was one of the few places I could let myself go. It was a lot of fun. Our director, Loren Wiebe, was a warm, fabulous, and an extremely knowledgeable and accomplished musician.

I'd made the choir in my first month at Biola and had been in it the whole year. That day in May, Loren decided to change the seating. Rather than sitting with the people who all sang the same part, he put us into quartets with a baritone or bass, a tenor, an alto, and a soprano. Each had two guys and two girls so that we could learn our parts in connection with theirs. I found a girl sitting in my new section whom I'd never seen before.

"Are you new?" I greeted her. (Remember, I was only nineteen and rather awkward.)

"No, I'm a sophomore," she answered. "Are you new?"

"No, I've been here since the beginning of the year. I don't remember seeing you before."

"Oh, I got really sick and had to go home." She extended a hand. "I'm Mindy."

"Oh, I'm Jon," I shook her hand meekly, then sat down and promptly started ignoring her as rehearsal got underway. For the next couple days, I kept wrongly addressing her as Wendy. (Groan!)

A week or so later, I was walking down the hallway in the music center when I heard a thunderous noise coming out of the concert hall. I looked in to see what was going on. Someone was playing the university's pipe organ. It was huge, and its music filled the space. The organist was playing Bach's B Minor Mass. When I looked to the organ, there was this little whirlwind at the keys. Her feet danced across the foot pedals, pulling and pushing stops with feverish precision. Her hands skipped over the keys in a blur.

"Who is that?" I whispered to someone in the back row.

"That's Mindy Fox."

I remember thinking she was really something, not realizing she was the same person I'd been sitting with in choir every day. It would be the end of the year before I put the two together. (Yeah, I know.)

Later, I saw her walking down the hall past me, holding hands with this big buff, Mr. Wonderful kind of guy.

That's not right, I thought. I immediately wondered where that thought had come from. I had no interest in her. There was no budding romance or even any sense of affection toward her. I shrugged it off.

The chorale made a final tour in May before the school year finished. We'd be up and down the West Coast for about two and a half weeks, singing at universities and churches and in various auditoriums. Mindy and I ended up sitting together on one of the bus trips. Without prompting, she told me Mr. Buff had just been drafted by the navy to go to Vietnam, so they'd broken up.

And then she told me that prior to him, she'd had a boyfriend who left to join the marines. I had no clue why she was telling me all of this. I'm not sure she did either.

"My life's a mess," she confided. "I don't think I was supposed to be dating either of those guys."

Remember, I was an introvert, so I was a better listener than a talker, so that's what I did. When we finished that concert, we ended up sitting with each other again. We continued talking for the rest of the tour. Then, back at Biola, we kept finding excuses to get together until it was time to part for summer break.

Rather than working at the nursing home again, I went to live with my aunt and uncle who pastored a church in Pontiac,

Michigan. Mindy went home to San Jose. One day, out of the blue, I received a package in the mail, containing a loaf of fantastic sourdough bread. It was from Mindy. I kept thinking about her all summer, and we wrote to each other regularly.

When we returned to school in September, it was—*Boom!*—romance.

Mindy and I were together constantly from that point, and she started coming to the Calvary tent on Sunflower Street with me; my roommate, Dan; and his girlfriend, Taffy (whom he would later marry).

By this time, Calvary Chapel had grown so fast that they'd moved their Sunday services into a large circus tent to accommodate everyone. I discovered that Mindy was as hungry for God as I was. Now two slightly rebellious Baptist kids were in love and in trouble with their familial root systems. It was a match made in heaven.

I wrote my parents faithfully through all of those years. That summer I wrote my mom about the girl who had mailed me homemade sourdough bread. Mom was immediately curious, and impressed. "Is she your girlfriend?" she asked.

"No," I wrote back. But when I returned to school that fall, I wrote again, confessing that Mindy was the girl for me. Mom responded, "Well, that's not good. We've got to meet her before you go any further. Can you tell us more about her?"

I replied, "Do you know a guy named Roy Rogers and his wife, Dale Evans? Supposedly they're famous. [I was clueless, having grown up in Japan.] They're her grandparents."

Mom shot back, "Do you remember the bedspread you had when you were five?"

"Yeah," I responded. "Wasn't it a cowboy on a horse with a lasso?"

Mom laughed. "Not just any cowboy. That was Roy Rogers and his horse, Trigger—your girlfriend's grandfather!"

In hindsight, I call it my "prophetic bedspread." Draped with the legend over me every night was a foretelling of coming under the "covering" of his family through marriage to his granddaughter. (Of course, at the same time, I probably wasn't the only baby-boomer boy who had a bedspread like that.)

After that, my parents *had* to meet her.

The first time Mindy met them, she wore a white blouse and a beautiful peasant skirt, and she had her hair all done up in soft curls. We met at a pancake house. Before we left the restaurant, both of my parents had fallen in love with her almost as much as I had. They immediately hit it off.

They spent about a week with us that first time. Besides meeting Mindy, I talked with them about what I'd been learning and struggling with between school and Calvary Chapel. I even talked my dad into going with me to hear Chuck Smith teach.

I remember sitting with my missionary father as the service turned from music to sermon. Suddenly a helicopter flew overhead and hovered above the tent. It kept crisscrossing, making it impossible to hear anything being said. Finally, it hovered right above the tent and showed no signs of leaving. "You know," Chuck said over the microphone, "the enemy will try all sorts of tactics to interrupt God's work. This noise—I'm feeling that this is one of those times. These helicopters have no business flying here and parking over our tent." He rose from his stool and set down his Bible. "Let's have a prayer, shall we?" he said.

He raised his head to the turbulence above him and prayed, "Lord, be kind enough to us and remove that helicopter from here—in Jesus's name!" The second he finished, the helicopter drifted away and never returned. The place exploded with shouts of praise, backslapping, and all manner of dancing.

My dad was blown away. "That was God," he said to me as we walked out.

"Yeah," I replied. "That was God, Dad. This is what I've been telling you about."

"Yeah," he said, scratching his head, "but I don't know. They're not even using hymnbooks in there."

We'd still be at odds for a while, but my parents proved to be less close-minded than I thought they'd be. Yes, they were deeply suspicious. But they seemed to be willing to let me work through my "phase." They must have figured that if it wasn't God, I'd eventually figure that out, and it if was, they didn't want to oppose it.

✦ ✦ ✦ ✦ ✦

Despite the minor win with my parents, things heated up in the classroom. By this time, as many as 200 to 300 Biola students were regularly sneaking off to attend meetings or concerts at the tent in Costa Mesa. It appeared things were getting beyond the control of the school administration, so they decided to unleash the professors on us.

I remember that one of my professors, Dr. Kurtanic, a really lovely man of God, was greatly bothered by what we were learning at Calvary Chapel. I took his class on the Pastoral Epistles—First and Second Timothy and Titus—and really liked him as a teacher. Nonetheless, he expressed his displeasure any time the subject of Calvary Chapel or the Holy Spirit came up. You could see the veins in his neck pulsing. He was so worried for our salvation; it was simultaneously shocking and admirable. He passed away a few years later. I often remember him, with sadness. I don't know if he ever came to terms with what God was doing in those days.

Into the midst of these happenings came an upperclassman named Owen Chamberlain. He affectionately told us he was a "Kiwi"—meaning he was a New Zealander. I'm not sure how he ended up at Biola, because he was wholeheartedly a Holy Spirit guy. We knew he carried some spiritual authority, though, because one night when we were all studying late, we heard someone start screaming. We all ran to the source to find Owen praying for a guy and casting demons out of him.

Here was yet another incident to feed our questions.

A couple of weeks later, my roommate Dan and I sat studying at our junkyard cable-spool table when we heard a quiet knock on the door. When we answered it, Owen popped his head around the corner, gently dropped a piece of paper on the table between us, and half-whispered, "Here are some Scriptures the Lord wants you to have. I'll be back in a week to hear your response."

Then he turned and was gone.

Dan and I looked at each other with raised eyebrows and picked up the paper that would keep us up until daybreak. It listed five passages:

> *"All authority has been given to me in heaven and on earth."*
>
> —**MATTHEW 28:18**

> *"Which of you fathers, if your son asks for a fish, will give him a snake instead? Or if he asks for an egg, will give him a scorpion? If you then, though you are evil, know how to give good gifts to your children, how much more will your Father in heaven give the Holy Spirit to those who ask him!"*
>
> —**LUKE 11:11–13**

> [Before Jesus's ascension.] *And with that he breathed on them and said, "Receive the Holy Spirit."*
>
> —**JOHN 20:22**

> [After Jesus's ascension.] *When the day of Pentecost came, they were all together in one place. Suddenly a sound like the blowing of a violent wind came from heaven and filled the whole house where they were sitting. They saw what seemed to be tongues of fire that separated and came to rest on each of them. All of them were filled with the Holy Spirit and began to speak in other tongues as the Spirit enabled them.*
>
> —**ACTS 2:1–4**

> *But because of his great love for us, God, who is rich in mercy, made us alive with Christ even when we were dead in transgressions—it is by grace you have been saved. And God raised us up with Christ and seated us with him in the heavenly realms in Christ Jesus.*
>
> —**EPHESIANS 2:4–6**

As Dan and I read these over and over, debating ideas and raising questions, I realized I was tired of dillydallying around over all these questions. I had to do something. *I had to have my thirst quenched!*

So we went to the library and started digging through some of the older books. We'd heard that R.A. Torrey and D.L. Moody had been friends and written about what they called "the fullness of the Spirit." We also knew there was a collection of Torrey's books in the library, because every year Biola had a spiritual emphasis week called the "Torrey Memorial Bible Conference." We knew that if our professors were against all of this and Torrey was one of the guys who had been part of Biola's forerunner institution, the Bible Institute of Los Angeles, they would have to respect what he had to say on the subject. What if, by some crazy chance, Torrey was a Holy Spirit guy as well? We had to find out.

So we found a couple of his books, one of which was plainly titled *The Holy Spirit*. As we read it, we remarked that it sounded exactly like the teaching we'd been hearing at Calvary—and contrary to what our professors had been warning us about. Torrey even wrote about the baptism of the Holy Spirit, the second blessing, and all of that "aberrant theology" our professors had been bad-mouthing.

We started checking out everything we could find on the Holy Spirit. Although many of the books were in the darkest, deepest part of the library, we tracked them down, read them, and shared what we were finding with our curious schoolmates.

This resulted in a run on these clandestine titles, much to the chagrin of the librarian. She reported the curious interest in the archival section to the administration. In a matter of days—*Poof!*—all of those books disappeared. We heard that they were not only confiscated from the library, but banned from any more perusal by us instigators. We found ourselves deemed *personae non grata* in the old archival sections of the library. (One of my greater achievements in life, methinks.)

In the midst of this, the next week, as promised, "Kiwi" Owen returned to ask us about the five Scriptures he'd left for us to ponder. We fired questions at him:

"Is the Holy Spirit in us, around us, upon us?"

"Do you have the Holy Spirit once, twice, or more times?"

"Do you receive Him completely when you are saved, or is there a subsequent 'blessing' down the road?"

"How do you know you've received the 'fullness of the Spirit'?"

"Do you have to speak in tongues?"

On and on the questions went.

Owen looked at us and answered, "What is your heart telling you that you are missing from the Scriptures you read?"

I still couldn't answer. My head contradicted everything my heart was telling me. I was confused and terrified.

I had lists of Scriptures that supported both sides, and I couldn't determine which was right. I was still starved for more of Jesus and all that He said and did. I couldn't believe that the Jesus of today would be so radically different from the Jesus who walked with the apostles—that Jesus was not the same "yesterday and today and forever" as Hebrews 13:8 tells us. A refrain of the '70s was "If this is so wrong, why does it feel so right?" and though the context was far different for us, the argument seemed to fit. *If all of the things happening at Calvary Chapel were "of the devil," why was God getting all the glory? Why were miracles happening? Why did we feel so much closer to God there than we did in Biola's classrooms?*

My desire for more of Jesus and the Scriptures fed my hunger for more of the Holy Spirit. Why was that?

Desperate, we turned to one of the leaders at Calvary, Ken Gulliksen. (Ken later founded the Vineyard Movement before John Wimber came on the scene and became its leader.) Mindy and I decided to bring our Bibles to him and ask him to convince us of what was right. While he confirmed everything that our Kiwi friend had intimated regarding the work of the Holy Spirit, he wasn't going to tell us what to do or what was right.

"We're Baptist kids, and we're really struggling with what to believe," we told him. "We're getting all this stuff against the Holy Spirit at school, and then we come here and all we hear from you guys is completely opposite. What are we supposed to believe?"

"I can't convince you of anything," he told us. "Only the Spirit of God can. You have to seek Him and ask Him to show you what is true. He's the only one who can teach you about the fullness He has for you."

A lot of help that was! But we sensed that Ken had a point. It was a different theological methodology than our professors at Biola were taking, and that impressed us as well.

We were teetering on the edge. It wouldn't take much to push us over.

✦ ✦ ✦ ✦ ✦

I was snapping on my bow tie and snugging my cummerbund into place under my tuxedo—it was concert time and Mindy was waiting—when Dan burst into our room.

"You can't go to the concert!" he proclaimed. "You have to come to church with me. They are going to pray for the Holy Spirit during the afterglow."

I must've looked at him like the proverbial deer in headlights. *Tonight, of all nights?* I was immediately caught between my scholastic obligations and my spiritual hunger. I hadn't fully realized until that moment that I wanted my thirst slaked so much that I would have done anything.

However, the first words out of my mouth were, "Not possible. I can't! Afterglow or not, Mindy is waiting for me, and this is a required concert."

He looked at me pleadingly.

The next words out of my mouth were, "Okay, but I need to let Mindy know first."

I called her while changing back into my jeans. Though she protested, she also knew what was on the line for me. I told her I didn't care about the ding I would get to my grades; this was the opportunity I'd been waiting for. It was time to find out if the baptism in the Holy Spirit was real.

The prospect thrilled me and scared me spitless at the same time. On the drive to the tent meeting, anxiety rose in my throat. I could hardly swallow. When fear rose, however, Luke 7:13 would come to mind: *"If you then, though you are evil, know how to give good gifts to your children, how much more will your Father in heaven give the Holy Spirit to those who ask him!"*

I was antsy and restless throughout the service.

Then, as the afterglow started, a parade of bright-eyed, berobed hippies invited people to come forward: "If you would like to receive the Holy Spirit, we'll pray for you." Dan and I got into line without hesitating. I was shaking in my shoes.

One of the big questions we'd discussed with Owen was, "How do you know you've received the baptism of the Holy Spirit?" Owen had told us we would know, but it was also common for one of the gifts to manifest when we received Him, the most common being speaking in tongues. As Dan was prayed for, he nearly burst his jugular trying to speak in tongues. To no avail. When Dan stepped away and the same group reached to lay hands on me, I noticed Dan looking on with jaundiced eyes, probably hoping I wouldn't get something he hadn't.

I couldn't have cared less about tongues. I was just trying to get my spiritual thirst satisfied. But as soon as they laid hands on me—*Bam!* A warm something—like an invisible oil—poured over head and oozed down my body to my toes. A rumble rose in my belly. Within seconds I was laughing uncontrollably, weak-kneed and loud! (This was all before the "holy laughter" phenomenon of the 1990s.)

They had to sit me in a chair while they prayed for others. For the next thirty minutes or so, I chortled, guffawed, and cackled uncontrollably. Dan sat there looking forlorn and neglected. (For the record, he did receive the Holy Spirit that night and spoke in tongues at a later date.)

The change after that was unquestionable. I had a new freedom.

Over the years, as I've mentioned before, a litany of destructive seeds had grown into a garden of "false truths" in my spirit. I was outwardly cheery and inwardly a broken young man when I had arrived in San Francisco in 1970. The enemy had dug his claws into an innocent heart. Thus, despite being born again, I was still deeply distressed and doubtful of myself. Deep depressions would sink in repeatedly for the next couple of decades as circumstances continually made me question my worth.

I walked into the tent that night to see if, maybe, God might bring me closer by filling me with His Spirit. When I rose from my chair, after being all but knocked flat by holy laughter, I was not the same person. Everything God does is redemptive!

The depression I'd acquired as a boy took a serious hit that night. True joy was in my spirit for the first time. While being born again in that leaky cabin on the Japanese coast had filled me with peace and begun the reconciliation process with my parents, being filled with the Spirit was an eclipse of the spiritual darkness I had grown up with.

A whole new world of spiritual possibilities opened to me that night, as I was filled with the Holy Spirit.

I was now officially a full-fledged inductee into the Jesus Movement.

UNVEILING YOUR FUTURE

Nurturing one's soul and finding one's identity—figuring out who you are—is the work of many years, though most of us would like to be able to figure it out in a weekend seminar. Answering the questions "Who am I?" and "Why am I here?" is still the deepest, most universal, and most human of quests. It transcends nationality, ethnicity, and culture. It's also difficult, because most of the work of forming our identities is unconscious. Growing up is a process of becoming more aware both of ourselves and the fabric of the world around us. Many of us tend to think of life as three phases: childhood, adolescence, and adulthood. But maturing as an adult is a much more complex process than turning eighteen and suddenly being responsible to make life decisions for yourself.

This is why five of Robert Clinton's six stages take place during adulthood, and those are about finding and cultivating our identity as unique individuals with unique destinies in Christ. It begins with a journey into the inner worlds of our hearts and minds. Then we pursue a career, whether in a church, a nonprofit, the halls of government, or business. We are created to impact our worlds, but that impact is rooted in knowing who we are in Christ and what our Gospel Identity is in relationship to the Godhead (knowing who each member of the Trinity is, what He has done, who that makes us, and what that means we should do).*

These stages are not always distinct. They overlap quite a bit as we wrestle with the questions of one stage, then the next, and then

* These four questions, multiplied by the three persons of the Trinity, create a twelve-box grid that identifies our Gospel Identity. (I have included a chart summarizing this on page 289.) For further reading, I recommend Jeff Vanderstelt's excellent book *Saturate: Being Disciples of Jesus in the Everyday Stuff of Life* (Wheaton, IL: Crossway, 2015), as well as my first book, *Unravelled: Reform the Church, Transform the Culture* (Castle Rock, CO: CityForce Media, Inc., 2018).

circle back to the questions of the previous stage. For me, I was answering the conflicts of the Inner-Life Growth phase while also seeing my Sovereign Foundations redeemed.

The Inner-Life Growth stage is a "light on the shadows" time in our spiritual development. No matter what you and I were deprived of, experienced, vowed, or cursed with in our formative years, our Father is always waiting for the invitation to "clean house." I have watched too many of God's people hide behind their pride and refuse to let their hearts be exposed. The longer one waits to "come clean," the more entrenched the pride becomes, resulting in deception, arrogance, and devastation in God's family. He is waiting for an invitation to come in and clean *His* house, after all!

It's better that we let Him do this work than try to do it ourselves.

While I wrestled through the Inner-Life Growth phase, I didn't realize I would soon be launching into my Ministry (or Career) Maturing phase—seeing how my gifts and talents and other inner strengths directed the work of my hands to touch the world around me. However, that didn't mean that the inner workings of my soul and spirit were completed. It just meant I was coupling inner-searching mode with doing mode.

At Biola, most of my work was inner and intellectual, but I would soon be focusing on figuring out what I should be *doing* in my life—trying to determine what my *vocation* should be, what I had been called to. The Inner-Life Growth phase is about the image of Jesus being developed within us, uniquely connected to who we are. The Ministry (or Work) Maturing phase is about projecting that image into the world. It's an apprenticeship phase, even though our title may be that of the leader (pastor, founder, president, etc.).

Resolving my personal crisis of the Holy Spirit's role in my life created room for larger questions and challenges. Being a freshly christened charismatic who still had a Baptist soul (and not wanting to turn my back on either group), I needed to find one unifying principle that would emerge over the next few years: For me it was the centrality of loving Jesus. If I had that, I knew the rest could be worked out.

I say all of this from the clear perspective of hindsight. None of it was that well-articulated at the time. I was stumbling over many things, just trying to at least fall flat on my face in the same direction each time so I could be sure of making some forward progress. I wanted to feel like I was figuring out why God put me on the earth. But I was still a long way from answering this question.

I did know that I was equipped with something, and that *"with God all things are possible"* (Matthew 19:26). It was time to start putting what I knew into practice.

PART TWO:

BECOMING JESUS-CENTRIC

THE HOLY SPIRIT UNDERGROUND

Coming back from winter break in January of 1972, I entered the second half of my sophomore year, and my twenties. I was on fire for God like never before. My attitude toward my classes also transformed. God's Word started to come alive for me, even in Biola's "dry bones" Bible classes. I now had a new teacher (the Holy Spirit), and the head knowledge I was getting in the classroom began to sprout into completely new and marvelous things in my spirit. All I wanted to do with my life was teach and preach (even though my tongue was still seriously tied). At the end of my sophomore year, I switched from music to going whole hog as a Bible major.

Though the applications of Scripture I was getting were still in the old wineskin of mainline denominationalism and taught from my professors' closed mindsets, the structure and discipline of working through all of the Bible and digging into each Scripture's meaning was an opportunity I took advantage of. Why wouldn't I learn about the history and settings of the Pentateuch and dig into the poets and warnings of the Old Testament prophets? I loved studying the New Testament, specifically the Gospels and the letters to the various churches (the epistles) by Paul, Peter, John,

James, Jude, and whoever wrote Hebrews. Not only that, but the library was a gold mine of supplemental materials we would never cover in class. Why not learn Greek? Why not take advantage of all available tools?

My outlook had changed. Now convinced of the truth and value of being baptized in the Spirit, I no longer needed to be combative. There was nothing to decide. I knew the validity of what I had experienced. I didn't need to fight with anyone to prove it. My professors could blab whatever they wanted; I knew they understood only part of the whole. I realized it was they who were questioning it, not me. (I would learn humility later.)

I went hard after the Scriptures, and I went hard after the Lord with Dan, Mindy, Owen, and a new friend, Jon Courson. The latter and I used to ditch class to seek the Lord together in the campus chapel. Dan and I spent hours in our room, around our cable-spool table, worshiping the Lord, talking Scripture, and sharing our hearts. It was a precious time. I'm still in contact with many of those people today.

After Mindy graduated in 1973, we got married (on June 23, 1973, to be exact). I'd had various part-time jobs during my years at school, starting with the gardener position I had at the retirement home. That second semester of my junior year, I was working at Alpha Beta grocers in the warehouse, stocking shelves and preparing deliveries to the individual stores. I worked the graveyard shift. About three weeks before the wedding, I felt the Lord asking me to quit the grocery store and trust Him for a job more compatible with the rhythms of new married life.

As you can imagine, that looked foolish to my parents, and my future in-laws. I was instantly barraged by calls from my father, father-in-law, and two close friends, chastising me about my decision: "You know you need to provide for your new bride, don't you?" Although they made a fine "traditional" argument, it was enough for Mindy and me that we agreed about what the Lord seemed to be leading us to do. On the day we returned from our honeymoon in Carmel, I was perusing Biola's job board when I noticed a posting for a local painter at a school district. "Experience necessary," it stated. I had zero. But I felt a nudge in my spirit, so I went in for an interview with the head of human resources, a Mr. Green.

He asked, "Have you painted before? Do you know how to use a brush, a roller, a spray gun? Anything?"

"Negatory," was all I could squeak out. After a few more unhelpful questions, long silences, and a series of confused expressions on his face, bewildered Mr. Green ended the interview with, "Okay, you're hired." I think he shocked himself!

It was totally the Lord! For the next twenty-five years, painting was the trade God gave me to make a living whenever we moved into a new location or I found myself between assignments. I spent the next year finishing my studies as a Bible major and learning the ropes of being a painter and a husband. Mindy took a teaching position at a small Christian school in the area.

Upon graduation at the end of that year, Mindy and I were invited to be "Deans of Counselors" at a camp in New Mexico for Native American children. We packed our things and ventured out into "life."

Once moved in, I was informed that I was to teach Bible studies on weeknights to the staff counselors. Because I was a graduate of a prominent theological institution, armed with teaching notes from my classes, the assignment made sense. There was one small difficulty: my still tied-up tongue. Despite all that I had learned and the deliverance I had experienced when filled with the Spirit, I still couldn't speak in front of others. (Later, I learned the condition is known as "selective mutism.") This "anointed" Bible teacher couldn't get a word out of his mouth while standing in front of a group.

I was in a new fix.

It was so bad that I graduated Biola three credits (three *speech* credits) short of my degree. (Yeah, I walked with the rest of my class, in my black robe, but received only an empty diploma case, a handshake, and a notice that I owed nine dollars in library fines.) I kept deferring those three credits, until I'd deferred them beyond graduation. They told me I'd need to finish those credits before I would get my degree. (I never did.)

I tried to take a speech class at the University of New Mexico in Gallup when we first arrived. The final blow was when I lost all the notes for a paper halfway through the class. I'd set them on the top of the car and promptly forgot about them. By the time I'd remembered, they'd been spread to the four winds. So I dropped out. As you can imagine, that brought my childhood discouragement and self-doubts back with a passion. The sense of rejection and failure started feeding the orphan spirit I'd grown up with, and I fell back into bouts of depression.

The only audience I felt comfortable with were the rocks and cacti I found while riding one of the ranch horses. All of this transpired in the first month in New Mexico.

God had a plan, however, as He always does. I think He let Mindy in on it before He informed me. (Something He did a lot back in those days.) In early August, I was caught between the proverbial rock and a hard place. I'd been assigned to teach a Bible study—something I wanted to do with all my heart, but I was unable to eke out even a few words. Mindy suggested, under the blaze of a New Mexico sunset, that we should "go to a meeting in Gallup tonight."

The meeting turned out to be a gathering of the Full Gospel Businessmen's Association. When we arrived, I was in a bad mood, stewing over my predicament and resentful of getting dragged out of the house. I just wanted to be left alone. [Note: When seeking to remain anonymous, never wear a red shirt.] I plopped myself down in the last row, ducking behind a rather large person to shield me from the front of the room.

The speaker was a Messianic or "completed" Jew whose topic was "Jesus in the Old Testament." He was eloquent, and his perspective on the topic was exquisite. He was showing how symbolism in the Old Testament, down to the almond blossom cups on the lampstands in the Tabernacle, all pointed to Jesus. I was just drifting out of my funk and into what he was saying, thinking, *Wow, I wish I could do that,* when he suddenly stopped and started looking around the room. His prophetic eyes zoomed in on me and he announced, "Young man—you, hiding way in the back, in the red shirt—please come forward."

I looked around hopefully, but there was no one else in a red shirt. *Groan.*

I stood and began walking to the front, my eyes fixed on the floor. When I was halfway down the aisle, he pointed at my chest, and yelled, "Open your mouth wide and I will fill it! Now, therefore, go and I will be with your mouth and teach you what to say. Take no thought, for in that hour, it shall be given to you what you should speak."

My only thought was, *Exodus and the Gospels in one breath?* Then my knees began to quake. I felt my whole body go wobbly.

"Furthermore," he continued, "there has been a curse on your mouth, and it is broken tonight! God is sending you as a witness to the nations, and your family won't be happy at first." Then he quoted Psalm 126:1–3: *"When the LORD restored the fortunes of Zion our mouths were filled with laughter and tongues with songs of joy, then it was said amongst the nations (and our families), The LORD has done great things for them....*" He prophesied that the displeasure of our families in our going to the nations would be followed by the recognition of what great things God had done for us.

My heart panicked. *I don't want to go to the nations! I've been to the nations! I have no desire to return to my missionary-kid roots. This guy has no idea what he's talking about!*

I was about to learn, however, that he did—and in some significant ways. I returned to my Bible studies with the camp counselors, my tongue no longer tied and my mouth free. My sole audience was no longer the cacti of the New Mexico high desert. I could unload my copious study notes onto the poor, bewildered camp counselors of Summer Park Ranch. When I held my first Bible study after the "miracle," you'd never guess I ever struggled to speak in front of others.

And if that part of what he said was true, what about the missionary stuff? I just stowed it away in the back of my brain and refused to consider it further.

The director of the camp was on the board of the local Baptist church ("local" is relative in New Mexico—it was about twenty-five miles away). He told the other board members that he had a young Bible school graduate on staff, someone who was great with the young counselors. They asked me to be their volunteer youth pastor. Eager for any opportunity to exercise my teaching gifts, I accepted. I have fond memories of our time teaching at the ranch and to that small youth group. To make things even sweeter, that winter, our first daughter, Amy Elizabeth, was born.

During the handful of months we were there, I unloaded my heart and what I knew about pursuing God at both the camp and as youth pastor. It was a wonderful time. Knowing that the camp and church leadership's doctrine was closer to what I'd grown up with (as opposed to what I heard at Calvary Chapel), I stuck to my Biola notes, though they didn't help much.

Adjoining the ranch was an authentic trading post that had been operating since the 1800s. The Vanderwagen Trading Post sat on the reservation line between the Navajos and the Zuni tribes and was run by Ernie Vanderwagen and his wife, Esther. They were lovely believers who talked openly about the Holy Spirit. They were some of the coolest people we've ever met, in love with the Native Americans and fluent in both Zuni and Navajo, which endeared them to the leaders of both tribes. Mostly they traded groceries, household goods, and other items for silver and turquoise jewelry or other things the Native Americans made. It seemed like something out of the Old West.

We would hang out with them in their huge home with its massive fireplace, spending time with God and feeding our hunger for Him. I still hungered to find who I was in Christ. During our last two years at Biola, "Kiwi Owen" gave us several Scriptures about being rooted and founded in Christ. As we fellowshipped with Ernie and Esther, all those verses began to make sense to me as we saw them walk them out in their lives.

Another neighbor, on the opposite side of the trading post, was Bluebird the witch doctor. He would leave lovely presents on our doorstep to remind us of his love for us: headless chickens and one time, a castrated goat. At other times, tails and reproductive parts were found to be missing from our camp horses. Demonic opposition is always a good reminder of the unseen battle raging around us.

The spiritual resistance continued. Early one January morning, while Mindy and Amy were bundled under a mountain of blankets in our cold little mountain cabin, I trudged out for my morning ritual of milking the camp cow. It was so cold that I had to break the ice on the top of the troughs with an ax so the cows and horses could drink. The camp director was waiting for me that day in the frigid milking barn. Without preamble, he gave me an ultimatum: "We and the board love you and Mindy and your teaching, but you have to stop fellowshipping with the *charismatics* at the Vanderwagen Trading Post." He said *charismatics* like it gave his mouth a sour taste.

I was floored. "What?"

Apparently, Ernie and Esther had caused a brouhaha in the little Baptist Church where I was youth pastor. Prior to our arrival, the former pastor was baptized in the Spirit and Ernie went on the warpath against him. He skipped the Sunday evening service to stay home, study the Scriptures, and prove his pastor had misinterpreted the Bible. He pulled out a long sheet of butcher paper and listed the Scriptures in "pro" and "con" columns, doing his best to contradict the pastor's new pro "baptism in the Holy Spirit" stance. By the end of his scholastic exertions, ol' Ernie, in a puddle of tears, slumped on the floor and asked the Father for the Holy Spirit He had promised His children, just as his pastor had. Ernie was honored to be the next derriere out the door of the Baptist church—just behind the pastor himself.

This ex-pastor and his wife often fellowshipped with us at the trading post. Somehow, someone had discovered this surreptitious gathering, and all heck broke loose. I later found out the camp director had been in on the decision to fire this pastor and instruct Ernie to leave the premises.

Now, emboldened by his past eviction experience, the camp director fired a salvo at me: "You have until May to comply. If you don't, we'll find someone else for your position." Then he spun on his heels and walked away. He'd done his job; the rest was up to me. Get "right" or get lost.

We got the same response the next Sunday when we showed up at the Baptist church. The elders were all lined up on the doorstep as we walked up. When they saw us, they pulled us aside and ushered us downstairs. Once we were in a private space, they lowered the boom: "We love you, the kids love you, you've been great—but we just can't have you hanging out with *those* people."

Fortunately—or unfortunately, perhaps—I'd already considered the ultimatum. While I initially received it with no pushback, I had questions this time. "I'd like more clarity on what exactly you are asking us to do," I queried. "You're asking me not to fellowship with God's people. Is that really what you're asking?"

One of the elders shook his head. "We wouldn't do that."

"But it sounds like that's what you're saying."

"No, no," another cut in, "we're asking you to stay away from people whose teachings are harmful."

"What's harmful about what they believe? They're some of the loveliest, God-loving people I've ever met."

"Well," another tried to explain, "it's just not the way we believe."

"Are you saying that these people are evil? That they aren't Christians? That they don't love and honor Jesus? They're not brothers and sisters in Christ?"

More hemming and hawing. "No, no, we're not making accusations," another said. "That's not for us to judge. We just feel what they are teaching about the Holy Spirit is in error."

"So it's not about their allegiance to Jesus. It's just that they don't believe like you believe? Are you saying those whom we choose to fellowship with must be based on what you all believe, not around Jesus?"

They glanced at one another. "Look," one of them finally said, "we just can't have you teaching our youth if you're hanging out with people who believe differently."

I was young, not even twenty-three, and a bit brash. "We can't do that," I told them flatly. "We're gonna meet with you guys; we'll meet with the other people. You are our brothers and sisters, and you have a difference of opinion theologically. But those people are our brothers and sisters too. We have Jesus in common, right? Isn't that what it's all about? What's the problem?"

The head elder had heard enough: "Okay, if that's the way you feel, then we need you to step down as youth pastor. You can attend the church, but you can't do anything else. You're not allowed to preach. You can't teach, and don't pursue the kids." The meeting was over, and they filed out. We returned to the campground.

Soon after, I informed the director that we'd be leaving in May.

The camp was under a mission organization in Flagstaff, Arizona. They sent their director to talk us out of our decision. "What can I do to convince you not to hang out with these people—and for you to stay on with us?" he asked.

"Nothing," I answered. "You're making it an issue of fellowship around doctrine and not around Jesus. I can't do that. Many people believe differently than Baptists do—and differently than I do, for that matter—but they all love Jesus. I can't break fellowship with them because they believe differently. How will we learn what's true if we don't hammer out disagreements together? The Bible teaches unity is in Jesus being Lord and Savior, raised from the dead to the right hand of the Father. We know doctrinal understanding is going to differ. We're going to stick with Jesus."

He didn't like that much. He got huffy and soon left for the train station.

Soon, Mindy's Baptist mom, who had been visiting at the time, heard that we had been asked to leave the camp. She disappeared unannounced into her room, gathered her things, and headed for the door.

Confused, Mindy asked her where she was going.

"I'm embarrassed and ashamed by what you've done to these good people," she stammered.

Mindy was in shock as her mother continued, "Our friends on the mission board got you this assignment in the first place, and this is how you repay us?"

She felt that we were breaking our word and running out on the job. We told her we were sorry, but we couldn't, in good conscience, comply with their ultimatum. After much cajoling, tears, and hot chocolate, she agreed to stay a little longer. (I think it was really that Amy was just too cute for her to break away.)

Come May, we'd loaded my father-in-law's Dodge pickup and our trusty, cherry-red Corolla with all of our earthly possessions. We were ready to go—kind of.

We said our goodbyes civilly and headed south to Gallup. When we came to the last stop sign in town, at the junction of Route 66, Mindy pulled the Corolla up beside me so we could pray. "Which way?" we asked the Lord.

We had nowhere to go. We had no plan, no job waiting somewhere, and no prospects. We stood at a literal crossroads, unsure what to do. So we prayed, "Which way, Lord? East or west?"

I felt a heavenly nudge. "West?" I asked Mindy.

She nodded. "West."

I turned left, she followed, and we headed toward the sunset.

UNVEILING YOUR FUTURE

That move to New Mexico was the dawn of a phase of leadership development that focused on our ministry calling and development. Clinton's Ministry Maturing phase is often the longest one. For me, it took place in three distinct sub-stages that spanned twenty years. (Our time in Gallup was the first part of the early stage.)

The beginning of this phase is marked by the revealing of new tasks, new gifts, new thinking, and new relationships. It is designed by God to make us depend on Him by breaking the power of unsanctified idealism and belief systems inherited through the effects of the indescribable pain often experienced during our Sovereign Foundations. Once cleansed, that idealism morphs into dreams that lie in our spirits, ready to embark on the lifelong journey of fulfillment. The healing of my selective mutism was not only a miracle, but also God's way of proving His faithfulness to me in the face of an impossible situation and an enemy stronghold. His deliverance released me into being the gift to His people I was meant to be. It solidified in my heart that He was truly with me.

I was learning I was nothing without Him.

Some people don't experience great pain in their formative years. Many have been raised in good homes where life is free of significant trauma and pain. Being "good boys and girls" has a direct effect on one's hunger for God. It often exposes a need for deliverance from religion and "being good" for its own sake—something that can distract one from being hungry for God because it breeds complacency. Goodness in the developmental years (without becoming familiar with the Spirit's work) often inoculates disciples against the need for a passion for God. Those who fall into this pattern often have unique wake-up calls. As I've already mentioned, you can't escape the unrelenting pursuit of God's love.

It's worth noting that not only those in "ministry" work—joining a church staff, working for a faith-based nonprofit, counseling at a Christian camp, or going to the mission field—experience this phase of leadership growth. You can also think of it as "Career Maturing." Those who launch positions in business or government should also be answering God's calling in their hearts. And if they are open to God's direction, they will face the same challenges, setbacks, and trials meant to develop them. Business and government need men and women with fierce determination to "do good," just as those answering the call to traditional ministry. The true purpose of business is far beyond making money, and the work of government is fundamentally flawed if it is used primarily to garner power. While Christians in such spheres may not talk about God and His callings and giftings with the same openness, God is no less in those places than He is in churches.

It makes no sense that the only true Christian calling is traditional ministry, while the desire to do anything else is just to make money to give to traditional ministry. We need people dedicated to serve as Jesus served in all arenas of life: arts and entertainment, business, education, family, government, media, *and* religion. All of these need the influence of good men and women, or they will fall into corruption and exploitation.

Thus, the same stages exist for all called to be a good influence in the world. Though the challenges, setbacks, and trials may differ, they are similar in purpose. God uses them to push us toward our callings and His will for our lives. Stepping into these other arenas also reveals our giftings and talents, and they should be considered no less prayerfully in secular work spheres than in traditional ministry.

MEETING THE PIRATE

On the trip west, I heard from the Verdugo Hills Nursing Home that Mr. Calaveras, the Greek man who had told me he would pray for me the rest of his life, was in poor health and wanted to see me. We drove straight there.

Upon entering his room, I saw my fragile, leathery friend, barely able to breathe. He waggled his finger for me to come closer and said in a raspy whisper, "I have not ceased to pray for you since the day I made the promise. Go and be a mighty man for God!"

I was cut to the heart and promised him that I would. A week later he'd passed away. I'd lost a friend but carried the impartation of destiny and commitment to prayer that he'd sown into my spirit through all his years of faith-filled prayers. I've never forgotten his example.

Now back in Los Angeles for a couple of weeks, we asked around about reconnecting with any of the crew from our Biola days. My class-skipping fellow Jesus seeker, Jon Courson, was still in the area and had heard of our demise in New Mexico. He was now a teacher at Calvary Chapel's School of Ministry, so he invited me to interview to fill a vacancy on the teaching team. The vacancy was created by John Wimber, who would become a well-known name in the Association of Vineyard Churches. John had been pastoring and teaching in the Calvary network since I'd graduated from Biola and was leaving the teaching team at Lake Arrowhead to plant a Calvary Chapel in Yorba Linda, California.

I was so excited at this prospect that I applied immediately. When I was granted an interview, I jumped into our red Corolla and headed to Lake Arrowhead. The interview went so well that I returned to Los Angeles convinced that I would be invited to join their teaching team, a dream come true. A second interview was scheduled for a week later.

I hit the road for Lake Arrowhead again, but I never got there. The Corolla's aluminum engine block exploded in the 110-degree heat of Riverside, California. It was dead—never to rise again. I found myself stranded on the side of the road. As I bailed out of the smoky car to avoid the fire erupting from under the hood, I questioned how such a thing could happen on the way to my destiny. Then I heard a whisper, *"Whose idea was this anyway?"*

Uh-oh! I recognized that voice.

In my excitement over the teaching job, I'd made one small omission. I'd forgotten to check in with my heavenly Father about what He wanted for me. It just seemed so right, so consistent with my dream, that I'd assumed the opportunity was from God. Apparently, it wasn't. I lost my car and my new dream at the same time.

I had no clue what to do next.

God did.

Mindy, Amy, and I piled into my father-in-law's Dodge pickup and headed north to San Jose to visit Mindy's family. When we arrived, I learned they'd arranged an invitation for us to take on an unpaid role as college pastor at their church, Calvary Baptist, Los Gatos. I spent the next year painting and getting my ministry fix by teaching and nurturing college kids. It was a fun and fruitful year.

But I should have known that any position with my old tribe wasn't going to last forever. In May of that year (1977), I got a surprise call to the pastor's office. I was even more surprised to see the associate pastor (whom I reported to) there as well. After some small talk, the pastor launched into the reason for the meeting. It was a familiar refrain: "We love your teaching, and the kids are growing in the Lord, but this Holy Spirit perspective . . ." I didn't hear another word after that.

How did I mess up this time? I wondered.

It turned out that while working through the book of Ephesians, I had exposited that we were to be "continually filled with the Holy Spirit." (It says it right there in the text.) I hadn't thought much of it; there were other Scriptures in Ephesians 5 that I wanted to emphasize more, so I breezed by it. I didn't even remember commenting on it. Before doing the class, I'd reviewed my notes with the associate pastor. He had run it through his Baptist theological filter and approved it. It also matched the Campus Crusade booklet on the text, so I'd gotten it from an approved source. Now, sitting with that same associate pastor, under the stink eye of the senior pastor, the associate pastor fervently denied ever giving me approval for "anything of the kind."

I felt set up.

The result: I was out, *again.* I felt betrayed and victimized by yet more narrow-mindedness. This was my third firing in two years. Unlike the Grinch's heart, which had grown three sizes when he decided to give back Christmas, I felt mine begin to shrink.

God didn't leave me in the lurch for long, however. Jon Courson had recently left the training center in Arrowhead and was going to plant a church with his brother in nearby San Jose. He called me out of the blue and invited me to join them in starting the church. (We wouldn't even have to move!)

It was a call to work in a church that wasn't going to kick me out for talking about the Holy Spirit. "Hallelujah!" I cried. "Spiritual freedom at last!"

Then came that whisper again: *"Why should I bless this new endeavor when you haven't forgiven My people in the last three places you've been?"*

Ouch! So I went to prayer. I forgave the camp director, every member of the church board of the Baptist church in Gallup, the senior pastor who'd just dismissed me (I can't really call it a firing, I guess, since I wasn't paid staff), and then the associate pastor who had just turned his back on me. (I came to call this "blessing backwards"—a principle that has been embedded in my heart and mind ever since.)

Jon and his brother Ben's (not his real name) church was called South Valley Chapel in the Santa Teresa area of San Jose. We set up shop and went to work. We started praying and seeking the Lord together as we had in our college days. They couldn't pay me, but I was used to that. My painting business was supporting us just fine. Salary wasn't a concern.

Jon was a fantastic teacher, and his brother was a bigger-than-life personality and a gatherer. After about nine months, Jon's teaching was so popular that the church had grown significantly. Cassette tapes of his teachings were being shared throughout the area. It was an exciting time, and I felt like I was finding my groove—finally doing what I was supposed to be doing with my life.

One day that fall, I was eating breakfast with some "bros" from South Valley, having a discussion on hearing and responding to God's voice. I was confessing my fear of sharing my faith, and I pledged that I would commit to obeying the Lord's voice in witnessing from that moment onward. They agreed wholeheartedly.

I thought I was being inspirational. Instead, I realized I had just drawn a spiritual line in the sand, and God was about to call me on it.

No sooner had we agreed to be bold witnesses for Jesus than the door opened, and the most despicable human being I'd ever seen walked into the restaurant. As I looked critically at his bruised and bleeding face (he'd been in a fight the night before), tattered clothes, wobbly demeanor, and flea-infested dreadlocks, the Lord seemed to be raising a divine eyebrow and offering me an opportunity to make good on my new commitment. I said to my boothmates, "Hey guys, I think I'm supposed to go talk to that guy. Who wants to go with me?"

Suddenly nothing in the world seemed to be as interesting as the eggs and pancakes on their plates. They wouldn't even look up at me.

Okay, I thought, *so much for bold commitments to witness for Jesus—wimps!* Of course, I didn't know what to do either. I needed to take it one step at a time.

I rose and ambled reluctantly from my brethren and toward the battered human sitting in a booth on the other side of the restaurant. I was praying the whole time: *Is this really You, Lord? This guy? Are You sure?*

The smell hit me before I could say, "Hey, can I join you?" Drunk, drugged, and barely conscious, he waved his hand for me to sit down.

He didn't introduce himself. Instead he said, "Are you one of those Jesus freaks?"

I must have blanched. "Guilty!" I responded.

"Then get your butt up and go back to your friends!" he barked.

"I can't do that. Jesus told me to come over here and talk to you."

He laughed unpleasantly. "Okay then, I guarantee that I'll make you see he was a fraud by the time we are done here."

I froze, speechless. I couldn't even blink.

He shrugged with a knowing grin and started looking over the menu.

His breakfast ordered, we began to talk. I found it fascinating that the longer we talked, the more sober he seemed to become.

By then, the guilt of abandoning me had landed on one of my breakfast buddies. He slunk over to sit with us. He didn't join in the conversation, though. He sat silently—white as a sheet and probably scared spitless. Or at least that's how I felt.

After his initial salvo, the man introduced himself. He informed me he was Porky the Pirate. "Yep," he said, "come out to my rig and I'll show you who I really am."

Reluctantly, my very pale friend and I went outside to a truck and trailer rig that looked like it had been on the set of *Grapes of Wrath*. I half expected Henry Fonda to climb out of the cab. It was laden with beer cans, road signs, and camping gear. It looked like a rolling garbage dump.

Porky proudly opened the trailer door to reveal walls plastered with pornography. "Come on in," he said with a sneer. I noticed that he had been limping badly and wondered if he was hurt. Seeing my gaze, he lifted his pants leg to reveal a homemade prosthetic leg.

"Like me leg?" he queried.

"Where'd you get that?" I asked.

"After I dropped out of my university professorship," he informed us, "my 'friends' invited me to a race track late at night. They pinned me to the ground and rolled over my leg with a steam roller." He said it as if he were bragging. I was sure he had concocted this story. (I later discovered there were numerous renditions of how Porky lost his leg, including a wall falling on it during an earthquake.)

"This beautiful leg is the gas spout of a high-performance race car. This here cap opens so I can put in my favorite drink." He reached into his shirt, pulled out a tube, and took a long draw from it. It apparently ran under his clothes down to the tank. "Today's flavor is *vodka*. Want some?" He held out the end of the tube for me to take a suck. Evidently, for Porky every hour was happy hour.

I instinctively turned to my silent friend to see how he was faring. Not well. He was gone.

Realizing I was alone with this madman, I suddenly felt God's presence descend on me like a warm blanket. As I stood staring Porky in the face, I knew I was in the center of God's protection. I could almost hear angels' wings.

Porky was now trying his shamanic best to read my aura, tell me my future and my fears. He wanted to convince me Jesus was a fabrication of religious brainwashing.

"You were rejected as a child and felt alone, so you turned to Jesus—a total sham!" he pronounced.

Although I had felt rejected and alone as a child, I couldn't give him the satisfaction of agreeing with him. "Your discernment on my past is no commentary on the truth of my present identity. I'm not lonely, because He is always with me."

He grunted in disbelief. "Jesus was a good man and he's dead."

I didn't respond.

After several more failed attempts to shake my faith, he said boldly, "I know what will change your mind!" He reached into a small closet inside the camper and produced a double-barrel shotgun. He cocked it and pointed it at my temple.

The gun wavered; I wasn't sure if he'd take off my head or my foot if he pulled the trigger. I soon realized that my concerns should be elsewhere—I should be paralyzed with fear that I was about to die—but for some reason I felt the "peace that passes understanding" instead.

"If you say another godd**n word about Jesus, I'll blow your brains out," he warned.

I looked him in the eye. "That's just not possible. Furthermore, if you pull the trigger, you will be painting a bull's-eye on your life, and God will never stop pursuing you to convince you of His love." My voice was so steady and confident, it surprised me.

He seemed to consider this. "Okay," he said, changing tactics, "I'm going to tell you a riddle. If you get the answer to the riddle wrong, I'll pull the trigger."

He began the story of his ex-wife's betrayal—adding as much graphic detail as he could. After sharing too much information, he paused, as if coming to a conclusion. "So," he offered, letting the word hang in the air, "who was right? My wife, *or me?*"

I sensed the trap. Both options were wrong. All that came to mind was *Help, Lord! Help!*

Then I heard myself speak. "Porky," I said, noting that his swagger was evaporating, "which is better: to be right or to forgive?"

A long silence followed. Finally, he dropped the shotgun. Quietly he said, "I can't get you, can I?"

I laughed nervously. "You got me way back at 'I'll pull the trigger if you don't stop talking about Jesus.'"

He laughed nervously.

"It seems, though," I went on, "the Lord is pursuing you despite your spiritualistic, atheistic beliefs and inner pain."

He sat on the running board of his truck. His head fell into his hands, and he began muttering to himself, "I don't know why I can't get you. I need some time to think."

After a moment, he turned and reached into his closet again: He produced something much less threatening this time, a large poster. As he unfurled it, I could see it was none other than Porky the Pirate wearing a Viking helmet with horns, clutching a cat-o'-nine-tails in one hand and a sword in the other as he hoisted his fake leg. There was a terrifying snarl on his face. I'm pretty sure he was saying, "Arrrrghhh!"

Then he dropped back to his seat, wrote something on the poster, and handed it to me.

It read, "To Jon, the first real Christian I've ever met. Your God is real!"

"Okay," he said, as if in surrender. "We need to talk again—but not now. When I am ready."

I nodded and gave him my phone number. He climbed into his truck and drove off. I wondered if I would ever see him again.

The next day, a "junkyard" rig broke down on the side of Highway 101 in San Jose. A car pulled up and the driver asked, "Do you need some help?"

The stranded man caustically informed the Good Samaritan that he was a mechanic and didn't need anyone's f***ing help.

"Okay," the man in the car said, "but what are you going to do about Jesus?"

"F**k!" Porky screamed. "Another Jesus freak!" But instead of resorting to more violence, he wilted. Falling to his knees on the hot California pavement, Porky the Pirate surrendered his life to Jesus.

That night, in one of our weekly services, I discovered that the man on the freeway was none other than our associate pastor, Ben. Then he came to the pulpit and told the story. Neither he nor I knew even half of each other's story until he began to share his encounter with Porky with the congregation. When he finished, I stood up and told the story from the beginning. The place went nuts!

UNVEILING YOUR FUTURE

In hindsight, I realized that the Lord used this seminal experience as a prophetic signpost, underscoring His plans for my life, which would parallel His intent for the church of that day. We wanted to reach the lost, but we couldn't accommodate the likes of Porky the Pirate in our current congregational cultures. People like that wouldn't fit in, even with the hippies. Yet it was obvious that God was inviting His unsanitized creation to His redemptive banquet table. Jesus is the only answer for God's fractured creation, and He was reintroducing His Church to the one who leaves the ninety-nine to find the one lost sheep on the precipice of the cliff—or, as I'd just experienced, in a roadside California restaurant.

At twenty-four, God was laying some principles into me that would be foundational to my future. One was that devotion to Jesus as the Son of God (not a set of doctrines) was the prerequisite for fellowship and membership in God's family. Another was that churches needed to be open to all types, the rough as well as the refined. There was no "clean yourself up before you come to the altar." It was "come as you are, submit to His grace, and obey His voice."

Unity in Christ is not a matter of conformity (especially external conformity). It's a matter of people coming together as they transform into Jesus's image. This allegiance crosses nationalistic, cultural, and ethnic boundaries, though I wouldn't see that more fully until I was entering my forties.

At this point, things I had learned and rectified in myself during my Inner-Life Growth were trying to find expression as

I launched into my Ministry Maturing years. Every experience fed development in both areas, though my work at the church was my major focus. At this point I thought it was "second star to the right and straight on 'til morning"—that I was in the place I was supposed to be and it would be relatively smooth sailing forward from there.

But that wasn't in the cards.

"NO MEASURABLE SPIRITUAL GIFTS"

The Jesus Movement and the charismatic renewal would continue to influence church culture throughout the 1970s and into the '80s and beyond. Most notable was the transformation of worship. From the formalism of the hymns of past generations to fresh, folky music rooted in Scripture and simple melodies, a reformation of worship was underway. It was intimate, grassroots, and contagious. Some churches were successful in blending older traditions with the new music, while some in the mainstream churches reacted strongly to the movement away from their tried-and-true hymnals and formal choirs. One pastor declared to me that this "irreverent insistence on songs that make you feel intimate with God" had to be extinguished. Another pastor said he would be overjoyed when the last guitar and drum were silenced in the church, then burned in hell. Nerves were on fire.

There were many tired opinions about how the invasion of this new "demonic African beat" was contaminating the solemnity and reverence of church traditions. Contemporary Christian musicians insisted they weren't joining the rock-and-roll movement, but "combating the negative influence of mainstream popular music." To defend their evangelistic efforts, they echoed the sentiments of

George Whitefield, William Booth, and other leaders of the past: "Why should the devil have all the best tunes?"

The beauty of hymnology was being supplemented with the "in-house" music from the hearts of these new street-level believers. One popular song was "Father, I Adore You" by Terrye Coelho, which is still sung in churches today. It was simple and contagious. Songs like this were weaving their ways into the hearts of God's people. Despite the religious objections, Jesus was unceremoniously bypassing stiff necks and using this new wave of music to heal broken hearts.

Such music made people lift their hands in intimacy with God. The little Baptist voice in my head would say, "Don't lift your hands; your mother could be watching." So I'd scour the congregation for my mother's look of evangelical disdain. *Oh yeah, she's in Japan.* Then I'd raise my hands. One beautiful old brother told me that Coelho's song was "unsettling and too intimate."

The witness of changed lives and the intimacy of the new worship music began to seep into more traditional churches. Mindy and I remember visiting her parents' church and hearing them singing our friend Karen Lafferty's simple, beautiful song "Seek Ye First," much to our amazement. (It wasn't in the hymnal! *Yet.*)

Even those who initially refused this new influx of misfits became less spiritually sterile as they opened their hearts to a variety of "unsavory characters" and their genuine and creative hearts. A bridge between church cultures was being built because it was just too hard for all God's people to argue against such radically changed lives. The desire for transformation was just too great.

✦ ✦ ✦ ✦ ✦

In the fall of 1977, Jon Courson left South Valley Chapel to become the pastor of what would become the Applegate Christian Fellowship in southern Oregon. Some of his teaching tapes had impacted a group of about forty believers there so much that they asked him to come up and speak one weekend. He fell in love with the group of hippies and business leaders—and the beauty of the area. When they asked him to be their pastor, he quickly agreed.

In Jon's stead, Ben stepped up as pastor, and I stepped in to replace Ben as associate pastor. I was elated. I was getting my first church paycheck, and now I could display my "anointed" self to the breathlessly waiting church members. I was having a blast letting loose my Scripture notes and blessing our congregants with all the fullness of the Word as I knew it.

But I was the one who was in for it.

Early in 1977, in the thrall of my new assignment as a *paid* minister and the joy of the arrival of our second child, Carrye Joy (born in December 1976), I was summoned to Ben's office. "Jon," he said somberly, "I have been watching you for the nine months since we planted South Valley, and I've concluded that you have no measurable spiritual gifts."

I blanched. *Zero, zilch, nada?*

"None. There's like, nothing there," he continued. "You should seriously consider going back to painting houses. I'm convinced ministry isn't your calling."

I couldn't speak.

"I want to be fair to you, so you have twenty-one days to tie things up. Then I want you to step down as associate pastor. Here's your severance check." He handed me a check for $400.

It cut deep. I had just been fired for the fourth time in three years, and this time I couldn't blame it on a doctrinal difference.

Now I was the problem. I was somehow deficient. I was being let go because my pastor was convinced I had no business being a minister.

You can probably imagine how I felt. I was done with this abuse.

On my drive home, I gave the Lord my notice: "I resign. Kindly don't call me again. I'm gonna do something else with my life."

When I returned home, Mindy greeted me with the obligatory, "Hi, honey, how was your day?"

"Great!" I answered sarcastically. "I was just fired and informed that I have 'no measurable spiritual gifts'! I was advised to go back to painting. He also mandated that I leave the office within the next twenty-one days. And oh, I got a massive severance check—*four hundred dollars!*"

I blathered on after that, castigating the man for his lack of discernment and the injustice of his small thinking. I felt I was entitled to a good grumble. I was gushing orphan spirit all over the place.

Without saying a word, she poked her finger into my chest, plopping me into a poufy lounge chair just behind me. She moved around it, laid a hand on my head, and said, "Dear Lord, please don't listen to a word he is saying!"

Splendid, I thought, *I can't even get sympathy from my own wife! I am out of work, we have a new baby, and I don't want to paint anymore! This isn't fair!* I was steaming.

When she was done, she went on as if it was any normal day: "Oh! There's a renewal conference at Cavalry Community Church this weekend. I think we should go."

You can imagine how I felt about that. *No way!* I'd just gotten fired and the woman wants me to restoke my religious fire, paste on a faux smile for a pack of rabid charismaniacs, and be pleasantly phony? It was the last thing in the world I wanted to do.

But, of course, we went.

When Mindy and I entered the church, we saw a placard that listed the menu of seminars. *Great!* I thought. *We can go to different meetings, and I'll just hide in the back and get through this.* All I wanted to do was sulk and lick my wounds.

She sweetly suggested, "We should go hear the guy talking on 'Unity in the Body of Christ.' His name is Floyd McClung. I hear he's good. He's a missionary too."

Unity, indeed, I thought. *And there's no way I'm gonna go hear a missionary speak.*

I had a thought. "We'll cover more ground if we go to different seminars. Why don't you go to that one and I'll find something else?"

Probably happy to be rid of Mr. Grumpy, she agreed and off she went.

As she left for her unity gig, I found a small seminar room with about thirty people waiting for some guy I had never heard of. *No one will see me in here.*

I sat in the back, folded my arms, and watched as the sound technician fiddled with the microphone. He was wearing a red parrot shirt, a white belt, white shoes, and had a white afro. He looked like a snowball on a stick. I couldn't help but chuckle to myself. *Where do they find these people?*

Then, to my chagrin, the old-fro-dude turned to the microphone and morphed into the seminar speaker. *Great!* I grumbled. This was too much.

He announced his topic: "Jesus the Rock."

Why do we have seminars? Who doesn't know Jesus is the Rock?

I was in bad shape. My heart was wailing, my attitude was bad, I was hurt, and I was angry. But there was no way of slipping out now without making a scene, so I settled in to sit it out. Maybe I could nap.

About ten minutes in, once I'd settle comfortably back into my self-loathing, the speaker suddenly stopped and started looking around.

Uh-oh.

This fellow was Dick Mills, a renowned Pentecostal prophet, now in classic prophetic mode. Who knew?

He found what he was looking for. His eyes locked on mine. The heat of understanding crept up to my cheeks.

"You!" he zeroed in, pointing at me. "You were just told that you have 'no measurable spiritual gifts.' You were given twenty-one days to clear out of the office. Furthermore, on your way home, you told the Lord that you resigned."

Has he been talking to Mindy? There is no way—

"God wants you to know that *your resignation is denied!* In six days, you will get your next assignment by phone, from the throne room of heaven!"

I hit the deck. Parrots and frizzy fro forgotten, I needed to repent. As I did, the laughter from when I got filled with the Spirit returned. I fell into hysterics, a puddle of guffawing on the floor.

I surrendered anew to the Father's destiny for my life. There was no escaping Him. I'd just been chased down again.

And Mindy had been right, *again.* (I have to admit, that was kind of starting to bug me.)

I had new questions to go home and figure out: How does one receive a "phone call from the throne room of heaven"? Just how does that work?

And why did God keep singling me out? (That was a question I would ponder for years.)

✦ ✦ ✦ ✦ ✦

I boxed up my things from my office at South Valley Chapel, said my goodbyes, went home, and waited.

The evening of the sixth day, Jon called from Applegate Valley. He was having incredible adventures. "Freaks" were coming out of the hills and encountering Jesus. (He'd even been invited to preach to a nudist colony living illegally on government land in the Siskiyou Mountains. After encouraging them to share their belief in Rosicrucianism with him, he reciprocated the next day by preaching "Jesus: The Resurrection and the Life." Many came to the Lord. [I don't even want to think about how they were baptized. Where do you put your hands when someone's not wearing any . . . oh, never mind.])

Jon apparently had no clue his brother had just fired me. "I want you to come up here and help me with the church," he said. "There are too many people coming from other towns. I need help from someone who can gather people in one of the nearby communities: Grants Pass."

The prophecy had been right-on. I shivered with the expectancy of God's direct involvement in this next step for our family.

Of course, I told Jon I'd be right up. A month later, I was on the road to Oregon and to "*freak*-dom." (At that time, southern Oregon was starting to become a refuge for those who wanted to "get back to nature" and escape the burgeoning metropolises of Los Angeles and the Bay Area.) My plan was to find a place to live before Mindy and the girls came up.

That prophetic word was the nail in the coffin of my doubting God and His call on my life. From that experience, I knew that all the rejection I had experienced over the years had brought me to a place of utter dependence on God. I knew that if I trusted in Him fully, He would guide my steps and open the right doors—even if they were doors I never dreamed of opening myself. I drove into

Oregon with a sense of precise, prophetic clarity that no matter what lay ahead, God was directing my steps.

I still remember the joy I had as I drove north on I-5, following the snaking Rogue River, and came around the bend to see the little community of Grants Pass for the first time. This would be the first place I'd feel at home since I'd left Japan. I was so excited to get started with whatever God had called us to do. Much of the essence of who Mindy and I are today was formed in that little town along the Rogue River.

Jon had successfully gathered a thriving community in the Applegate River Valley, about forty-five minutes from Grants Pass. He arranged for me to meet with a beautiful couple, Chris and Phil Hyatt, who had been commuting to Applegate Community Church from Grants Pass. I drove straight to their house because they had agreed to help me start looking for a place to live. I was hoping to find a rental, but there weren't any that were suitable. A week later, I was getting ready to climb in the truck and drive back to Sacramento to tell Mindy there was nowhere to live when a Realtor friend of Phil's called and said, "I've got a house that's for sale."

I replied, "No dice. I can't buy a house; I don't have any money. I have two hundred bucks—that's it."

"What can it hurt to go look at it?" Phil asked. "Let's just see if the Lord's in this."

We jumped in the Realtor's car and took off for the east side of town. I couldn't believe it when we pulled up. It was a funky little house this guy had built himself. It sat on an acre of fruit trees and grass and had a beautiful view overlooking the whole Rogue Valley. There wasn't a right angle in the whole house, but I loved it.

So we went to talk with the owner, a Mr. Warner. I'll never forget him. He was a dear man whose wife was dying of cancer. They needed to get in a smaller place with hospice, and they had prayed that the Lord would bring a young Christian couple to buy their house.

As I got up to leave, I told him I didn't have enough for a down payment and thanked him for his hospitality, and for showing us his place.

He asked, "How much money do you have?"

"I have two hundred dollars."

He scratched his chin. "Okay, I'll take that as a down payment if you can come up with ten grand in sixty days."

"I've never seen ten thousand dollars in my life."

He smiled. "Well, let's trust God. If you're the ones to buy this, the Lord will provide the money."

What did I have to lose? We shook hands in agreement.

I called Mindy and said, "I think I bought a house. The only caveat is we need ten thousand dollars in sixty days."

"Well, we'll have to trust God," she said. *My wife!*

So we did—and He did. Before the sixty days were up, we paid the ten thousand. We and the Warners shared the joy.

Mindy and the girls returned with me to Grants Pass, and we began commuting to Applegate Christian Fellowship. Soon, we started a Bible study in Chris and Phil's home. It began with about a dozen curious people, and then it started to grow—twenty, thirty, fifty, and so on. It was quite a group: From the warmth of a faithful old sister, Grandma Reed, to Byron Bouquet, a mop-head who played the guitar, our meetings filled with hungry hearts. We were home.

Applegate Christian was a fair drive for those of us in Grants Pass, so it wasn't too long before people started talking about finding a place to plant our own church in Grants Pass.

We eventually moved into a slightly bigger house, but that filled up quickly as well. Then the owner of the Riverside Restaurant and

Inn started coming. His place was downtown, right on the river, between the bridges for the town's two major thoroughfares. He said, "I have some property that you might be able to use." He took us to see a barn on the southeast side of town, which had previously been used to dry tulip bulbs. It was funky, funky, funky. It needed *a lot* of work, but it was a place where we could meet, and there was a massive vault where we could hold our kids' Sunday school classes.

Perfect.

He said if we'd fix it up ourselves, he'd let us use it for free. (Eventually he deeded it to us.) That was a deal we could swing, so we agreed. Once we did the renovations, we started meeting there and calling ourselves The Barn Fellowship.

In less than two years we grew to between 200 to 300 attendees every Sunday. At that point, we got into all sorts of trouble from the city, because the place wasn't coded as a church: We had too many people in a place that was a bit of a firetrap. So we switched again, to a junior high school on Redwood Highway.

We were heading into some of the most adventurous years of our lives among the hippies and the spiritual hunger of southern Oregon.

Again, I thought I had it all mapped out. (When would I learn?)

UNVEILING YOUR FUTURE

I've always thought I should get a plaque made to celebrate being fired from four ministries in three years—a dubious badge of honor. Those painful rejections repeatedly decimated any visions of ministerial grandeur I might have let dance in my head.

At the same time, God was keeping His promise that He would never leave nor forsake me. (See Deuteronomy 31:6, 8.) His repeated, amazing prophecies kept me on the road toward my destiny, despite wanting nothing more than to quit. Despite my inclinations, I wasn't getting out of any of this so easily.

If you look, you will see a pattern in my story of a prophecy or a "word from the Lord" foretelling each new season. After the incredible word through Dick Mills, we moved to Oregon. I have seen that the Lord often gives a sign (a prophecy, a Scripture, and a word of counsel) of a pending shift before the change results in a new assignment. I've also learned the more spectacular the word from God, the rougher the seas ahead are likely to be. He wants us to have no doubts that He's called us there and would be with us, even though it woud seem like He was nowhere to be found. Usually there is a "boundary phase" between a change in seasons, calling, or life assignment. These transitional periods allow us to change gears, get our hearts and emotions aligned, and be better prepared before we move into the future.

This shift was not just in assignment and location for us. We were also shifting phases again. Moving to Grants Pass was a shift from the early Ministry Maturing phase of my development into my middle Ministry Maturing phase. (For the record, the move into my latter Ministry Maturing phase would also include a change in mission and geography—one I never considered possible when we set up house in the Rogue Valley.)

In my early Ministry Maturing, I often faced outside forces beyond my control. They tested the resolve of my calling and my convictions. Would setbacks drive me to deeper dependence on God or harden my heart to the point I'd quit? (I wouldn't exactly call this a choice, but I also know, despite feeling like I wanted to quit, my initial commitment to serve the Lord always won out. Even though God intervened dramatically on more than one occasion, I don't know how far away from that I would have gotten if He'd been less emphatic. I'm glad I never had to find out.)

My middle Ministry Maturing challenge would be to find out what would happen if things started to go awry when I was "the man in charge." Before that happened, we were going to experience some amazing things. Let me tell you about some of those before we get into our next phase transition.

DESTINY CONFIRMED IN FREAKDOM

The Barn Fellowship became a story factory. In the nearly five years we spent in Grants Pass, Mindy and I inherited a lifetime legacy of incredible adventures and strange occurrences. Such was the nature of the Jesus Movement in the second half of the 1970s, and we were at the heart of it. Tons got saved. Praying for the sick was a regular part of our church activity, and we saw everything from people being healed of cancer to kids recovering from colds, rashes, headaches, and nightmares (something I had a great affection for, as you might guess) in record time. We also saw a lot of emotional inner healing, and more prayer for demonic oppression than you would ever imagine would be needed in small-town America. It was beautiful to watch God move.

There were angelic visitations and remarkable miracles. Vans and "flower-power" buses were everywhere, carrying freaks to unknown points and spreading Jesus's name. Long hair was "in," much to the chagrin of our conservative contemporaries. "Freaks" who caught anyone wearing a tie summarily chastised the poor soul—in jest, of course. Silly external biases, though separating some, were an opportunity for fun repartee exchanged in the spirit of unity found only in Christ.

One of the most amazing Jesus People stories I heard during this time was of a strung-out hippie who was introduced to the Gospel by Jesus in the middle of an LSD high. He came to his senses immediately, got delivered, and is now the leader of one of the largest ministries in California.

In Grants Pass, we had midnight baptisms, deliverance of the demonized, weddings in tree houses and teepees, babies born in tents (don't these people believe in hospitals?), and—*Poof!*—The Barn was at 500 people. As a shepherd to an unorthodox generation, I performed twenty-seven weddings before I performed one in a traditional church building. Those teepees and tree houses, along with the occasional golf course (the fifth hole was a favorite), were popular wedding venues. The Rainbow People, a '70s cult, loved to come out of the hills, sit in the back row of our Sunday meetings, and give me a weekly update on the color and nature of my aura. A real blessing indeed. (It was diagnosed to be radiant blue.) They saw me as some sort of guru or shaman. All I could do was keep loving them toward Jesus.

My old Biola roommate, Dan Johnson, along with his wife, Taffy, joined us to minister in Grants Pass. Having such close, longtime friends around always had an important impact on anything I was doing, and I was learning that we needed more than doctrinal alignment to do the work of being a church.

Following my principle of being Jesus-centric in my leadership, I based much of who would become elders and staff at The Barn on friendship. I felt that friendship would outlast tests of doctrine or disagreement. I thought this would allow us more leeway and grace in faith and ministry experiments—especially if things went awry, as they were sure to do from time to time. When hearts are joined in friendship and pursuing God above all else, changes are more easily tolerated, and I hoped that would leave us room to grow wiser together. As I had seen, when things were based on beliefs alone, personal growth was often pushed to the side and new understandings or mistakes brought divisive consequences with them. I learned a great deal about how important friendship and maturity was in my time leading The Barn. (Unfortunately, the lack of the latter would cause us problems.)

Josephine County, of which Grants Pass was the county seat, did what it could to deal with the influx of people "getting away" from the metropolises of California, seeking a place to just "be" in the rural, natural surroundings of Southern Oregon. (The Rogue Valley was a happy medium between sunny California and the gray, Pacific "rain forest" climate of the Willamette Valley.) The traditional Methodist church in town showed *Brother Sun, Sister Moon*, a Jesus Movement "cult" film (it told the story of St. Francis of Assisi) that tried to portray a Christian message hippies could identify with. The place was packed with Rainbow People sitting cross-legged on the floor. The bewildered pastor was very welcoming, but none of the "freaks" could relate to his clerical robe and classical church building. At least they tried.

I eventually had a scintillating conversation with Gabriel, the leader of the Rainbow People. Apparently, he was awarded this name by the angel himself—a moniker that gave him great authority to accomplish his mission on earth. Gabriel was flanked by his younger brother, whom we affectionately named Rainbow Bob, or R.B. for short. R.B. came to Jesus in the days that followed and continues to follow Him today.

The Jesus Movement at this point was nomadic, creating a viral effect on conversions to Christ. Vans loaded with young believers made pilgrimages to festivals and concerts. Slogans and symbols such as the *ichthys* fish (an early Christian symbol), "One Way Jesus" T-shirts, and Maranatha ("the Lord is coming") appeared in many forms of artwork. There was a deep belief in Christ's imminent return, fueled by a strong premillennial emphasis from teachers such as Chuck Smith and Tim LaHaye. What they lacked in stability and doctrinal foundation, they made up for in a rabid hunger for more of Jesus. Jesus was the center of everything they did, and they spread His name everywhere they went.

Not long after our weekly attendance grew to 500, I started visiting with other churches and pastors in the area. Together we started a Grants Pass pastors' prayer group. It was the first time anything like that had happened. These churches, both large and small, had historical grievances among them, but we found a way to come together to pray for each other, and for the region. For some reason, at the ripe old age of twenty-six, I was the catalyst for this unity. I'd come in my overalls and they would come with their suits—one guy wore a three-piece, sporting a bouffant hairdo and white shoes. He was in a town filling up with hippies, and he looked like Pat Boone straight out of a 1958 movie.

✦ ✦ ✦ ✦ ✦

We held concerts in the woods, where hundreds of freaks and their young families would gather to hear the new sound, always followed by testimonies and the preaching of the Gospel. Hundreds came to Christ through these concerts, and many were baptized—often immediately, as there are many rivers in Southern Oregon. (Thank You, Jesus!) These were very spiritual, but "non-religious" events. I was particularly taken when the popular band Daniel Amos struck a fantastically salient chord on their guitars, and the glasses they were wearing sprung little fake eyeballs—*Sproing!* Not your typical church hymn fest—especially with all those little kids running around buck-naked.

Two beautiful Barn "members" (we didn't have anything so official, but they came faithfully), John and Jennifer Wooliscroft, opened a "commune" on A Street in the heart of town. A steady flow of new converts visited their ministry house. We concocted a policy that ensured that every new convert would be encouraged to enter into water baptism immediately upon acceptance of faith.

Soon after that brilliant decision was hatched, my phone rang at 2:00 AM, informing me that a couple of guys had just come to Jesus. Could I meet them down at the river for a baptism?

"Of course," I replied.

I arrived to the strains of worship tunes, prepping the atmosphere. I headed to the boat ramp and into the icy April runoff. Then I saw the behemoth they expected me to baptize first. He was huge! To get the proper leverage on this giant, I moved into water up to my armpits. At "I baptize you in the name of the Father . . ." I slipped. I lost my balance and headed with great speed toward the Pacific Ocean. As I fought for my life, I heard the music stop and a bewildered voice in the darkness ask, "Where did they go?" My baptismal partner and I, now thoroughly immersed—Wouldn't John the Baptist be proud?—were miraculously rescued by a couple of low-hanging branches, mere apparitions in the inky night. In a few more yards we would have been into the rapids without life jackets.

I was quick to nix the new baptismal policy after that. There was no reason we couldn't be patient and at least wait for the light of day.

✦ ✦ ✦ ✦ ✦

The people we ran into every day were very raw. One "new age" seeker argued with me about the Gospel and accused me of "mind f***ing" her. I assured her the pressure she was feeling was the Holy Spirit inviting her to surrender to Jesus—and the enemy was fighting it with everything he had. Eventually she slumped, bowed her head, and gave her life to Jesus.

For the most part, we were an untrained bunch equipped with nothing but the simple Gospel. Thank God He was with us in our enthusiasm and ignorance. His Spirit was ever-present, allowing us to draw hungry people to His heart by His amazing grace. Little time was given to examining our ecclesiology or our forms of church government. We were simply riding the current moving us forward and trying to remain upright in its power.

✦ ✦ ✦ ✦ ✦

In 1978, a Youth With A Mission (usually referred to as YWAM, pronounced "Y-WAM") bus broke down outside of Grants Pass. A wild, sandy-headed young Kiwi named John Dawson and his bedraggled, wild-eyed, short-term missionary team came to us for help while the bus was being repaired. It would be a few days.

"Perfect," I grumbled, "fifty rabid, virginal missionaries all wanting food and lodging for who knows how long! Stupid YWAM buses!"

But I was soon rebuked by their kindness. To "earn their keep," these "kids" served our church people, mowing lawns, raking yards, fixing broken plumbing, witnessing on the streets, and engaging in other outrageous benevolence. John and I became fast friends, lazing along the gurgling Rogue River and discussing what God was up to in YWAM, and beyond.

"What does the Kingdom of God look like in daily existence on the earth?"

"Why are we here now, during this move of God? How are we supposed to participate in it?"

And so on and so forth . . .

Having grown up as a missionary's kid, with constant pressure to take the Gospel into all the world, I enjoyed thinking beyond our small lumber town, even if just for a little while. It stirred the international strings of my heart, planting a seed that would eventually bloom into our next stage of ministry.

When John left, he hugged me and said, "I would really love to work with you someday."

Not gonna happen, I thought. I didn't mind talking missions, but I still had no interest in ever *being* a missionary. Once they pulled out of our parking lot with that ramble of do-gooders, I just logged it away as one of those God encounters that pass through your life and feed your soul a bit. I wouldn't understand the true significance of that incident until a few years later.

✦ ✦ ✦ ✦ ✦

There was also a lanky, long-haired dude named Doug (not his real name) who got radically saved. After he was baptized, he asked me what he should do with his "three hundred thousand–dollar garden."

"What garden?" I started to say, then realized any garden worth that much couldn't be of the legal variety. So I tried launching into a short biblical treatise on leaving the past behind, when Doug interrupted: "Can we have a burn party? I want to break with my criminal past publicly."

I remembered burning our magazines and albums in Japan as a sign of starting anew, so I said, "Why not?" I should have given my answer more thought.

We headed off with a prattle of patchy-looking new converts (my suspicions on full alert) into the breezy night to find the hollowed-out section of forest where Doug had become a wealthy farmer. It suddenly struck me, as I looked nervously around: "We're talking about mixing burning pot and baby saints here!"

Instructions were given to test the direction of the wind. Then the witnesses were herded to assemble just upwind of where the smoke would blow. There was some residual reluctance to deny "just one more whiff" on the part of some of our wobblier mendicants, but we held firm as a group. The plants were uprooted and piled high. Then Doug set a torch to it. Our entourage erupted in shouts of praise and rejoiced as the smoke drifted into the sky. I realized they were serious about leaving their pasts behind after all. I learned something new about active repentance that day.

✦ ✦ ✦ ✦ ✦

Part of my routine while living in the Rogue Valley was to go to a rock outcropping I had found on an isolated mountain in the lower Siskiyous. It provided a magnificent view where I could be alone, pray, and prepare my sermons. I'd sit there and listen to tapes by Jack Hayford, Campbell McAlpine, and Chuck Smith, among others, taking notes and following along in my Bible with the Scriptures they quoted.

In the midst of my meditation one day, I heard that holy whisper again: "*You're not right with your former pastor in San Jose. You have to go back and get it right.*"

I realized that even though Jon's brother Ben had hurt me and I had tried to forgive him, God wanted me to do more. He was a brother, and we needed to be restored to one another. I also realized I was holding something in my heart against him. My attitude still wasn't right toward my four firings, and that pastor most of all.

I'd heard that South Valley Chapel had started floundering after Jon and I left, and I realized (with conviction) that I'd been secretly glad about it. Meanwhile, both of our churches in Southern Oregon were flourishing. I saw that I'd abandoned supporting a work of God, with the excuse that I'd been forced out and wasn't wanted. I had secretly reveled in their hardships, but I should have still been blessing them and praying for a work I'd been part of, a work the Lord loved.

The whisper came again: "*You need to get in your car and go. Like now.*"

So I jumped in my car and drove to Grants Pass. When I got home, I shouted at Mindy, "Road trip! See if you can find someone to watch the kids. We need to go down and see Ben." I didn't even take the time to call and see if he was available. We just jumped in the car and began the seven-hour drive to San Jose.

We arrived at his house that evening and walked to the front door. We knocked, the door opened, and when Ben saw me he launched himself to embrace me. We tumbled down the front steps and landed on the sidewalk together, his arms around me and his head buried in my chest. Over and over, he said, "Can you forgive me for what I did? Can you forgive me for what I've done to you?"

We must've been a sight.

"I forgave you on the way down here," I told him. "It was a little hard, but I do forgive you. The Lord's forgiven me for so much; how can I not forgive you?"

After that we had a fantastic time of reconciliation. We prayed, cried, and, finally, laughed together.

✦ ✦ ✦ ✦ ✦

During a warm, sunny Sunday a couple years into our time leading The Barn, I sat nervously on a wobbly stool at Indian Mary Park, surrounded by 300 hippies and many curious campers who strolled by wondering what was going on. Decked out in my Sunday best overalls, held up by little more than one of baby Carrye's old pink diaper pins, I took my honored place as the leader of this rabble. I was more nervous than usual because my "proper" little missionary mother sat, lotus-style like the rest, sandwiched between two large, long-haired hippies with full beards. Nestled in the shadows of this mass of cross-legged freaks, she looked like a visiting alien, conspicuous in her page-boy haircut, trim missionary-issue tweed suit, and perfect little Mikimoto pearl brooch.

Mom was visiting the family and wanted to hear me preach for the first time. She was in town because our third child, Andrew Jon, had been born in April of 1979. At this time, I was twenty-seven.

Under the tall sunlit Oregon pines, with the Rogue River roaring softly in the background, I launched into an exposition of Ephesians chapter one. When I introduced verses 15–18 as "my life Scriptures," I saw my mother jerk and her eyes fill with tears. I was instantly attacked by insecurity and tried to stay focused on the rest of the group. But I couldn't escape the thought: *I have never seen Mom cry. This must be the worst teaching she's ever heard. Did something I say offend her?*

I plunged on dutifully, but slightly detached, through the rest of the service. We baptized some new converts in the chilly river (at least it was daylight), as we usually did at the end of each meeting. Then we headed home.

In the car, I tentatively asked my mother about her crying.

She looked at me, her eyes beginning to glisten again. "As you know, before we left for Japan, the doctors told us we wouldn't be able to have children. So I prayed, like Hannah did, that if God would give me a son, I would dedicate him to the Lord like she did, no strings attached."

As she went on, her voice trembled, "When you were born, I asked the Lord for your name—it would be Jonathan: 'one who lays his crown down to make others great.' Then I asked the Lord for a guiding Scripture I could pray over you throughout your life."

She stopped and took a breath, tears streaming again. "The Lord gave me Ephesians 1:15–18: *'that you might have a Spirit of wisdom and revelation in the knowledge of Christ.'*"

In shock and now crying myself, I pulled the car over to the side of the road and held my mother, both of us weeping like babies. It was some time before I could pull safely onto the road again.

Sometimes destiny sneaks up on you; other times it smacks you in the face. This was definitely the latter.

UNVEILING YOUR FUTURE

This phase (the late twenties into the thirties for most) is the decade of learning to be with God, to listen, to be contemplative, to immerse oneself in the Word, and to be shaped into His image. These years reveal that failure is a friend to coax us to exchange our finite dreams for the dreams God gives us, yet doesn't reveal before their time. For once, God showed restraint in giving me too much vision for the future. He waited until I was healed of the rejection that had clouded my sight in the past and caused me to overcompensate for my spiritual impotence.

Unfiltered idealism and unchecked ambition in young leaders tend to cause them to overinflate the importance of their current ministries, making it difficult to see the beauty of bringing every vision to the foot of the cross. They accept the present as a given, and the future as more of the same, only better. They are not what we are to build our identities upon; we are to do that on Jesus. For dreams and visions of the future to live, they must be surrendered to the Father and hammered to the cross. Only then can they be resurrected to the true life God planned all along. Many times they have to die and become something completely different to fulfill what God intended them for. The key is to stay in relationship to Christ first—what we do for Him is always secondary to that.

One of the ways God confirms our destiny is through a variety of challenges. In Grants Pass, we experienced myriad events that tested my confidence and maturity. The middle Ministry Maturing years are God's great smorgasbord. We get to eat what's good for us, not just what we like or are comfortable with. We get to try new things and see how our gifts work in new circumstances.

The variety also includes painful and distasteful (yet healthy) options that we either embrace or ignore. I hated conflict in those years and avoided it with fervor. One soon learns that avoidance is an enemy, and it brings painful consequences in the long run. Deal with it! I heard one preacher say, "I embrace trouble like a bowl of granola—crunchy but healthy! Bring it on so I can be more like Jesus!"

You may have heard yourself using "surely it can't get any worse" language, or the ever-popular "I can't take any more" mantra that "graces" the lips of too many disciples of Jesus. Why are we so consumed with measuring our pain and monitoring our suffering at the expense of everything else? Because we have a fixed mindset defining everything by current capabilities and ignoring our ability to grow, we have not surrendered ourselves to being a tool in the hands of Christ, to use as only He knows. Jesus told us we would have to pick up the "cross of Christ." (See Matthew 10:38 and 16:24.) It *can* get worse and we *can* endure more pain and suffering *because He is with us*. His goal is not our comfort, but our transformation to His image—and that will always be a fiery ordeal!

This is also the season of life when young leaders should be willing to be exposed to everything, including opportunities outside their comfort zones. Nor it is yet the season to come into your primary calling with power and authority. Serve with abandon and don't worry too much about it being your gift, fitting into your "sweet spot," or being "the man" (or "woman") in charge. *Serve!*

Early in the Ministry Maturing phase, we discover our primary gifts. From the moment the Lord healed my speech handicap, I knew I was called to preach and teach. The Barn's ministry was built largely on my teaching gift, a pattern I now discourage in my spiritual sons and daughters. God has blessed us with wonderful gifts, but they are not to be the only foundation upon which we build His Church. My leadership was dangerously validated by people's attraction to my teaching, while my character and knowledge base still needed more deconstruction and reconstruction before I could more fully be used of Him. It's too easy to let what you're good at distract you from what God wants you to work on for your wholeness and the Church's health.

Those years in Grants Pass—in the middle of my Ministry Maturing—were a good reminder that you don't have to be a grizzled veteran or have all your ducks in a row for God to use you. You just need a heart for Him, and a willingness to obey even the oddest of His still, small whispers. Fortunately, the solid foundation I'd gotten at Biola and at Calvary Chapel saw me through things that shipwrecked others. For this, I'm very grateful.

We are all on a journey, and the more we meld our hearts together on that journey, the safer we all are. But the more we get out on our own and think it was all about our own unique, special gifts, the more we set ourselves up for running our ministry onto the rocks.

THE END OF A GOOD THING, THE BEGINNING OF ANOTHER

Near the beginning of our third year leading The Barn, there was an incident with two of our elder (I'm tempted to put that word in quotes) families, which created a problem we would spend the better part of the next two years suffering under. It taught me some important things about leading a church, as well as important things about what biblical church eldership should look like.

As you already know, The Barn was a church built out of hippies and other hungry young people. Most of us were still in our twenties. Knowing I needed to "share" the leadership of the church with my congregation, but not really knowing how to do that, I appointed elders—some of the people who had helped us get started and had the most energy for pushing us forward. Thus I appointed other eager young couples like Mindy and me who wanted to see the church succeed.

At first it was great. There was a lot of energy and willingness to try new things, but there's a reason Paul uses the word "elder" for these positions and not "fellow leaders." "Elder" implies a level of maturity and wisdom. It doesn't mean they can't be young, but they shouldn't *all* be young. And just because one spouse is called to leadership, it doesn't mean both should be. What happened was an incident that revealed our eldership was lacking in those two key ingredients.

It all started when the child of one of the elders hit the child of another while waiting for the school bus. It was certainly a matter that needed to be addressed, but it got too personal way too quickly. In the heat of defending their child, one elder asked the other, "How can you be an elder, when your boy hit my boy at the bus stop? What kind of parent are you, anyway?" This gnarly little snit planted a seed that would reproduce like dandelions.

Another problem we had was that our elder board members had little in common but their relationships with Mindy and me. While I valued friendship as a basis of leadership, I'd missed the step of helping my elders build relationships with each other. Each had loyalty to us, but not to one other. Nor did they have an equal commitment to affection and truth-telling among themselves. I had become the lynchpin of our unity, and when this little disagreement turned into taking sides, I was expected to favor one over the other, rather than being an instrument of reconciliation.

The pain of misunderstanding, blame, immaturity, and spiritual idealism (that "if we are mature Christians, we will have perfectly behaved kids and a rosy lifestyle of one blessing after another" and so on) began to unravel the blessing of what we had built. It's unreasonable to think that kids will always be angels, no matter who their parents are. (We'd learn that later when our own kids became teens.) Things do need to be dealt with, and making excuses for bad behavior doesn't help. These accusations burned deep and were not aimed at everyone getting closer to God, but at one set of parents taking more authority in the church than another. The seeds of great ugliness soon began to sprout. People were accused of having "Jezebel spirits" and other demonic influences. I knew things had gotten away from me. There would be no easy way to restore peace.

I found myself in a tug-of-war between factions. Division was taking hold, and I didn't have the maturity to properly bring both sides in and hash things out, though I did try. The fellowship overall was protected from this disunity for the first year of it, but then the ugliness began to spread beyond the leadership. Lines were drawn, sides were taken, and the church began to shrink in size and passion.

To make matters worse, this brought back many of the "orphan spirit" thoughts connected to my rejection as a kid and a teen: *I'm alone. I'm unlovable. I'm deficient. I'm a screw-up and worthless. There's a reason I got fired four times, and I'm going to fail at this as well.*

It's really hard to recognize such things as enemy lies when they sound like you are the one saying them and they feel so true. I was in a tailspin, though far more confident of my calling than I had been when I gave God my resignation in San Jose. Still, it made me question a lot of things about my viability as a leader, as a husband, a father, and a human being. Mindy and I would lie in bed and cry, because we were not only losing our friends, we were losing all we had built. *Had we really missed God so badly?*

Early in this strife, Mindy and I went to a pastors' conference at Mount Herman, one we attended every year. The usual speakers were Jack Hayford, Loren Cunningham, Darlene and Ron Howard, Joy Dawson, and the like. This year, there was a new speaker: missionary Floyd McClung, whom Mindy had heard speak while I had unsuccessfully tried to hide from God by going to the Dick Mills session. Mindy talked constantly about how impressed she was with Floyd, so I was interested to hear him.

Floyd was a big guy, about six-seven, and he spoke with a powerful humility. He was candid and honest as he told us about how, through his own pride and attempts to be "the man" in Holland (where he was a YWAM missionary), he had contributed to nearly blowing up the ministry in Heidebeek (a YWAM training center in the Dutch countryside). He transitioned from that into speaking about the importance of unity and how to find it, despite hurtful circumstances. I'd never heard anyone speak so openly and honestly before. I wondered what advice he might have for me, given the crisis at The Barn.

Of course, after he spoke to the hundreds present, dozens wanted a moment of his time afterward. Rather than press in (which has never been my style), I waited while others talked with him and shook hands. After finishing with one woman, he looked up and surveyed the crowd. His eyes found me. He motioned for me to join him. Mindy and I approached, and he asked, "What's up, brother?"

I stammered, "I'd love to—doesn't need to be right now, but before you leave—I'd love to catch a coffee with you and talk about some of stuff we're going through at our church."

"Why not right now?" he responded.

"Sure," I said, in shock.

He turned and led us across the stage to a door in the back. There was nobody in the green room, so we went in. He shut the door, and we sat at a table. For the next two hours, we told him about what we'd been going through. He listened attentively. Once we had finished, he shared what he thought.

He was so compassionate and so helpful. At the end, we still weren't sure what to do, but we had a much better perspective on things. We were so grateful. I felt the intense need for a mentoring presence like his in our lives, something we didn't have anywhere in sight.

He seemed to sense the desire for attachment as well. "Wouldn't it be great to work together someday?" he said, grinning broadly.

Missionaries! I thought. *No, that ain't happening. I'm not doing the missionary thing.*

But I smiled and nodded. "I'm really more of a church planter and pastor," I said, "but if the circumstances were right, why not?"

But I was thinking, *Never in a million years.*

Why not indeed.

His advice greatly helped for a short time, but I was still too timid to step up and speak the truth as was needed. Things continued to escalate. About a year later, as events started causing real friction and people started leaving in packs, a friend suggested we seek the counsel of a more mature and spiritually insightful couple in Portland. It was amazing how God used them. Our friend had told us, "Just go sit with them." So we drove up and did just that.

They knew how to counsel people to receive inner healing and to overcome personal spiritual strongholds. When we prayed with them, the wife "read my mail": "This point in your childhood is where your depression entered, and when this happened in your family, this is what went on." I remembered the things specifically as she described them and saw their insidious connection to what I believed about myself—and the depression those thoughts fed and how that had eroded my confidence as a leader.

"You've had demonic encounters in your life that have traumatized your soul," she told me. "And you've had beautiful acts of God in your life that you are rejecting as false. You're now at a point where you must identify the lies and denounce them before you can move on. You need to let the Lord continue to bring you into your sonship. He's been with you through it all, and circumstances aren't His rejection of you, but simply challenges He wants to redeem for you and turn into strengths."

As we prayed, I remembered two significant teachers in my teens. They told me, "You'll never amount to anything," because of my performance in their class or my poor attitude. And I was certainly no sexy Mr. Wonderful like some of the other leaders I'd met over the years. I was low-key and liked the shadows over the limelight. But in the midst of it came these thoughts: *I will never this* or *I can't that,* and the devastating lie, *You'll never be good enough to be like so-and-so.* Despite all of the damaging programming that I'd suffered, I needed to forgive those who'd spoken negatively about me if I was going to push on toward my destiny. I needed to sever connections with these entangling thought patterns to be free to move on.

The couple laid hands on us and prayed. I forgave those who'd spoken caustically about me. I rejected the lies that my past told me about myself. It was one of the most important steps I would take as a young leader—to see that I was loved by God and He was calling me to be His son. It would take time to learn to plug in to Jesus and the Holy Spirit more fully. When we left that day, depression had been dealt another reeling blow. While a quiet experience no one else knew about at the time, meeting with this couple was another turning point for me. What they had said and prayed for us released me to fall in love with the Holy Spirit and Jesus all over again. God was continuing to create a new narrative for me.

As the situation in Grants Pass grew darker, Mindy and I promised the Lord we would never leave there, no matter how ugly things got—unless He called us somewhere else, of course. We would always obey His call.

After coming back from Portland, we were better, though the church was not. We still weren't sure what to do next, but we were standing stronger together despite our uncertainty. We knew we'd find a way to weather the storm, somehow.

Then, Chuck Smith invited us to join him on one of his annual pilgrimages to Israel, with about 300 others from Calvary Chapel and elsewhere. We were reluctant to leave the mess at home but felt compelled to go. It might be the break we needed to come back with better answers.

Having been born in Japan and not having been beyond the States for a while, I was ready to renew my passport, fly across an ocean, and get beyond the forested walls of the Rogue Valley. As I stepped off the plane into an unfamiliar country, I began to detox from the caustic nature of the church situation. It was such a little thing. We had a chance to unpack some spiritual baggage during the trip, see some sites, and eat some different food. It fed my soul in a way I hadn't experienced since the last time I'd been with my parents to purchase squid out of a fisherman's net.

As part of the trip, George Otis Sr. invited our tour to visit "The Voice of Hope" radio station on the "Good Fence": the northern boundary of Israel, shared with Lebanon. While listening to Lebanon's Maronite Christian military leader, Major Saad Haddad, in full dress uniform, brief us on the war in Lebanon, I was moved by the stories of rockets being lofted between Lebanon and Israel and the mounting casualties. I was especially moved by the report of an errant missile hitting a Lebanese school full of children. It was grim.

This tug on my heart seemed to release something in my spirit. During the major's talk, I heard the near-audible voice of God for the first time: "Go home and resign. I'm calling you to the nations." Jolted, I looked around for Mindy and saw she was with a circle of ladies twenty yards away, unaware of the tsunami that had just hit my shores.

This can't be right, I told myself. *I'm a church planter and pastor, not a missionary. It's not for me.*

And yet there was that tug to do something other than pastor in a small town. There was nothing wrong with my calling; I just felt suddenly like I needed to do something that could make a difference for an area of the world that was really hurting, a place beyond the comforts of the United States.

Maybe it was just a bad shawarma I'd eaten earlier, however. *I'd better confirm this with Mindy,* I told myself.

As we headed back toward Jerusalem at the end of the visit, the bus chatter lulled into a sleepy silence. I told Mindy, "I think I heard the Lord back there."

"Yeah," she said, "so did I."

My eyes widened. "On the missionary thing?"

"Right, on the missionary thing. I think we're supposed to go home and resign and get ready to go to the nations."

So it hadn't been the shawarma at lunch—it was God. Mr. "I'll never be a missionary" was in for an adjustment. Mindy had been right (*again!*) when she made me agree we might one day be missionaries. I had more crow to eat.

Of course, there was still the "How?" question. Maybe God would ease us into it.

"Why don't you call J.D.?" Mindy asked me.

"John Dawson?" I answered. I hadn't talked with him in a while.

"Yeah," she said. "Maybe we should call him when we get back?"

I said I would.

When we returned, we debriefed the church leaders who had managed to steer clear of the division the church was experiencing. They asked us, "Do you have anything to share with us after your trip?"

I nodded. "I think God is calling us back to the nations."

Before I could say anything more, one of them offered, "The Lord told us the same thing—He is calling you away from The Barn."

It was confirmed. God was calling us away—*but to where?*

I called John Dawson. Excitedly, he told us that YWAM's founders, Loren and Darlene Cunningham, were preparing to open a Leadership Training School in Kona, Hawaii, and their first session would be in April. (This was in February 1981.) "Can you close things up there, pack up, and be in Hawaii to be part of that inaugural class?" he asked.

My heart leapt. "Yes, I think we can," I told him, even though I had no idea how.

I resigned my pastorate at The Barn. We were able to hand the church over to a fine couple, Tom and Kristin Lynch. Tom and Kristin were a little older and a little wiser, just what The Barn needed to move into its next phase.

We packed in a hurry, jamming most of our earthly possessions into thirteen boxes and shipping them ahead of us. The Grants Pass Petersen clan made it to Kona in the nick of time and with our hair on fire—much to the chagrin of the YWAMers who received us. (Most of the attendees where young and single. They weren't sure what to do with us.)

We arrived at the door of our new one-room accommodations, a battered old hotel on the side of a volcano in Kailua Kona. YWAM had bought the nasty, moldy building, hoping to turn it into the Pacific and Asia Christian University. According to Loren, it was to be founded "on biblical principles that equip students to serve in all spheres of society and in all nations by teaching students to think biblically, discern spiritually, and apply scriptural truth to every area of life." There we were with our three little towheads—two, four, and six at the time—and a ton of residual pain.

Our "going to the nations" was underway.

UNVEILING YOUR FUTURE

Thinking I was done with the legacy of failure, I charged into Grants Pass full of faith and zeal for God and humanity. Almost five years later, I was sucker-punched again, and out of another job. It felt like a failure, *again.* I couldn't blame others, because no one had fired me this time. I'd been knocked down, again, and didn't want to get up off the mat. I wanted to lie there and let the ref count me out.

Indicative of the middle part of the Ministry Maturing phase, it was time to keep partaking of God's buffet table: honing gifts, learning about church government, chocking up relational wins, and experiencing losses while keeping a teachable spirit during times when pain can blind you to your growth and success (in God's eyes, if not the eyes of yourself or others).

One of the primary lessons for Mindy and me in the Grants Pass years was the need for spiritual parenting. We were insecure, idealistic. We needed wisdom and counsel from those who had gone before us. We had no one like that at The Barn.

Many young leaders long to be coached and mentored. The Lord brought me short and sweet inputs from various leaders like Jack Hayford, Campbell McAlpine, and Chuck Smith over the years. Though it was often from the distance of a pulpit while I sat in a conference pew, the impartation of the Word, Spirit, and legacy of "lives well lived" were invaluable to me. The introduction of key mentors, long- and short-term, is one of the primary relational components of this phase of personal and leadership development.

Fathers and mothers in the faith were vital to the early church. The Church was designed to resemble the family, and a family comprises multiple generations. When God starts doing amazing things around you, you can start thinking you are a special gift to humanity. Spiritual parenting puts our ideas, attitudes, and actions in perspective. Being in alignment with the heavenly Family—Father, Son, and Holy Spirit—will align us with His Family on earth—mothers and fathers, sons and daughters, sisters and brothers. The "me and Jesus against the world" days are over. We need to be seated in a multigenerational family, with all the spiritual perks and natural challenges that brings. If you are missing this fabulous component in your walk with your church, ask the Father to align you with His Family plan.

At the same time, we've seen "spiritual parenting" lead to excess and abuse. The problem comes when leaders feel entitled to take authority over their sons and daughters in the faith, as if they have the right to do so based on age, knowledge, and experience. Leaders who operate this way are lording it over their sons and daughters, not serving them as Jesus demonstrated.

Demanding loyalty is often the hallmark of a twisted human relationship. All unity in the family or church starts with equality, not authority. Jesus, on behalf of the heavenly Family, became like us and laid His life down for us. This gave Him authority over us—but He never takes it without *our* invitation. We give Him loyalty because of His great love and wisdom. Jesus's servant heart wins us over, His ransom releases us from the "kidnappers," and we run from our hellish prisons into His open arms. His lavish love "forces" our surrender, and we give Him permission to exercise His will in our lives. This is the template for church leadership: We submit one to the other, always looking for the other's best.

Spiritual parenting is exercised by serving, loving unconditionally, and waiting for your charges to reciprocate. We parent-types must be invited in (as with our biological adult children). It is often a painful process because until sons and daughters need you, and aren't afraid of the threat you represent to their blossoming identities, they won't come calling. They're responsible to God for their decisions, not to us. We can't hear God for them. We need to wait for them, just as the Father waited for His Son to return to Him! (God the Father is ever the pattern for good parenting!)

Remember that we're talking about a family relationship, not an organizational one. The distinction is critical. In an organization, the goal is to lead and be led, do the task and produce an outcome that satisfies the leaders' vision, so the organization can thrive. The corporate leader hires people to ensure his/her vision is fulfilled, leaving one's sense of value in the hands of the leader's evaluation of one's performance. Corporations tend to employ the many to fulfill the vision of a few.

In God's family, the leaders are parents who value maintaining a unified relationship over performance objectives, a vision of Jesus over ministry accomplishments. Such leaders exhibit tenacious loyalty in the face of monumental failures by their disciples. One is assigned value independent of performance and perfection. In the light of failure, fathers and mothers do not patronize, yet they are committed to tell the truth in an atmosphere of grace. The goal is always helping each other grow closer to God.

I longed to have a parental voice like that in my life, but nothing was on the horizon. What do we do in cases like this? We pray and wait in faith, knowing that isolation from the ideal is preparation by the Father to bring the right relationships to us in His time.

The Barn was mainly a movement of young people, and with "elders" all in our twenties, our immaturity eventually led to trouble. That trouble would end our days in Grants Pass. We were being "pushed" into our latter phase of Ministry Maturing—and more blessed redemption! The Father was about to bless us with spiritual parenting (discipleship) that would see us through the next twenty years.

PART THREE:

JESUS ACROSS CULTURES

THE DREADED "MISSIONARY THING"

In the course of our training, Loren and Darlene had us share the still-too-fresh burden of our failure in Grants Pass and the years immediately preceding that: all five of our "failures."

After we'd prayed about it, Loren put his arms around Mindy and me and pointed into the sunset: "See that rough patch of land in the back of our property?"

There was a rise beyond the hotel, and the hillside was covered with black lava rock and plumeria bushes.

"I have an assignment for you," he continued. "Every afternoon for the next three months, when you're not in a class, with your family, or on work detail [there was a lot of work to do on that old hotel to turn it into a university], I want you to sit on that patch of land and talk to God. Ask Him for understanding about what has happened to you. Then, listen to what He says."

It sounded crazy, but I felt like I needed a little crazy. I did just as he said.

For the next twelve weeks, Mindy and I attended classes, worked on cleaning and repairing the hotel, and took our kids swimming in the afternoons. While they splashed around in the surf, we walked on the beach and talked. Whenever I wasn't in the midst of this routine, I'd head for my hill. I sat up there and prayed, asking God about what had happened, why it had happened, and what it all meant. Sometimes I'd cry, sometimes I'd yell, sometimes I'd laugh, and sometimes Mindy would join me, because we had a lot of processing to do together. It brought up questions about myself again and about what I was supposed to do with my life. I needed time to deal with it all. This wasn't something I could claim deliverance from by faith; there was work to do. First, I needed transformation and healing. There were things that needed to be laid before the throne of God and left there—not to be concerned with again until He gave them back to me, if He ever did.

This season underscored a lifelong principle: Prayer is the engine of transformation. I'd never been much of a pray-er, but in the desperation of that season, it became as natural as breathing. Transitions and failures need to be fed a high-calorie intake of fervent prayer. This lesson has stuck with me through both personal and collective crises in all the years since.

I remembered the words of our shop teacher from that night at summer camp: "You can't run from the love of God." There was no escaping it. Whatever bad happens, He comes after you to redeem it, and then gives you another assignment to stretch you even further.

It felt like I was on an upwardly mobile trajectory by being downwardly mobile in ministry "success." The more pain you go through, the more you rise—not in the sense of rising to the top of the ladder, but rising in God's purposes for your life. It is all commensurate with the amount of cross-bearing that we embrace.

As I saw this, and that I had never been outside God's plan, I felt a new wellspring of hope rise in me. There was a world out there to take on, and God had been taking all the bad that had been happening to me and using it to build my character, and my dependence on Him so that I could be part of His redemptive plan. Bigger things were ahead.

One evening as we neared the end of our twelve weeks of training (much transformed and rested by my hillside musings), Mindy and I were walking along the Kona coast, watching the sun sink into the Pacific. It was the typical idyllic Hawaiian evening, complete with a troop of dancers traipsing by, all in Hawaiian regalia: grass skirts, leis, and lilies in their hair. The men sported *haka* tattoos on their broad chests, and they were walking down the beach to a luau, chattering and giggling like schoolchildren. It all blended into a stunning sight.

When we looked back to our path down the beach, we saw a large, slightly familiar form coming our way. It was Floyd McClung, all six feet, seven inches, walking toward us—the same Floyd McClung we had spoken with about a couple years earlier at the Mount Hermon Pastors' Conference.

Mr. "Wouldn't it be great to work together someday?"

Yep, that Floyd.

I told him, "I don't know if you remember us, but—"

He laughed. "Not only do I remember you, but I remember what we talked about, and I remember saying, 'Wouldn't it be great to work together someday?'"

"Yeah," I replied, "I remember that too. And I remember thinking, *Never happen, dude. I'm not going into missions.*" I shook my head. "Now look at us! Here we are at a missionary training center on a beach in Hawaii, open to whatever God has for us next."

He smiled. "Let's go to dinner." (When uncertain of your future, eat!)

We agreed.

So he and his wife, Sally, took Mindy and me to a beautiful beach restaurant with tiki torches and Hawaiian regalia. We sat on a balcony overlooking the ocean, listening to the waves lap on the beach. It was a perfect evening. By the end of the night, we were on our way to working with the McClungs among the junkies and prostitutes of Amsterdam.

Like the call to go to Grants Pass, it was clear to both Mindy and me that this, again, was not a call to a place, but a call to people, to friends, and to fellowship. God had orchestrated a connection to Floyd and Sally, not Amsterdam's red-light district, where we would spend the next dozen or so years. It was a call to building friendship, not to doing ministry. It was never about what I was supposed to do as much as with whom I would do it. Once that's figured out, *what* you are supposed to do comes into focus. It's a collective discovery that comes out of praying together and laboring side by side.

I would eventually get a call to Amsterdam, and we would be there even after Floyd and Sally went elsewhere. But that was not what God led with. Floyd and Sally were the call first—the spiritual parents and mentors we had always needed, even if we didn't know it.

✦ ✦ ✦ ✦ ✦

At this point, we found ourselves at the crest of another wave of God. The 1980s would see a renewal of missions work around the world, a renewal that owed much of its origins and vigor to a gathering of 2,400 evangelical leaders from 150 nations in Lausanne, Switzerland, in 1974. The International Congress on World Evangelization was the brainchild of Billy Graham, who perceived the need for a global congress to reframe Christian missions in a world of political, economic, intellectual, and religious upheaval. He had developed a passion to unite all evangelicals in the evangelization of the world.

Time magazine described it as "a formidable forum, possibly the widest-ranging meeting of Christians ever held."[7] Speakers included some of the world's most respected evangelical thinkers, including Francis Schaeffer, Ralph Winter, and John Stott. The Lausanne Committee reported:

> Those who attended remember with gratitude God's presence and favor on those ten days of prayer and planning for global mission, which galvanized the church in three major ways:
>
> 1. a theological foundation for global mission,
> 2. targeting unreached people groups, and
> 3. embracing holistic mission (societal domains).[8]

The Church, Graham said, had to grasp the ideas and values behind rapid societal changes (not something we were very adept in back in the day).

The Lausanne Conferences, in 1974 and again in 1989 (in Manila), not only fueled new mission thinking, they also served to hoist a canopy over the Church's collective participation in global church planting and evangelization. This resulted in the '80s being the greatest explosion of global partnership in the call of God in human history: Leaders and churches from developing nations began to reverse the direction of missionary involvement, resulting in a global shift from "the field" to "the force."

My father's generation was steeped in the notion that they represented a missionary "army" coming from Western nations to the "primitive" inhabitants of the "field": Africa, Asia, the Middle East, etc. The 1980s were a tipping point in the other direction. The developing nations—for centuries considered the "pagan countries"—were now sending more missionaries from their nations than the Western nations were. This cross-pollination raised new questions about what was essential to preaching the Gospel and discipling, and what were simply cultural forms and biases.

✦ ✦ ✦ ✦ ✦

The training school on Kona would wrap up at the end of June, so we had July and half of August to get home and either sell or rent our house and do something with the stuff we'd left behind in Grants Pass. Since the first place we'd bought was in town, I subdivided the acre and sold it off, making a thousand-percent profit in the process. I fleetingly thought I might have a future in real estate investment long before house flipping became popular. (Um, no, I didn't.)

I took that money and bought five acres at the foot of a mountain southwest of town. With the help of our congregation, we built a log cabin there, big enough for the five of us. These festivities felt a lot like a barn raising you'd see in a western. Once we finished it and moved in, it was a place of peace and rest. Idyllic. We had deer stroll through the yard regularly.

But as Mindy was looking out the window one day, she heard the Lord say, "This is My gift to you. Enjoy it. You'll be gone in six months."

That word was right-on. Now here we were, back at that house, packing what we wanted to take to Amsterdam and getting the rest ready for a big yard sale. Rather than selling the house, we decided we wanted to rent it so that we could return someday. (We were such dreamers!) Of course, before we could tell our Realtor this, the house had already sold!

We couldn't host a yard sale from a house in the middle of nowhere, so one of the church members—remember Grandma Reed?—offered her front lawn. She was one of those iconic sweet church ladies who always baked cookies to bless others. We loaded everything up and displayed it in her front yard. It's amazing how much stuff you can accumulate in four years when you have three young kids!

As soon as the sale began, chaos ensued. People were coming and going. They bartered like we were in a Third World country, and we did our best to get rid of stuff but not lose too much money in the process.

One woman came over from a house somewhere across the street and seemed more interested in what was going on with our move than buying anything. "What are you doing? This is a really big yard sale. What's going on?"

"Yeah, we're from up the hill," I told her. "We've been here for five years, but we're moving to Europe."

"Where in Europe?" she asked.

"We're moving to Amsterdam."

She made a face. "Not the Amsterdam with the red-light district? The one with all that ugly, hard, sinful, bad stuff?"

"Oh yeah, that's where we're going."

She spun and walked back across the street without saying another word.

I shrugged and returned to bargaining.

At about 5:00, we were starting to put blankets over what was left, closing down the sale, and making plans to give away the rest. Here came the woman from across the street again. She strutted up to me and pointed her finger at my chest. "I've been thinking about what you just told me about moving these three little babies into that den of iniquity," she said.

Our kids had been playing in the yard with friends and neighbor kids who'd wandered in all day for all to see. They were really the cutest things to watch.

"You have no right to take your children into that hellhole!" she went on. "You're leaving a country of safety, you're taking them away from their grandparents, and you're subjecting them to who knows what kind of dangers!" She went on like that for a bit, and then punctuated it with, "You're a fool!"

Then she spun and strutted back across the street.

The first thought that came to me was, *You're right, baby. I'm a fool for Jesus.*

Mindy and I knew we were doing what God wanted us to do, but we weren't ignorant of the dangers. There would be spiritual work to do to keep our kids protected in the years ahead, and we would face some ugly stuff. But God was calling us, and I knew that no matter what happened, He'd be with us because of how He'd been with me through the depression and oppression of my past. I realized He'd been preparing us for this mission for a long time.

There was no going back now. We'd jumped off the cliff. It was time to launch into the dreaded "missionary thing."

UNVEILING YOUR FUTURE

Upon the move to Kona, the fear of failure was so great that I had no way to go but up—up to the Father. Prayer became integral to every step we took. After years of attempting to pray (the discipline of prayer, quiet times of prayer, and other prayer "boosters"), I found beauty in the way pressure and desperation drove me to my knees before my Father. I found truth in "the desperate [fervent] prayer of a righteous man gets a whole lot done in the Kingdom enterprise" (James 5:16, severe Petersen paraphrase).

Moving to Kona was also a loving rebuke to a son who had told the Father the he "would never" multiple times. "I'm done with ministry!" *No, you're not.* "I'll never be a missionary." *Et voila!* I'm doing something that suspiciously resembles missionary stuff. Maturing as a leader brings a boatload of lessons about overcoming fear and projecting "imminent disaster" if "such and such" happens in our lives. Gideon had a bad case of "Who me?" and "I can't do that!" Moses said, "Sorry, Lord, You have the wrong guy—seek Aaron for the talking parts." Israel stood on the border of the Promised Land and convinced themselves they wouldn't be able to enter. Reluctance and bold declarations of "I will never" need to be summarily buried in the deep blue sea of His wisdom and foresight.

Seeing Floyd's large silhouette on Kona's beach was not only a shift in direction for us, but also a foundation stone that would be laid in our lives. *Whom you are with is more important than where you are or what you do.* God's guidance is relational first and transactional second. Jesus chose His twelve "to be with Him," mentored them, and included them in His adventures. Eventually, He released them to carry on His mission. I encourage those seeking God's direction to ask, "Whom am I being called to be with?" rather than "What do You want me to do?" One prayer depends on being "hooked up" with the right people; the other prayer is often our way of validating our independence or feeling valued, based on some "spectacular" assignment. (Makes a good newsletter but breeds a discipleship vacuum.)

Growing in leadership often means growing resistance and disapproval from friends and family. We certainly experienced this from our immediate friends and family—and my strutting "neighbor" at the garage sale. This resistance is critical to refining our callings from God. If the voice of parents, boyfriends, girlfriends, other leaders, and their unredeemed expectations for us interferes with our decision-making process, we need to stop, drop to our knees, and roll away from any voice that isn't the sweet voice of the Father. Resistance hones our listening skills and is designed to deliver us from the fear of human beings.

Geographical changes can be scary. Getting detoxed from one culture to minister in another is like going through a sheep dip: It removes the *fear* of the wolf, the annoyance of *fleas*, and *friction* with others. What is preferential gets replaced by what is essential. For some it is a switch between ethnicities or geopolitical entities. For others it may be leaving single life to get married. It might be a change in corporate culture and workplace. Why doesn't the Lord give us more warning or foresight into major changes in our geography or calling? Because, in the immortal words of Jack Nicholson from *A Few Good Men*: "You can't handle the truth!" Really, a hint is usually all you get until you really need to know.

Those of us who've manifested "Premature Information Addiction" (PIA—Okay, I just made that up) need a serious stay at the Jesus addiction clinic. We're always looking for a "word" to get insight into our futures, but that's seldom the way God operates. (And if He does, it usually means rough seas ahead—believe me, it's usually better *not knowing*.) Besides, we aren't entitled to know anything He isn't willing and prepared to reveal. I've seen more peace compromised by good folks raising questions for which there are no immediate answers, or giving ultimatums and deadlines to try to force God's hand. Good luck with that—surrender and enjoy your ignorance! You don't always have to know all of the details. That is part of the substance that trusting God is made from.

When I counsel younger people on their journeys—in ministry or some other vocation—I see them struggling with the same feelings and doubts, whether their experiences are lesser than what I experienced or much worse. These self-doubts and questions about purpose, mission, and calling are identity questions we each need to answer and resolve, through the conviction of biblical truth and Holy Spirit learning. They are challenges the Father will use to change the issue of our lives from trying to refine ourselves to experiencing an exchanged life—ours for His. The goal of leadership development in God's family is teaching us to live "from Jesus, the center," and to hold tightly to that, no matter what else is thrown at us.

AMSTERDAM

On August 16, 1981, we arrived in Amsterdam with even more stowage than we'd taken on our Hawaiian escapade. In addition to all of our stuff, people graciously sent us off with financial gifts to help us get settled on the other side of the pond. Our parents, now in full support, were our first prayer team, along with lifelong friends in Grants Pass.

We are going to need that prayer, I thought as Floyd introduced us to our new 350-square-foot "home" in a 200-year-old building just over a *patatkraam* (french fry shop) that served the neighborhood dealers and junkies (at all hours, it seemed). Suddenly the hotel on Kona didn't look so bad. Thankfully, it was next door to our ministry center, Samaritan's Inn, and across from the train station. Commuting and getting around wasn't going to be a problem.

Samarian's Inn had once been owned by the Salvation Army. After that, it had fallen into the hands of a cult called "the Children of God." It was in poor shape when Floyd and his team had bought it a year and a half before. Bob Pierce, a well-known Christian leader in those days, had seen the building, talked with Floyd, and contributed a significant amount of the down payment to help us purchase the building. The location was great, but the building was bargain basement–priced for a reason. Many of the floors were so dilapidated that they had holes in them—there was one toilet you could sit on and see two floors down. We had our work cut out for us in getting this dowdy edifice into useful shape.

The *Zeedijk*, where we now claimed our domicile, was the most prominent and populated street in Europe for drug trafficking. We were adjacent to the original city gate, now the official entrance to the 600-year-old red-light district. As we learned more Dutch, we were soon able to distinguish the current price of the drugs as we lay in bed each night, trying to shut out the street chatter and the aroma of the shop below so we could sleep. When I think of that place, I still smell the oil and frying potatoes. It would take a few years to get used to that. We would also hear the fights and people swearing at each other at all hours. We were, indeed, in a "den of certified sinners."

Maybe I *was* a fool.

Mindy's movie-star grandmother, Dale Evans ("The Queen of the West"), was so excited about what we were doing that she'd flown to Amsterdam ahead of us and was with Floyd when he met us at the airport. Grandpa Roy? Well, he was less than supportive. He would snort, "Don't we have enough damn bad people in America for you to need to be traipsing off to some foreign country?" (Again, I think the real issue was seeing the great-grandchildren more.)

Two years later, on our first furlough, Roy struck up the mantra again while we were sharing our stories in his living room with a circle of their friends. With Dale shooting her famous "look of disdain" in his direction, I pontificated, "We went to Amsterdam because the inner city had virtually no access to the Gospel or a vibrant community of God's people. We go where believers ain't."

Roy threw up his hands and said, "Okay, why didn't you say that the first time around?"

Got to love that man.

As we were moving into the apartment, Grandma Dale was so elated that she took pictures of everything out of our windows, to show to Roy and their friends back in Apple Valley. When we left the building a little later, we learned that it's usually the police taking pictures out windows—to document drug deals in the streets. We were met by a disgruntled group who demanded that we hand over our camera. Things threatened to get ugly, fast. Fortunately, they all knew Floyd and he was able to appease their concerns.

Poor Grandma Dale! She nearly fainted when she realized what she had done. Floyd was really gracious. He told her, "You know what? Taking pictures like that is just something we can't do. We're trying to build trust here. We don't want people thinking you're an undercover cop."

"Me?" she responded. "I ride horses."

All the same, Grandma Dale agreed not to take any more pictures.

Welcome to Amsterdam!

✦ ✦ ✦ ✦ ✦

The first two or three years in Holland were not about being missionaries as much as about our family acclimating. Mindy and I healed slowly from the meltdown at The Barn, and what lingered from the four firings I had experienced before that. (It's one thing to forgive and put those things behind you, but it's another to remove the negativity from your mind and really have confidence in yourself as a beloved child of God.) I spent a lot of time painting and fixing up the Samaritan's Inn. (We eventually put a statue of the Good Samaritan in the entryway, along with the words "Let your heart be pierced with the things that pierce the heart of God"—a phrase Bob Pierce was well known for.) One of the first things I remember doing was building a triple-decker bunk bed set for the kids.

Floyd and Sally had no intention of rushing us into anything. We were now in a place where we could help by fixing things up. We could chill out, put our hands to what needed to be done, and let the new culture seep in.

Since most of the YWAM team were so young, and we had a revolving door of kids coming to do short-term missions stints, we received a strange respect as "seasoned" pastors, even though we still were only on the verge of our thirties. Given our backgrounds in music, we were also treated like professional musicians. After seven or eight years of multiple-church ministry (and attending many conferences), we knew people who were becoming prominent national leaders back in the United States. We were special in the eyes of the kids coming through, but we knew better. Regardless, the instantaneous respect built our confidence even further.

Floyd informed us that we were YWAM's first urban-focused ministry. The organization was deeply rooted in the 1960s and '70s and seemed to espouse the belief that God was fundamentally communal and preferred idyllic countrysides. YWAM "bases" to that point had reflected the Jesus communities of the '70s. They were simple retreat centers, not outposts near "dens of iniquity." It was not unusual to get resistance from many in the church, as well as in YWAM, to the idea of moving teams into such dark places as the red-light district. Despite that opposition, we were grateful for the encouragement of prominent Dutch icons such as Corrie ten Boom and Brother Andrew, and the Chicago-based urban ministry innovator, Ray Bakke. Those were pioneering times.

Along with Floyd's team of forty YWAMers, we moved in and fell in love with the people of Amsterdam and those we ministered with. It was wild and wonderful. We were never sure what might erupt.

During one night of rage, soccer enthusiasts from England and the local Surinamese drug dealers got into a squabble that escalated into cobblestones being lifted from the pavement outside our window and hurled at the other party, with accompanying expletives. One errant brick crashed through a window in the kids' bedroom, missing little Andy's head by inches. That brick became a memorial in our living room: a "thank You for Your protection, Jesus" artifact. On some days, we would approach our outside door and need to knock from the inside to give a "neighbor" on the outside the opportunity to cease any urinary administrations before we pushed it open.

In repairing the inn, someone found an old picture of the building from its Salvation Army days, noting that there was once a sign atop the building, reading, "Jesus Loves You," and "God Roept U"—Dutch for "God is calling you." When people saw it, they thought it would be cool to restore the sign to commemorate the building's history, and the fact that the Samaritan's Inn again stood for those same principles. The national Christian television station offered to erect new signs. They held a big event to raise the needed funds. They brought in a former astronaut to speak at the fund-raiser. It seemed an odd marketing ploy, but I've never known much about branding and things like that. Thankfully, the campaign was a success.

Then about a year later, we got a phone call from a father from South Holland. He told us, "I just want you to know what a blessing your sign has been to our family. My daughter recently ran away from home, fighting with our belief system. She was so angry that she decided to seek her fame and fortune in Amsterdam.

"When she came out of the train station, she looked up and saw that sign across the street on your building. Conviction hit her and she fell to her knees and repented of her bad attitude and the way she'd been treating us. She turned around, jumped back on the train, and came home." There were tears in the man's voice: "I got my daughter back because of your sign."

Okay, I thought, *I'll never criticize "wasting" money on that sign again.*

Through incidents like that, I learned how God honors communities of faith who pray day and night for interventions of the Holy Spirit. He touches people unexpectedly. We dove more deeply into prayer, and God started opening even more surprising doorways.

✦ ✦ ✦ ✦ ✦

I'd been put in charge of supervising the inn's renovations. I oversaw the working crews—teams from around the world helped us bring that disaster of a building up to code, make it livable, put YWAM offices in the bottom, and a nice big apartment for Floyd and Sally on the top floor. I soon fell into the routine of YWAM, whose mantra was "evangelism, training, and mercy ministries." I learned to do street evangelism, which I did not enjoy. I didn't like confronting people with a religious message, but since the New Testament guys did it all the time, who was I to disagree? I wanted to be subtler, more behind-the-scenes, but many of my colleagues had quite a flair for it.

One of those was a "wild-eyed" evangelist named John Goodfellow, who, while running from the law in England, had encountered a YWAM street team and gave his life to Jesus. He asked Floyd several times, "Can I build a coffin and go into the streets and proclaim, 'Jesus is the resurrection of the dead'?"

Floyd thought the idea was nuts. He told John, "Under no circumstances are we going into the streets with coffins. That's ludicrous!"

Then, one day, Floyd walked by the prayer room and heard, "Dear God, change his mind, change his mind. I believe You want me to do this." It was John Goodfellow praying that Floyd would warm to his coffin idea.

"I surrender," Floyd later told him. "Make your crazy coffin."

John got some guys to make a pine box with a lid, then painted the "coffin" black. He got his mates together as pallbearers, all dressed as mourners. John would climb into the box. Then they'd hoist him and the box onto their shoulders and march him slowly to the center of town—Dam Square—singing a Gregorian-sounding dirge they'd created for the occasion. The square was about three-quarters of a mile from our building. There, they'd place the box in an open area and gather in a ceremonious circle around it.

This square was truly Amsterdam central. Members of Parliament often came walking through. People were everywhere: tourists, the homeless, office workers having lunch or tea, addicts smashed out of their minds, children playing. The whole world seemed to converge on Dam Square.

People couldn't help but gather around the box in curiosity as the "pallbearers" stood there silently with their heads bowed and hands folded. Once a sufficient crowd had gathered, John would pop out, dressed all in white and preach "Jesus, the resurrection of the dead" and "He is risen!" As ridiculous it sounds, it worked! John and his team led people to the Lord through this crazy stunt all the time. (We used to tease John that he was "scaring the *hell* out of them.")

✦ ✦ ✦ ✦ ✦

For our community in Amsterdam, regular street evangelism outreaches were the norm. Our teams were on the streets nearly every day, preaching and augmenting the message with music and dramatic presentations that creatively depicted biblical truths. *Toymaker and Son*, an allegorical depiction of Jesus's death and resurrection, would often be performed at Dam Square and elsewhere in the city.

Keith Green was one of the most memorable Christian musicians and evangelists of the '70s and early '80s. He had a strong prophetic tone and loved evangelism. Keith and his wife, Melody, visited our base in Amsterdam in the late spring of 1982. That trip to be with us and other European YWAM bases deeply impacted Keith and Melody. They returned home determined to challenge believers in America to go and reach the lost and needy everywhere. This set the stage for a fall concert tour to spread the message.

Keith never performed the tour, however. He died in a plane crash with eleven others (including two of his children) on July 28, 1982, just a couple of months after his visit to Amsterdam. Melody, at home with their youngest daughter (and newly pregnant with their fourth child), decided that their Last Days Ministries would still fulfill Keith's desire to carry the Great Commission, via the Keith Green Memorial Concert Tour, which happened as scheduled that fall. (You can still find the video of that tour on YouTube by searching for "Keith Green Memorial Concert.")

This first tour inspired future efforts to call America's emerging generation to "go to the nations." In his final concert performance, Keith passionately reminded American youth, "He told you to go—you need a call to stay." He often said there were more

Avon salespeople per person worldwide than there were Christians trying to reach the lost. This burning passion in his heart fanned the flame that motivated more than 300,000 from 110 cities to "go." YWAM founder Loren Cunningham observed, "I don't know of a time in history when more youth were presented a missionary challenge." Operation Mobilization and YWAM's training schools exploded with students because of those concert tours.

Various YWAM leaders, including yours truly, were invited to crowd the concert tour bus on a road trip that engaged thousands of hungry young disciples. I spent two weeks on the tour bus with several other missionaries, going from city to city with Keith's message. My father's missionary world would never have imagined thousands of non-seminary youth being launched into the world of short-term missions in order to fulfill God's dream for the nations. It was holy pandemonium!

✦ ✦ ✦ ✦ ✦

The early years in Amsterdam were some of the best of our lives. We were surrounded by a radical team of pray-ers, evangelists, and "sold out" families, representing various nationalities, along with an increasing number of Dutch friends. Floyd regularly took time to sit with me for hours and let me pour out the pain and self-doubt from my ministry failures of the '70s. Then he would direct me to the Lord's promise to *"repay you for the years the locusts have eaten"* (Joel 2:25).

Feeling depressed and monkish during one of our earlier meetings, I entered a large YWAM staff meeting and promptly placed myself behind a pole that obscured me from Floyd's sight onstage. You would think I'd have known by then that such tactics don't work. During the "response" time after his teaching, he walked down off the stage, past 300 people, crawled over ten chairs in my row, knelt down to look in my eyes, and spoke God's message to me: "I'm going to get inside of you."

I melted. It's what I longed for and was terrified of all at once. Every heart needs to be pursued past the point of comfort, where love is not contingent on behavior. Such unconditional affection needs to be repeated until the subject surrenders.

Under that grace, the roots of my healing sank deeper into my heart.

The Lord continued to restore our confidence and clarify our calling, preparing us for bigger things than we could have ever imagined. We found ourselves doing anything and everything, from renovating Samaritan's Inn, to serving in the coffee shop, serving Christmas meals to street people, and praying through the red-light district while fending off curses from Satanists.

We prayed for the impossible no matter what our eyes told us. We didn't see many results from those prayers initially, but then things started to change, as if we were reaching a spiritual tipping point. I know that the foundations of prayer we laid in those years led to the breakthroughs we were soon to experience.

It's amazing how God can take one small thing, one conversion, and affect so many—and then do that again and again and again.

UNVEILING YOUR FUTURE

After moving to Amsterdam, it was obvious that the buffet table of ministry opportunity was still set, but the fare had changed. Now there were ethnic foods: new cultural lessons, experiences, and relationships. Changing cultures is a fabulous and frustrating process. Everything is different: smells, customs, language, pace, taboos, etc. This introduction to new things is all part of keeping the learning leader fluid, non-static, and dependent on God. Those early years of learning to acclimate to the culture were a type of detox and "wipe-the-slate-clean" season.

Nobody really knew Mindy and me when we moved to Amsterdam. Any arrogance I might have had about my "stellar teaching gift" and "church planting prowess" were quickly doused by the obscurity of serving our team in the "shadows," even in spite of the immediate respect we got as "veterans" from all the visiting teams. It was the perfect place for us at the time. It gave us a chance to detox from negative self-talk and be distracted by the craziness and surprises of adjusting to a foreign culture.

We can't always tackle the next assignment on the success of the prior one. Sometimes we have start from scratch.

We set our hands to renovating Samaritan's Inn. The work was therapeutic. In some ways, it was great to be out of the pressure cooker. In other ways, it felt like a demotion. In obscurity, in the dark, life is formed and potential is gestated. This was certainly the case during those initial years in Amsterdam, where I began developing a clear ministry philosophy and the beginnings of an ecclesiology, learned another language, and developed skills in Deliverance 201, prophecy, and power encounters.

God will expose young leaders to myriad experiences as a filter system to appreciate what others are better at and to highlight what their primary skill set is on the road to their destiny. During this time, I learned I'm not a youth pastor, an associate, an administrator, or even an evangelist, yet I still performed as all of them. That introduced me to all of those worlds as part of the shaping of my character and my toolbox of skills—serving others without being noticed, and yet progressively coming to understand what my primary gifts from God were.

The middle to latter Ministry Maturing phases seem to be universally dedicated to teaching us how to hone our primary strengths, get along with people, function in healthy teams, grow in strategic and organizational understanding, and maintain a burning passion to serve God and one another. I was learning to trade efficiency in getting things done for building foundations by "moving at the speed of relationship." Thus, out of this "backstage" time, I learned one of the most important lessons in my life: "slow down and make friends first."

PRAYER AS "THE AIR WE BREATHE"

In 1983, we got word that the Billy Graham Evangelistic Association (BGEA) wanted to host an International Conference for itinerant evangelists in our city. It was a wild time. Three-fourths of the 3,871 attendees were from developing nations, and most of them had never ventured beyond their own villages. Now they were staying in high-end hotels, meeting at Amsterdam's massive RAI Convention Center, and facing one of Europe's darkest, most immoral cities. Their senses were assaulted by the decadence and depravity.

They were also thrust into a bewildering cross-cultural "soup." These precious brothers and sisters knew little of Western conference protocol. Many were ordering room service and dry-cleaning willy-nilly and charging it to the BGEA. Others were unsure how to navigate our toilets. (They tossed their soiled toilet paper in the wastebaskets; that was normal for them.)

Despite the cultural learning curve these dear brothers and sisters faced, they flooded our streets with pure Gospel fervor. What a blessing to have nearly 4,000 rabid evangelists unleashed on the city you love, live in, and pray for each day.

The 1983 conference was so successful that they did it again in 1986, when more than 8,000 evangelists from 173 nations descended on our city. It was a holy free-for-all, as my international brothers and sisters preached Jesus to many bewildered Amsterdam-ers.

The plan for global evangelization birthed in the 1970s significantly affected how churches were going to be planted overseas in the 1980s. In 1980, the Philippines hosted the Congress on Discipling a Whole Nation (DAWN). The world was hungry for a more communal and effective model for church and discipleship, and people needed information on the current state of the nations and ethnicities of the world. "New wineskins" were needed for informed prayer about places that many people were unaware of.

In that spirit, our Amsterdam team used to gather underneath a massive wall map of the world. It was at least twenty feet long. One day, as we were praying over the map, we noticed someone had added tape forming a rectangular area. Curious, we asked our resident missiologist, Jim Mellis, about that box on our "holy" map. That's when Jim introduced us to the "10/40 Window." I learned about unfamiliar nations and people groups as we "prayed through the window." The Lord was speaking to our staff (and others throughout the world) about "the window," and many responded to the need.

This region of the world was previously known to Christians as the "resistant belt," a term coined by the Lausanne II Conference in Manila in 1989. In 1990, Luis Bush, the CEO of Partners International, introduced research that led to a meeting with the developer of the first PC-based GIS software. They analyzed the region using a box located between 10 and 40 degrees north latitude. Accordingly, it was dubbed the 10/40 Box. A few weeks later, Luis's wife, Doris, recommended renaming it the 10/40 Window, denoting a "window of opportunity," not a "resistant belt."

The "Window" represents an area that in 1990 was said to have the highest level of socioeconomic challenges and the planet's poorest access to the Gospel and Christian resources. Roughly two-thirds of the world population lives in the 10/40 Window. It is also populated by people who are Muslim, Hindu, Buddhist, animist, Jewish, or atheist. Many governments in the 10/40 Window are formally or informally opposed to Christian work of any kind within their borders.*

Several of my friends were arrested in the 10/40 Window, and one even lost her life near Sulaymaniyah, Iraq. The intensifying activity in these new frontiers was birthing new methodologies for getting the Gospel to these isolated people. There was a rush of Bible translation missionaries, radio, medical relief efforts, new technologies, and new mission thinking. In this flood of information and new strategies, I eventually saw the master pattern. It was all about the Father wanting to reveal to His Church the numerous children of His creation, who were hidden and had been denied knowing the beauty of His loving intentions for them.

And once we saw them, what were we going to do about it?

Our battle cry became, *"This gospel of the kingdom will be preached in the whole world as a testimony to all nations, and then the end will come"* (Matthew 24:14). With the turn of the millennium in sight, the 1980s and '90s boosted the idea of getting the Gospel to "the frontiers," and to "bring Jesus back." This spawned endeavors like "Praying through the Window," the AD 2000 Movement, and the "Global Congress on World Evangelization" (GCOWE-1995).

---

* If you and your church family are interested in "praying through the window," I recommend Jason Mandryk's *Operation World: The Definitive Prayer Guide to Every Nation* (Downers Grove, IL: InterVarsity Press, 2010), an introduction to each nation and its prayer-worthy needs.

In its history, the Church has developed more than 700 plans for global evangelization. Jim Montgomery, founder of DAWN, developed a "closure strategy" that was different from most. He emphasized the multiplication of congregations as the key to seeing the world evangelized by the year 2000. He predicted that seven million more churches were needed before 2000 in order to fulfill the Great Commission. Montgomery defined DAWN as an attempt to mobilize the whole body of Christ in a whole nation in a strategy for discipling that nation. By 2000, church planting was the norm in global mission strategies, though Montgomery's goal of seven million churches was not realized. Regardless, DAWN and other collaborative endeavors faithfully continue their efforts toward that goal.

✦ ✦ ✦ ✦ ✦

For our Amsterdam team, the 1980s were the decade we also became convinced that church planting was God's way of making disciples and impacting a city with the Gospel. We believed that the foundations of new churches could be built only through prayer. Amsterdam was increasingly becoming a heterogeneous, pluralistic society. Africans and those from the Middle East were constantly filtering in to receive political asylum or obtain guest-worker status.

In addition to our Middle Eastern immigrants, nomadic European youth continued to pour in for the "free lifestyle" of Amsterdam. The hippie movement of the 1970s was aging out and being replaced by punk music advocates, with their mohawks, spiked bracelets and chokers, tattoos, and leather jackets.

Dave and Jodie Pierce, two of our YWAM leaders, began visiting punk clubs, hangouts, and domiciles. After World War II, laws had been drafted to protect those living wherever they could find housing, and those laws had never been changed. Thus, punks had "license" to take up residence in abandoned buildings, without fear of eviction. Amsterdamers call these people *krakers* ("squatters"). I'll never forget talking to Dave and his team after they'd spent more than a year ministering to hundreds of Amsterdam punks. He showed me pages and pages, bearing the names of every punk they had met. They were discouraged; not one had come to Jesus.

So, as was our way, we turned to prayer. Then as we prayed, a slightly different tactic was inspired: When all else fails, throw a party! That party was held on our floating ministry barge, formally known as "The Ark," and now the home of *Steiger* (Pier) *14*, featuring an inimitable band called "NLM," which stood for "No Longer Music." So many punks came for the party that we feared the barge might sink! (Thankfully, it didn't.)

That night launched Dave and his team's dream to evangelize and plant a church among the punk culture. Their first convert came to Christ that night, and many followed in the ensuing years. The Lord used the *Steiger 14* team to plant a community of faith on that barge, while NLM went on to tour Europe, helping to spread the Gospel to countercultural youth.

During a visit by my parents, I introduced them to two or three punk kids who had joined our ranks. My dad's eyes grew as big as saucers. He later confided to me, "God can't be glorified by this."

"Do me a favor," I countered. "Take those three guys out to coffee. Just talk to them."

He took me up on it—I'm sure with the thought that he was going to straighten them out.

So he had coffee with these twentysomethings. When he returned, I asked, "So, how'd it go? What did you think?"

"Wonderful young men!" he exclaimed. "They're fantastic kids! They've asked me to counsel and pastor them."

I smiled. "They're gold, aren't they? No matter what they look like on the outside?"

He smiled. He knew I had him. He patted me on the back and said, "We're meeting again next week. I look forward to it." (I love my dad for that kind of thing. He might have seemed a little starched sometimes, but when it came right down to it, he loved people more than rules. He was always willing to learn when he saw the glorification of Jesus leading the way.)

This success among the punks, in one of the darkest cities on earth, convinced me of the Lord's absolute desire and commitment to go to the lowest of the low and invite them into His Family—*His* Church. There is no person, no group, and no nation outside Jesus's redemptive power. Jesus is always prepared to move in mercy and power to those who have willingly abandoned all self-protection, reputation, and worldly thinking. Jesus has commissioned us to plant churches to disciple all people and nations, inviting them into His Family. The rich tapestry of God's plan includes weaving in those hopeless ones who have been left on humanity's garbage dump. He wants to create the image of His Son out of the tangled threads and torn cloth of their broken lives.

The Father is always willing to go low to find His lost family. For this to happen, His redeemed family needs to enter others' "zones" and interpret the Gospel for their cultures. The only way to do this is by being *with* them, getting to know them, to serve them and earn their trust. We need to do more than show up, preach on the streets, and encourage converts to join local churches. We need to pray, then inject ourselves into their culture, and as people in that culture come to Christ, to walk with them as leaders to make more disciples. We need to "move at the speed of relationship"—basing discipleship on friendship, not the other way around.

So, like Paul, we learned to become *"all things to all people so that by all possible means* [we] *might save some"* (1 Corinthians 9:22).

Our "punk missionaries" looked like punks. They visited punk bars and were indistinguishable from the punk culture—except that they loved Jesus. We were learning that function trumped form, that the Gospel had to "become flesh," and that no one is outside of Jesus's redemptive love. For me it was the birth of evaluating, and sometimes challenging, my notions of what "church" was. Growing up, I'd always thought of it as an organization, but it was really more about people relating with other people as they all tried to relate to and do the will of God.

✦ ✦ ✦ ✦ ✦

These adventures into "weird" church planting were not unique to the '80s. Up to that point, the American church had grown increasingly isolationist. Thus, missions work had a distinct nationalist flavor. Due to the increased cultural disconnection among denominations and independent mission agencies, the task of taking the whole Gospel to the whole world required a new approach, a new biblical paradigm, and new direction from the Holy Spirit—a new "wineskin," you might say. The realization of the magnitude of the Great Commission seemed to foster a truce of old dissent and birthed an increasingly amicable spirit among global church leaders, movements, and agencies. Unity and strategy were being found only via prayer. As I had experienced the power of prayer on my little hill in Kona, Hawaii, I was about to experience the power of collective prayer on a more international and boundary-breaking scale. Even then, the foundation for this had been being laid for some time.

Throughout the 1970s and '80s, God's people were turning to a fresh dependence on prayer, rather than organizational strategies. In Papua New Guinea, the Enga churches were in a desperate spiritual state. Prayer meetings began among pastors, missionaries, and Bible-college students. It spread to villages. Some villagers agreed to pray together every day until God sent new life to the church. So it was that:

> On 15 September 1973, without any prior indication, simultaneously, spontaneously, in village after village as pastors stood to deliver their normal Sunday morning messages, the Holy Spirit descended bringing conviction, confession, repentance, and revival. Normal work stopped as people in the thousands hurried to special meetings. Prayer groups met daily, morning and evening. Thousands of Christians were restored, and thousands of pagans were converted. Whole villages became Christian, and the church grew not only in size, but in maturity.[9]

Meanwhile, spectacular growth was occurring in Argentina through the fervor of praying Argentinian believers. Jose Luis Vasquez saw his church explode from 600 to 4,500, then to a constituency of 10,000 members in five years, following a visit from Carlos Annacondia. Omar Cabrera started his church in 1972, with fifteen members. It grew to a combined membership of 90,000. Hector Gimenez started his church from zero in 1983. His congregation grew to 70,000.

In the mid-1990s, I visited Argentina several times with Harvest Evangelism. (I'll tell a few stories about these trips later.) I witnessed firsthand the immense dedication to prayer in all of the churches mentioned above. At their events, two tents were erected for evangelistic meetings, one for the preaching of the Gospel, and one for the deliverance of the demonized—a noisy and joy-filled tent it was! Prayer was the foundation of all the meetings—before, during, and after each event.

I first heard Dick Eastman, international president for Every Home for Christ, speak on prayer at one of the pastors' conferences in Mount Hermon, California, in 1978. I read his book *The Hour That Changes the World* and was radicalized for a lifestyle of both personal and collective prayer.

The National Prayer Committee (NPC) was founded in 1979, and it spawned many prayer initiatives in many nations. The NPC began as a subcommittee on prayer at the International Congress on World Evangelization held in Lausanne, Switzerland. Out of the Lausanne gathering came the US Lausanne Committee (now Mission America) and America's National Prayer Committee. Global mission strategies and partnerships were snowballing quickly.

Peter Wagner (co-founder of the World Prayer Center and author of some remarkable books on prayer and missions) has intensely investigated what lies behind such effective ministry. He concluded that powerful intercessory prayer is the chief weapon. Although much of this intercession was happening in Pentecostal and charismatic environments, believers of all stripes were finding power, not in mission strategies or pet doctrines, but in dependence on unified and focused prayer.

Wherever this prayer first principle was invoked, amazing things happened. In 1982, Christians in East Germany started to form small groups of ten to twelve who committed to meet and to pray for peace in Germany. By October 1989, 50,000 people were involved in Monday-night prayer meetings with this purpose at the top of their prayer list. By year's end, when those praying people moved quietly into the streets, their numbers quickly swelled to 300,000, as many of their countrymen joined them. Though a factor unseen by many, I have no doubt this prayer was a big reason why "the (Berlin) wall came tumbling down." Things often need to get settled in the courts of heaven before they change in the halls of government on earth.

Then came "March for Jesus," which began as "City March" in London in 1987. It emerged out of the friendship of three groups: Pioneer, led by Gerald Coates; Ichthus Christian Fellowship, led by Roger Forster; and the British arm of Youth With a Mission, headed by Lynn Green. These three friends came together with worship leader Graham Kendrick and led a prayer and worship movement that, over the next three years, spread across the UK, Europe, and North America—and eventually around the world. Hundreds of smaller marches emerged in its wake. In 1994 the first Global March for Jesus covered every time zone and involved more than ten million Christians from more than 170 nations. It is estimated that by the final "Global March for Jesus" (in June 2000), more than sixty million people in 180 nations participated.

My first Amsterdam "March for Jesus" prayer parade occurred on a cold day in May of 1992. Nearly 15,000 believers marched, holding banners, singing songs, and praying for God's blessing on our city. While not a fan of large, aggressive endeavors like this, I was drawn in by the unity of so many brothers and sisters, and the hope that God gave us. It was an event that was a decade of worldwide prayer in the making.

In Cuba, as the 1990s were dawning, an Assemblies of God pastor, whose congregation never exceeded 100 people, began praying with other leaders once a week. He soon found himself conducting twelve services daily, for 7,000 people. They started queuing at 2:00 AM and even broke down the doors to get into the prayer meetings. Asked to explain these phenomena, Cuban Christians say, "It has come because we have paid the price. We have suffered for the Gospel, and we have prayed for many, many years."[10]

Globally, the church was learning that it was more important to pray than to organize. We were learning the same thing as we followed God's ideas into the depths of the red-light district to touch the lives of punks, druggies, and prostitutes.

UNVEILING YOUR FUTURE

Few leadership lessons are as pervasive and lifelong as learning to pray. To live a lifestyle of communication with our God, to fulfill the mandate to stand between heaven and earth and petition the Creator for His will, is sobering—and fun!

This is one of the lessons that runs through all the leadership phases, and it increases in potency, effectiveness, and routine through our lifetimes. Knowing the Word, hearing God, and loving each other are lifelong pursuits. What differentiates the prayer of a young leader and a seasoned leader is how the latter's influence becomes the conduit of his or her prayer life. As the Church engages cities, nations, governments, and business realms, leaders can be assured that their level of influence as ambassadors will be increased by their faithfulness to prayer.

But where does it begin? Day one. The journey begins with our first prayer. Your first Bible study, mission outreach, effort to help the homeless, or whatever God is calling you to do gains traction through prayer. The lessons learned in the "small days" build our prayer muscles for larger tasks. We learn to pray alone, then with friends, then in public. In time, prayer becomes like breathing.

Prayer-oxygenated Christians are dangerous to the kingdom of darkness.

In this section, I hope you've seen how God seemed to link prayer with His global initiative in the 1980s: reaching ethnicities (10/40 Window), church planting (DAWN and Steiger 14), national and international prayer movements (various prayer initiatives like Global Day of Prayer, etc.), and "prayer-walking" (March for Jesus, Lighthouses of Prayer, etc.). All of these were birthed and sustained by communicating with the Father, Son, and Spirit.

Conversely, prayerlessness, assuming God will bless our plans (rather than seeking His), flippancy, and airy "religious" prayers are an affront to God. He wants prayers from potent ambassadors, not impotent spiritual wimps looking to impress their hearers. When Jody and Dave Pierce prayed for the punks to come to Jesus, they meant business, and God answered. We prayed daily for nine years for our first prostitute convert. After the first one, however, the barriers began to crumble and many came to Christ. We had evil bureaucrats oppose us, but we prayed. *Zap!* Satanists cursed us; we blessed them in prayer, publicly. Walls in the East that wouldn't fall—after global, unified prayer—*Boom! There they go!* Evil despots over nations? Petition the King of Kings. *Deposed!* In Argentina we walked a city of 180,000 people, every street and every business, three times in three weeks. Hundreds were saved, crime rates fell to nothing, and the Church grew.

The older we get, the more we depend on the Lord's voice. As we grew more confident in the Lord's ability to joyfully answer our prayers, our spiritual influence swelled and we saw cities and nations changed.

Want to secure your destiny? Be freakish in prayer!

14

RED-LIGHT JESUS

All three of our kids reached school age in the mid-1980s, and there was only one primary school in the area they could attend. It sat in the middle of the red-light district. It was a little Catholic parochial school run by two nuns, Sister Peters and Sister Nefkins. It was very traditional. Students got their hands smacked with a switch if they misbehaved. The two nuns wore black robes with green trim. I don't know which order they were part of, but they loved all of their students, most of whom came from single-parent homes. One year, our Andy was the only one in his grade with married parents. A lot of the students were the children of prostitutes; they didn't know their fathers. Others were orphans. Talk about a cultural shift from Southern Oregon! It's no wonder that our dozen or so YWAM kids were a blessing at school—educationally, socially, and spiritually.

To get our wee flock to school, we "YWAM parents" would trade off shepherding them from Samaritan's Inn across four different canals (and through the red-light district) to the school.

Each day, our kids walked by live sex show theaters and sex-toy stores, with all the erotic paraphernalia on display. The movie theater posters often depicted people in various sexual acts without a thread of clothing on—nothing was held back. Interspersed between these were the "shop windows" where the scantily clad prostitutes worked. Sitting behind glass doors, patrons would "shop," then be ushered into a little chamber in the back. Later, the women would return to their windows, targeting the next customer.

However, when they saw our innocent kids walking through the district, these women would transform from vixens back to the girls they actually were. They would wave to the kids and offered them candy. They wanted to befriend them. We quickly realized that our children were our greatest evangelistic tools in this realm.

Of course, we had to practice great care. We trained the kids to guard their eyes and keep their hearts right, and to see these women as human beings and not sex objects. Adults always accompanied the kids to school, due to the area's rampant oppression and demonic activity. All the same, the kids became some of our finest prayer warriors.

When Amy and Carrye became teenagers, they learned how to do manicures and pedicures and were equipped to join a team of about eight of our missionary ladies. They went from door to door (or window to window) and offered to do the women's nails, for free. As they did, they talked and found out about other ways they could help them. They learned to care for these women in tangible ways in order to open up trusting relationships with them.

People soon learned that if there was a need, they could go to the building with the big sign proclaiming, "Jesus loves you" and they would find help.

✦ ✦ ✦ ✦ ✦

Late one blustery night, we heard a frantic pounding on the door of Samaritan's Inn. Robie, an Indonesian pimp, was jumping around, yelling, "You have to come help her!"

Knowing only that "her" was probably a young prostitute that Maria Scheepers, one of our South African staff, had befriended, we felt compelled to follow. He led Herma, a Dutch staff sister, and me into a small, filthy brothel and up a narrow, dark flight of stairs to a tiny attic room. As we entered, we saw a limp body, sweat-covered from fever, lying on a filthy futon. It was a young woman we called "Yopie" (spelled "Joopie"). Next to her was a cardboard box, containing a baby boy wailing hysterically and wallowing in his own feces.

"Help her!" Robie shouted again.

Robie's mother, an Indonesian witch, had lined the room with several small Buddhas, with nooses around their necks. In her tradition, these were believed to bring healing. Herma and I immediately invited God's presence into the room, neutralizing the demonic activity that seemed to permeate the air, and commanded the darkness out of the oppressive environment.

Joopie, who had been "trained" as a prostitute by family members at the age of thirteen, had given birth to two children by the time she was seventeen. Though she had been in a near coma for days, passing in and out of consciousness, she suddenly sat up, healed, looked me directly in the eyes, and said, "I had a dream. I saw a large hand come out of the black clouds and offer to lift me out of the stormy sea. Do you know who that was?"

Yes, I knew who that was.

Her journey to God, though long-delayed, had now begun.

Joopie, as we found with all the prostitutes and junkies we encountered, struggled to accept our community's love. They had been betrayed and mistreated by so many people, trust was not even in their vocabulary. Seeing the need, we once offered to set up a babysitting rotation for her kids while she was working. In a fit of frustration over our unrelenting kindness (sometimes that can be annoying to people used to everyone trying to take advantage of them, as odd as that may sound), her anger boiled over and she cocked her arm to punch me in the nose. I wanted to duck, but something made me smile at her without flinching.

I said, "If you hit me, I'll only love you more."

She screamed in frustration, lowered her fist, and fled back to her brothel.

Our community persistently prayed and tirelessly served Joopie and her children, as well as anyone else who would let us. About two years into this, we had gathered at Christmas to give "gifts to the Lord." This was an annual YWAM tradition of singing songs we had written, sharing art we had created, and giving financial gifts to worthy causes (including one another). In the midst of the celebration, Joopie sauntered in, wearing skintight leopard pants and sporting poufy platinum-blond hair teased high on her head. Strangely, she seemed at peace. This was not the norm for her.

She walked to the front and said, "I have a gift for the Lord today." She paused and then announced, *"Me!"*

We went berserk. We shouted joyfully and pressed around to hug her in a holy scrum as she publicly surrendered her life to Jesus.

In the midst of that celebration, I asked myself, *Why on earth had I ever resisted becoming a missionary?*

✦ ✦ ✦ ✦ ✦

Our team had access to the girls in the windows because they were on public display, but not those in the live sex shows. They were shut up in theaters, so our women started praying and asking God for ideas on how to reach them. They eventually developed a simple plan.

In addition to Samaritan's Inn, we had something of a halfway house in the red-light district, which we called The Cleft. It was about a ten-minute walk from the inn. The Cleft was a place where women could get help and addicts could come to get free. We had a small team who lived there—people who could deal with the intensity of the area. Coming together to address this concern in prayer, The Cleft team, along with a few staff members from Samaritan's Inn, were the ones who concocted the strategy.

On Easter, they would go to the back doors of the theaters and knock, asking the proprietors if they could give each of the women a rose and a small Easter gift, to celebrate the life that Jesus can bring us. Each gift included a card with our contact information and the address of The Cleft. The results were better than we expected.

One of the proprietors, who seemed to have no idea what Easter even was, allowed our women access to his theater's changing rooms. No one had ever asked to do anything nice for his girls, and this small act made a real impression on him. Once inside, the girls were so touched by this kindness that many of them broke down and cried. It had been so long since any of them had been shown genuine love. The proprietor was blown away.

He called the owner of another "sex club" and said, "These real cool ladies are running around and giving out cards and roses to my girls—my girls love it! Would you like them to come by your place?"

Our reputation continued to grow.

✦ ✦ ✦ ✦ ✦

After Joopie's conversion and other small successes, it took many years and lots of daily prayer before we saw the dam break among the prostitutes. Much of that, again, would come through a source many had overlooked.

Lura Garrido was a widowed missionary to Columbia. After her husband died, she moved to Amsterdam to be close to her daughter and her grandchildren. After a few attempts to join various mission agencies, she found none who would employ a "retired old single woman." Then she applied with YWAM. Floyd recruited her on the spot to be his personal secretary.

Although Floyd kept her busy, Lura started "sneaking" out of her office when she could, heading to the red-light district to pray for the girls. Fluent in Spanish, she was drawn to the many Hispanic women who had been trafficked away from their families in Central America to fill the shop windows, sex shows, and brothels. Prayer was followed by acts of kindness, then Bible studies.

In time, Lura became "mother" to a gaggle of Hispanic prostitutes. After several gatherings in Lura's apartment, where she regularly taught and preached the Gospel, a young woman (prophetically?) named Grace was the first to accept Jesus. Then, suddenly, we had forty Spanish-speaking prostitutes come to Jesus, after Grace shared how God had changed her life.

As still more women turned to Jesus, Lura came to me one day, wearing a concerned frown. "I'm not a pastor," she said. "I'm only a woman. I don't know what to do with all these ladies who are growing in Christ. I'm also too old."

"Lura," I told her, "you are it! We'll figure out the theological, gender, and geriatric boundaries later, but, for now, we declare you leader and chief pastoral advocate for these precious ladies." Somewhat reassured, she pressed on, and her impact was heavenly. It continued for several years.

Many of these women had been trafficked to Amsterdam against their will, always leaving families behind, sometimes even children. As we learned their stories, we encouraged as many as we could to return to Latin America.

This didn't make us popular with their pimps, as you can imagine. We were removing from circulation women who had made them a lot of money. As a result, we had new oppression to face. One of our team members even had a knife held to his throat. But we continued to press in, bless, and pray for protection, and God continued to answer those prayers.

Then a strange thing started happening. The women we'd sent home to Latin America returned to Amsterdam with their families. The Spanish-speaking churches we'd helped plant started to grow and multiply. The Holy Spirit was afoot again.

When I returned to visit Amsterdam in the mid-2000s (some twenty years later), I had just finished speaking to a network of pastors and intercessors when I felt a tap on my shoulder. I turned and saw a round, beaming face grinning extravagantly. "Do you remember me?" she asked.

"Grace!"

We flew into each other's arms.

Over the course of those twenty years, the Spanish-speaking churches planted in Amsterdam had spread into the rest of Europe, with the sons of those returned prostitutes (now ex-prostitutes, of course) as their pastors.

And Lura was still there, sitting in the back row by the door, wearing glasses as thick as Coke-bottle bottoms, blessing all who walked by. It gave a whole new meaning to the term "Mother Superior."

✦ ✦ ✦ ✦ ✦

In all of this we were learning the power of living out Jesus's admonition to be *"servant of all"* (Mark 9:35). We could never have reached into these places without hearts looking to serve and love first, and *then* bring people out of their bondages. Prayer always greased the wheels of these transformations. It ran counter to most of what we saw happening in the church around us, but it was a lesson we learned in myriad ways. I came to understand the idea of Jesus as a servant who upended power structures not by toppling them, but by subverting evil's hold on them through acts of service. Talk about grassroots! Learning to lay down our lives and our moral superiority in a really wicked city, despite heavy criticism from our own families (and from the church in Holland), was a challenge to each of us.

Every day our senses would be assaulted. The smells were horrid. People would knock on our door, sporting open sores. They vomited on our doorstep and swore at us threateningly. We had that one sudden breakthrough with the sex-show proprietor, but nothing else came easily. You must go low to lift up others, and we were constantly stretched by just how low you sometimes have to go. It was a constant struggle, and we constantly had to repent of our hesitancy and rededicate ourselves. Forgiving those who broke into our building to steal or harm our staff was a continual battle.

One of the best examples of this was dealing with a Satanic church in the red-light district. Their building was only two doors down from The Cleft. Dressed in Druid-like hoods and robes, members of this church would surround the Samaritan's Inn on the three sides open to the streets and sidewalks. It was like a scene from a horror movie. They would hurl curses at us, and the spiritual atmosphere would become so charged that our kids, especially Andy, could feel it. He reported things moving in his room on a number of occasions.

When we prayed about it, God always told us to bless the Satanists. That took our servanthood to new levels. It was one thing to ask God to bless them; it was another to reach out and do it ourselves by bringing gifts to the door of their "church" at times. That was spirit stretching, to say the least.

✦ ✦ ✦ ✦ ✦

As a former hippie pastor, I openly resisted administration and organization. But I had been called upon to help this organization with buildings, budgets, and 360-plus missionaries to house, feed, and coordinate. (I should note that about 140 of those were kids.)

Once things started humming more smoothly, however, I started to enjoy it. Floyd appointed me operations director for the base. I went from a hippie guy wearing overalls held together by diaper pins to a preppy in khakis and penny loafers, ready to interface with the Dutch public and government officials at the drop of a hat. Occasionally, I had to stop and wonder, *What's happened to you, man?*

Through all of this, the Lord taught us we could bless even our most aggressive opponents, and we had no shortage of those. Journalists wrote horrible things about us. We had to continually deal with the Satanists and with government officials who saw us as interlopers, sticking our noses where they didn't belong, interfering with the lucrative operations of Amsterdam's permissive society. Eventually, the Aliens Police came down hard on us and one day started denying visas for our incoming short-term missionaries. They also tried to block our current staff members from renewing their visas. People with valid documents were turned away at the border. They were told their papers were no good, and they were sent away. It got ugly fast.

Then we received a letter from the government, telling us that all *sects*—that was the term they used for nonprofit charitable organizations, so we and the Satanists were in the same boat as far as the government was concerned—had thirty days to prove we were of value to the nation or we had to leave the country. Can you imagine that? Thirty days! There were approximately 200 foreign nonprofit organizations operating in the area, all of which were suddenly in risk of deportation.

We owned property, we had Dutch staff, and our group included many foreign missionaries. All would be in jeopardy if we couldn't prove that we were good for the Netherlands. So what could we do?

Back to our knees. We prayed.

With appeals and deferrals, we would be embroiled in the issue for the next year. Our team visited churches around the country to solicit support, inform them what was going on, and ask for prayer. We spent much time discussing the work we were doing and why it needed to continue. If the nation was going to start shutting down nonprofits, it was going to cost everyone dearly. We called everyone we knew, including Brother Andrew, the famous Dutch Bible smuggler. All of our allies supported us.

Then we finally got our day in court—before the minister of justice.

Our Netherlands directors at the time, Jeff and Romkje Fountain, headed down to The Hague with our lawyers to represent YWAM in this final hearing. Speaking through our lawyers, Romkje said, "We believe we have ample proof of our benefit to the nation." At her signal, carts of mailbags were rolled into the room, bearing letters from around the country—Christians and non-Christians, businesses we'd worked with, prostitutes, drug addicts, homeless people we had helped—all telling the court, "We would not be where we are today without their help. We're so very grateful." A clerk took one of the bags, and with a flair that would have made William and Catherine Booth proud (who had quite a knack for dramatics in dealing with government themselves), emptied it on the table until the letters spilled onto the floor. We'd received thousands of letters.

As it turned out, we were the tip of the spear. We took most of the heat for the other nonprofits. In the face of the overwhelming evidence YWAM presented, the minister of justice ruled in favor of our staying, and the cases against other nonprofits began to drop in quick succession.

For a short time—a very short time—we were heroes throughout the country.

The government even came down on the Aliens Police for denying our visas and making life difficult for us. The Ministry asked us how many visas we would need for the next ten years, so that they could get them ready in advance. We prayed, "Lord, what number should we give them?"

Our profile in the country changed. Suddenly, we were front-page news. New doors opened to preach the Gospel, teach, and train staff and volunteers. The police and other local authorities cooperated with us in all of our efforts. It was an amazing turnaround, and it all happened because we focused on serving rather than looking for power. Whenever opposition came, we lifted those people or organizations up and prayed for those who harassed us. It became as natural as breathing, and the results were always incredible.

We soon learned why God had trained us to do this. He wanted us to take these values into His next mission for us: spreading the Gospel into Eastern Europe after the fall of the Berlin Wall.

UNVEILING YOUR FUTURE

Joopie's conversion, victory over Satanic curses, prayer-walking daily, street evangelism, church planting in Amsterdam among punks and prostitutes, and overcoming bureaucratic resistance were all the result of hearing God's voice and obeying His instructions.

The Ministry Maturing phase is usually heavy on aligning our attitudes with Jesus's attitudes toward the culture, to love as He loves. Righteous indignation makes it so easy to take offense at the world around us, including the culture we are embedded in. From the 1970s to the 1990s, Christendom grew antagonistic toward the outside world, over issues like abortion, gay marriage, and drug legalization. Traditional evangelicals waved their Judeo-Christian flag at secular society. Some in the church were more eager to condemn the world for its shoddy morality than to pursue lawbreakers with a greater law: the law of love. Many believed that having faith meant holding these moral lines politically and never surrendering to cultural pressure. There's some truth to that, but there's also a greater truth—the one summed up in John 3:16: *"For God so loved the world that he gave . . ."*

As leaders we are invited to be like Jesus. He never *approves* of our behavior as "sinners," but He *accepts* us "in the beloved." After all, sinners sin. That's our nature, until we come to Jesus. Even if we could remove all social and moral ills from a nation, it's not like everyone would suddenly come to know Jesus. We would be proud of our achievement but stranded on *Isla Humana* without a Savior. *"For God did not send his Son into the world to condemn the world, but to save the world through him"* (John 3:17).

Jesus taught and demonstrated a better way. His love and servanthood were always unconditional. People didn't have to repent of their sins to get Him to love them. He didn't instruct us to bless only those who agree with Him: "*While we were still sinners, Christ died for us*" (Romans 5:8). We should follow His example of preemptively blessing. The greater the opposition we face, the greater the blessing should be. That's the kind of love that "*never fails*" (1 Corinthians 13:8). Yes, this approach takes time, a lot of humility, and is far from easy. People might refuse the gift, but we can never cease making it available to hungry hearts.

This is how our Father measures our love for Him. This is the essence of being a leader in the image of Christ.

During this growth phase, to my horror, I discovered I had a profound organizational gift that eventually landed me as the "operations director" for the base. (I thought administration was of the devil before that.) Grants Pass had been my solo show. Now I faced a decade of expanding my serving abilities, for the benefit of a twelve-member leadership team (whose hearts were being knit together) and for our deeply committed staff.

Not only that, but our prayers for spiritual parenting came to fruition in the form of Floyd and Sally. In my early years in Grants Pass, I had prayed, "Lord, what do You want me to do for You?" Now my prayer had changed to, "Lord, whom are You calling me to be with?" Floyd and Sally were a direct answer to that prayer.

I share this principle regularly with young leaders who come to me seeking to know what their ministry will be. It is my joy to tell them that you can't know your destiny without being knit into a spiritual family where people can champion each other into nurturing the spiritual gifts God's graced them with. He calls us to a family who love each other so fervently that it inspires great acts of Kingdom mischief. We are called to be relational before we are transactional. Our natural drive is to know the future and be "the man (or woman) of power for the hour." This false idea is doomed to be challenged by our loving heavenly Father because it keeps Him and His Family out of the equation. He endorses very little that hasn't first been wrought with Him in prayer—once again, relationship first.

This was a high time for us. We were maturing in our ministry. But there was more to learn and do. We had a few more years in our latter Ministry Maturing phase before we transitioned into the fog of the next season.

WALLS COME TUMBLING DOWN

In 1986 I arrived late for a gathering of hundreds of leaders from across the Netherlands, representing a variety of church traditions. It was dark outside, and the lights in the large room spilled into the night. As I walked toward the large, waist-high windows, I was puzzled by the silence and the absence of human presence. There was no one to be seen. Had I gotten the wrong location? The wrong night?

As I peered inside, I saw where everyone was: A sea of bodies—either kneeling or prostrate on the ground—covered the floor. Some were crying, some rocked back and forth slowly, and others were hugging each other. Was I still in "religiously stiff" Holland?

Tiptoeing in, I queried the gentleman at the door. "What's going on?"

"Eenheid!" he whispered. *Unity!*

The message for the evening was the impossibility of a nation being blessed if the Church was fractured by competition, kingdom-building, and animosity. As these precious leaders responded to the Holy Spirit's conviction, it felt like a victory cannon had been fired, announcing the advent of a new spiritual shift in the nation. I love the Dutch and get all "wiggly" inside just thinking of their tough exteriors surrounding spongy, compassionate centers. Floyd used to say, "Give me one tough Dutchman with a heart broken by Jesus, and we'll change the world."

Amen, I say.

This was happening as a new wave of foreigners were being called to partner with the Dutch to church-plant, pray, and encourage the Body of Christ throughout the Netherlands. Pastoral unity groups began to blossom, and intercessors were raised up. When we had arrived in Amsterdam in 1981, there were barely twelve churches preaching the Gospel, and none of them with more than 250 members. Today there are hundreds of churches in Amsterdam, with some numbering in the thousands. The African-immigrant churches in Amsterdam began populating each subway station daily, praying for those commuting to and from work. It was a new day for the city. I'm convinced that this historic "unity" meeting was the engine that fueled this phenomenal growth.

On YWAM's international front, Mindy and I found ourselves involved in Leadership Training Schools, shuttling between Amsterdam and our old stomping grounds, the Pacific and Asia University (soon to be the University of the Nations) in Hawaii, where Floyd and Sally had first invited us to join them in the Netherlands. On one memorable trip, our international leaders were gathered in a Polynesian longhouse in Kona for a week of meetings. Joy Dawson had just announced that she would be speaking on "spiritual blindness."

Oh boy, I thought, sensing divine intent. *I'm not sure I'm ready for this.*

After speaking for a few minutes, Joy turned to her husband, Jim, and asked, "Is everything okay between you and me?"

"Yes, honey," Jim replied.

She went on, and then, after a few minutes, she turned to Loren Cunningham and asked, "Is everything okay between us?"

Loren said he was sure they were okay.

Then she announced that she was losing sight in her left eye, and she wanted to ensure that unresolved relational issues in her heart weren't the cause. Soon, however, she had lost sight in both eyes.

All the doors were closed, and the massive space grew dead quiet. As Joy continued to speak, a bird rose mysteriously out of the center of the room. It seemed to appear out of nowhere and began to dive-bomb some of us. Eventually, the bird made a beeline for me, and I grabbed it out of sheer reflex, then handed it quickly to one of my colleagues, who walked it to the door and set it free outside.

A few minutes later, Loren (who had stepped out to answer "nature's call") returned and told Joy, "The bird that was in the room is outside flying around the trees like it is drunk. I think *it* is actually blind!"

The fear of the Lord fell on the room, and we all hit the deck. The rest of our time was dedicated to responding to God's obvious demonstrations through Joy's blindness and the bird's erratic behavior—and of our own "blindness" in trying to live by our own strength rather than Jesus's revelation. As soon as Joy finished speaking, the leaders laid hands on her and her sight was restored. It was quite a night; no one left that building unchanged.

We had been called to be alert in the Spirit for what the Lord was about to unleash on the earth. Our walls of self-righteousness needed demolition by the wrecking ball of a jealous Father.

✦ ✦ ✦ ✦ ✦

Upon returning to Amsterdam, we realized we were physically exhausted. We longed for a furlough focused on an intentional study of God's plan for our future. I ached for input at all levels. I was thirty-nine and felt starved for wisdom and context in the greater scheme of God's Kingdom. Up to that point, I had held seminaries in low regard. I believed they were obsolete and inappropriate for pioneers like myself. So—you guessed it—God called me to attend seminary.

And I loved every minute of it. The School of World Mission at Fuller Theological Seminary was offering a master's degree in Intercultural Leadership Development. After all the years of giving out, I was now feasting on the amazing content provided by seasoned missionaries and leadership gurus in a multicultural circle of global "lovers of Jesus." Though I couldn't stay for the full two-year program, I received much material in my studies that would enhance my work with leaders in the future. I love how God is unimpressed with our ridiculous biases. He got me good once again.

We returned to Amsterdam refreshed and ready to face the new decade.

✦ ✦ ✦ ✦ ✦

Just a few months after we returned from California to Amsterdam, on November 9, 1989, the Berlin Wall came down. We had been alerted by a few Dutch intercessors that this might happen, and that we should be prepared. In our meeting room in Amsterdam, we had been faithfully praying over our gargantuan map of the world, country by country, for years by that time. We always expressed a heart to see the Eastern Bloc released from Soviet rule. Throughout the '80s, we learned of new groups being formed on both sides of the wall that were praying for it to come down. That day all of our prayers were answered.

While a wonderful event, it only marked a new beginning. As the wall was being dismantled, we renewed our prayers for Eastern Europe. I remember standing in front of our big map during that historic week and asking the Lord, "What do we do now? How do we respond to this?"

God directed us to target seven former Soviet Bloc cities with our prayers, and then to visit each one. Within the year, I and several others had visited all seven cities, agreeing with the believers there for a visitation of the Lord—and to discern how YWAM Amsterdam should serve those countries' churches.

On one trip, Paul, a Filipino-American, and I headed to Sofia, Bulgaria, without any preparation. We didn't know anybody there, so we were surprised as we waited at the baggage carousel to see a fellow jumping up and down on the other side of the glass and waving at us. He displayed a sign bearing my name.

"Curious," I said to Paul. "Do we know that guy?"

As we exited baggage claim, the man ran over and said, "Jon Petersen, I've been waiting for you."

I wasn't sure if he was KGB or an angel.

"You don't know me," he rambled, "but I heard you preach in Frankfurt last year. Last night I had a dream, and the Lord told me to get to the airport to meet you. This way, please. A number of people are at my house, waiting to be ministered to."

What could we do? Off we went and found an eager gathering of Bulgarians stuffed into a miniature living room. (By the way, don't nod your head up and down in Bulgaria if you mean "yes," because to Bulgarians it means "no." I learned this cultural nuance from a brown-eyed, seven-year-old Bulgarian sweetheart. She was very kind in her correction of my faux pas.)

Two of the people in the room had had a long-standing fissure in their relationship. A prophetic word was given that got to the heart of the problem and the two were reconciled with hugs and tears in front of their house group. After an unusually powerful time of prophetic ministry to this hungry group of believers, we were whisked off to a church office and introduced to a room full of dour-looking, drab-suited Bulgarian Pentecostal pastors. They were gathered at a conference to ask the Lord's blessing on their nation, which was still in the clutches of Communist rule. Suspicious of us, they asked why we had come.

"To pray for Sofia and the church in Bulgaria," I announced.

As though they didn't hear me, they queried, "Did you come to speak in our conference, bring or ask for money, start a ministry, or what?"

"No," I said. "We are just here to pray and bless the church and your beautiful city."

Surrounded by this sea of bedraggled gray suits, we, in our blue jeans, were sent off with our new friendly "jumping bean" guide to bless and pray for Sofia.

Bursting with excitement, our friend led us to the *Nezavisimost* (Independence) Square, home of the Communist Headquarters and a mausoleum containing the embalmed body of Georgi Dimitrov, Bulgaria's infamous communist founder.

What do we do now? we wondered.

We looked at each other. *Pray!*

And so we did, for the next hour or so, inviting God's presence into the square.

Once back in Amsterdam, I received a phone call from our wildly excitable Bulgarian escort. Holding the phone back to preserve my right eardrum, I was told an amazing story. Shortly after our departure, the communist building had been burned to the ground and an edict came out removing the body of old Georgi from the mausoleum and having it be cremated.

Wow! Such a strange set of coincidences right on the eve of our visit.

We could come to no other conclusion. "Prayer works!" he cried.

And we had made some new (and very good) Bulgarian friends.

✦ ✦ ✦ ✦ ✦

Life went all a-fuzzle after that. Prayer and evangelism teams flew in all directions. Students with a heart for Eastern Europe were filling our schools, and we were becoming well known in the Netherlands and Europe as a hub of God's work.

I remember having lunch with YWAM's Europe, Middle East, and Africa Councils, when one of our team said, "I feel like we need to pray for Romania—*right now*." I hardly knew where Romania was, much less that Bucharest was the capital.

As we prayed, I got the picture of a large predatory bird with its talons embedded in the brain of the nation's communist leader. We entered into a powerful afternoon of warfare prayer. I'd never heard of Nicolae Ceaușescu, nor did I understand the nation's spiritual or political climate. One week later, we received news that Ceaușescu had been deposed in an uprising led by a pastor from Timisoara. (Though it's doubtful he'll be in any of the history books—in a quick look online, I couldn't find any mention of him in connection to these events. But it was fascinating to hear him tell the story at a conference some time after the events. He was a bit of a folk hero in our circles. A humble, unsung hero we'll probably never hear the full story of until we get to heaven.)

So, true to form, we jetted off to the chaos that was presently Bucharest and stood in the center of the main square during a miners riot that turned ugly and violent. We took clandestine pictures and prayed like fire.

During that trip we also experienced the beauty of the East-West reconnection of God's Church. It brought such joy to the Romanian believers to be reunited with their brothers and sisters in the West, those they'd never been allowed to talk to before. It was an incredible time. God was doing so much in so many places.

We also visited the mansion where Ceaușescu had lived while ruling the nation. It was opulent to the point of decadence—so cold and overdone it was actually ugly. Our guide told us to take sticks and tap the pavement in the huge square outside the entry. As we did, we could hear the hollow resonance of a maze of tunnels beneath our feet. She told us those tunnels were used to secretly traffic political dissidents around the city. Ceaușescu also used them to send his forces from one part of the city to another without anyone knowing. When the uprising happed, the "liberators" found those tunnels and used them to infiltrate the mansion.

✦ ✦ ✦ ✦ ✦

Later, back in Amsterdam, I was standing alone in front of the aforementioned "gargantuan map," when I laid my hands on a prominent Middle Eastern city. I felt the Lord whisper, "Are you prepared to go there and lose your life for My sake?"

It shook me to the core. I had never contemplated laying down my life, other than in a spiritual sense, but this seemed more literal. I remember the sweat beading on my forehead, as I said to the Lord, "I really don't know." I didn't know if this was a prophecy or more of a general invitation and inquiry into my willingness to obey.

After a few moments of silence, I said, "How can I not lay my life down, for all You've done for me and for those in this nation who don't know You?"

Now, whenever that Middle Eastern city is featured in a news report, I renew my vow. Verbally declaring that you are willing to die a physical death for the Gospel has a curious purifying effect on your perspective. Smaller issues lose a lot of their troublesomeness.

For me, the 1980s were about global missions, the power of prayer, and lessons in relational ministry. I was coming to grips with the magnitude of our King's sovereignty over the realm of His rule—the nations of the earth He so loves. I was living the "ministry dream" and hoped it would never end.

But once again, God had other plans.

UNVEILING YOUR FUTURE

One of the major threads of growth during the Ministry Maturing phase is training and development. From that first Leadership Training School (LTS) in Hawaii to my time at Fuller School of World Mission studies, those years were crammed with formal and informal learning. That ranged from evangelism training, to developing organizational skills, to seminars on strategic planning. Through the school of hard knocks, I learned how to raise kids in a foreign land, how to use personality tests to assess team health, and so on. The table He sets during this growth phase includes the many learning opportunities that shape our lives.

Avail yourself to as much as you can stomach!

Thirtysomethings should expect a lot of variety in their experiences—a good deal of change and some success. But they need to remember that present realities may not reflect the fulfillment of their ultimate dreams. What we do in our thirties is rarely, if ever, an expression of our ultimate calling. (Of course, Jesus was an exception to that rule, as are, in all likelihood, those cut off in their prime as we saw happen to Keith Green.) There are still character issues to be decided in our thirties, as well as issues of ministry philosophy and biblical clarity that the Father is busy deconstructing and reconstructing during this stage of life. The immense variety of lessons and experiences in the twenties and thirties set the stage for a deeper work of God in the years that follow.

"Ministry" was never designed by God to be a goal or a matter of "climbing ladders." Accomplishments are part of a process, not destinations in and of themselves—a process of knowing Him more completely. During my twenties and thirties, I was convinced God was preparing me for bigger and better ministry—until I realized God was using ministry to prepare me for more of Himself.

I was about to enter the next phase of my "growing up"—the Life Maturing stage—something that happens in the same years that many call their mid-life crises. This doesn't surprise me. It is a phase in life where we reevaluate everything that has come before from a new depth of understanding and perspective on what really matters. With our identities more established in Him than in what we achieve, everything looks different. It's like God flips on a switch and suddenly we can see color where we formerly only saw black and white. Areas of our life we formerly thought were separate and distinct come into an orbit of new correlations with one another. New universes of possibilities emerge as we see the interrelatedness of all God had previously been up to in our lives.

In the next few years, I would go from the height of being a minister to nations with all its fanfare to coming back down to earth—*hard*. God re-grounded me. Once again, God was getting me ready for something bigger—though not something bigger by human standards, but by His.

PART FOUR:

BECOMING THE FAMILY...

AND THEN EVERYTHING CHANGED...AGAIN

I believed deeply in discipling my children (note: that's "discipling" not "disciplining"; while that's important too, it's a different context), not just raising them to be "good Christian boys and girls." As our kids got older, though, I felt hopelessly inadequate as a parent, on so many levels. Mindy and I had been married for more than twenty years, but I often felt like *we* needed parenting, especially when our own kids came along.

When we first arrived in Amsterdam, I was already feeling like I had dragged them through so much. Frustrated with my parental ineptitude, and knowing there were harder days ahead as our kids hit their teens, I ditched a mandatory YWAM meeting while in Mayrhofen, Austria, and drove high into the Tyrol Mountains. I pulled over at a small park, found a tired old glacier, and sat on the ancient ice.

I prayed, "I'm not leaving until You give me something to help me father these beautiful kids. I need hope, a dream, a word—*something!*"

Graciously, the Lord gave me key guiding Scriptures and a "picture" of the destiny for each of my children. Amy was to be a strong woman like Abigail, who had tried to divert the results of her husband's disastrous decision to take on King David. I saw that Amy's destiny would be to stand before kings and fools. (Many years later, she served as personal assistant for US Attorney General John Ashcroft.) For Carrye, I got Jael, the woman who defeated the leader of Israel's enemy by putting a stake through his head. I knew she would be a strong intercessor and bring victory to whatever assignment God gave her. The only references to Andrew in the Scripture are those of him bringing people to Jesus, unlikely ones. That's my son. He loves and shepherds the brokenhearted in a natural, non-religious way.

All these years later, those images of our children, as destined by God, allowed us to weather the storms each of them experienced. When things got dark and out of our control, we remembered the promises God gave me for our kids, promises that served to stabilize Mindy and me through the joyful terror of being parents.

It was worth the frozen fanny.

In the late '80s, as I was taking on more of a leadership role in Amsterdam, Mindy and I realized that our kids needed more parental attention. We had ministry responsibilities morning, noon, and night. The demands of the red-light district never slept. We couldn't even go to the grocery store without someone seeing us and trying to get help:

"Do you know where Marissa is? I need to talk to her."

"Can we come to the thing next week? We need clothes. I know you have the open clothes distribution."

"When are your girls giving mani-pedis again?"

"Can you pray for me?"

I was driving and flying all over Europe. We had outreaches. We ran coffee shops. We had all this stuff going constantly. Plus, there was the old nemesis—addiction to ministry achievement—much like people have in their careers. It was "workaholism" in spiritual robes. It's the old danger of slowly becoming "so immersed in the work of the Lord that we neglect the Lord of the work." It's far too easy to start seeing our accomplishments as our significance and start neglecting our primary role as sons or daughters of God. It's a Satanic bait and switch.

Many parents hit the stride of their careers in their thirties to find that's also when their kids need them most. Constant pressures in the office pull them away from their families rather than allowing them to spend more time with them. Caught up in the thrill of doing God's work, we can become deceived that we are irreplaceable in His processes. So much of our identity becomes tied up in what we *do* rather than who we *are*. We mistakenly believe that our work responsibilities are more important than cultivating the relationships in our homes not only because that's what pays the bills, but it's also where we get most of our accolades. It's easy to get things out of balance. I saw how hard it was for me and my team members to give up ministry time and spend it with family. When our children were seven, nine, and eleven, it was evident that something had to give, and it shouldn't be our kids.

Amy struggled with any physical touch from a man (including me). Carrye was so spiritually sensitive to the strongholds in the red-light district that she suffered from insomnia and depression. From time to time, Andy saw demonic manifestations. Eventually, he was tempted by Amsterdam's drug culture. Mindy and I knew we had to do something to intensify our active discipleship in their lives.

I approached our leadership team and "suggested" that I would be unavailable most weeknights for the foreseeable future. "You can have two-thirds of my waking hours, but the other third is for my family," I said. Then I started "dating" my kids and Mindy weekly. I skipped out on evening ministry three times a week to spend a designated weeknight with each of the kids, and I took a fourth night with Mindy, who, of course, chose "shopping night," when the stores in Amsterdam stayed open late. We'd dine out at their favorite places. We'd hang out and talk, walking along the canals in the less spiritually oppressive parts of the city.

My example affected the whole YWAM Amsterdam community. More and more of us began finding great ways to spend time with our families. It was a little controversial at first, but it quickly gathered support. In time, my decision not only established a template for my family, but for many of our team's families. It paid off!

We also resolved to make our kids part of our ministry team, as much as we could. They joined outreaches, feeding programs, and trips to foreign nations. It was one of the "takeaways" from my years as a third-culture kid. I recalled how I felt more like an appendage to my parents' ministry than a part of it. Despite the rigors of school and everyday life, we tried to find ways to incorporate Amy, Carrye, and Andy into our world through mission trips around Europe, and into the Soviet Bloc countries. We sent them on King's Kids trips and included them in the circle of our YWAM and Dutch friends in Amsterdam. It might sound exotic and expensive for a family of five with no money, but the old adage springs to mind: "Where God guides, He provides." I still don't know how it happened, but somehow we always had the money for these trips. God was showing His love to my kids.

I couldn't have asked for a better discipleship strategy for Amy and Carrye than the free mani-pedis they did for the ladies of the red-light district. They ministered and grew through service as integral parts of the team. That didn't keep them from facing tremendous pressures in public high school. (They eventually aged out of the parochial school with the nuns.) Public secondary school provided a new set of challenges. Some teachers were known to recruit students into alternative sexual lifestyles. (Amy was targeted at one point.)

Despite the oppression and temptations, the girls learned to stand in the strength of their faith as they journeyed with Jesus to learn His ways.

His promises for my kids held true. I had a breakthrough with Amy in the middle of a tantrum, and the Lord calmed her fear of physical touch. Sobbing in my arms, she asked if she could sit on my lap "for the rest of my life." *Done deal.* After years of depression and insomnia, Carrye had a demonic encounter that led her into rebuking the lies that had terrorized her heart. She won and the spirit lifted. Andy, still spiritually sensitive, fought off substance abuse and is now free and thriving in his career. These were all hard-won battles that took years of faithful prayer and love, though. Victories might have happened all at once, but it was always a battle getting to those points.

✦ ✦ ✦ ✦ ✦

In 1990, a few months before we got the letter with the "prove yourself or leave the Netherlands in thirty days" ultimatum, Floyd invited me to be the director of YWAM's work in Amsterdam, so that he could attend to growing global responsibilities. "Under one condition," I negotiated, "that you stay in Amsterdam." After Floyd's assurance that he had no plans to do otherwise, the Lord promptly called Floyd and Sally to return to the United States, after nearly twenty fruitful years in the Netherlands. Mindy and I would miss our friends and mentors. After a stubborn response from me (and a swift rebuke from the Lord for cowardice), I capitulated. When the McClungs moved on, Mindy and I were commissioned to take over for them and move into their old apartment on the top floor.

After some perfunctory grumbling, I eventually grew excited by the new challenge and the amazing team of extreme missionary friends. I learned more about leading cross-culturally, managing ministry finances, prayerful strategic planning, purchasing real estate, understanding personality types, and team building. With the Berlin Wall down, I was traveling throughout Europe, and to Africa and the Middle East. I got tremendous jollies from it. Man, I was good—and increasingly arrogant. So was my team. We were now well-known throughout Europe—and we were getting cocky.

In 1990, I arrived at our annual fall strategic planning meeting, ready to lead the process of coordinating the goals, objectives, and budgets of our burgeoning and fruitful ministry teams. Outreaches were going bananas in Eastern Europe and in Holland, and new works were being targeted in Africa. It was intoxicating.

As I opened my mouth to dispense wisdom as an opening for the meeting, someone had the audacity to ask if we could read Isaiah 41 and meditate on it before we began. Being the man of the Word that I am, I nodded sheepishly and led the Scripture reading. With that behind us, I tried to launch our three-day strategic extravaganza again, only to be interrupted once more. My friend John "the coffin guy" Goodfellow declared, "I have to confess, my heart is not right. I came to this meeting to compete against the rest of you for my team's budget." He fell to his face on the floor and started groaning. The rest of the room went silent. *Oh, shoot,* I grumbled to myself. *Hijacked by someone's conscience.*

After John, others followed suit. Some began crying, lying prostrate on the ground, and asking God and others for forgiveness.

Foiled again, I thought. *But how long can this last, anyway?* I was sure it would be over soon and we could get down to business.

Instead, it lasted the full three days.

By the end of that "planning session," I, too, was swept away by the current of conviction. We all understood that we had been seduced to believe our own press. We had failed to lead the community in a way that reflected God's heart. We agreed that we needed to publicly confess our failure at our staff meeting the following Friday—a day that would be remembered in the annals of history as "Black Friday."

For four hours that fateful day, we leaders blubbered our confessions, one by one. Our staff sat stunned, unsure how to react. One dear sister came to me afterward and said, "Thank you so much for sharing your sins. It put everything in perspective for me." I waited, anger rising, but remembering that the Lord had warned to avoid "convicting" any of the staff. He would do it in His time. *Rats!* She went on joyfully, "Now, I know why so many of us are in a mess—you guys have been completely out of order."

Great, I thought, convinced I had just shot any confidence in our leadership squarely in the foot. *So much for identifying with the sins and weaknesses of others.* I normally love finding people to commiserate with about my sins and weaknesses, but this?

It was a full two months before any conviction manifested itself among the rest of our staff. Our leadership team never did get to the ministry planning for that year. Each time we gathered, we met God and touched each others' hearts. In late November of 1990, one by one, our staff began to come under God's conviction for a variety of their own offenses. The move of the Spirit was on again.

In early January 1991, we received two brothers from the United States, men with a reputation for strong prophetic ministries. *Right,* I mused, *we'll see about that.*

We were sitting in a circle in the basement of Samaritan's Inn when they arrived. After some nervous introductions (no one wanted to sit by them for fear of having their "mail read"), one of the men declared that the enemy "had been made to reveal himself" as he sat in the taxi and that he was "planning some major mischief in the city within three days." He said it would be a sign that the Lord's Spirit was about to move.

I had no idea what to do with that bold assertion. So we went back to prayer.

Three days later, I stepped out of a restaurant on the Dam Straat and felt a blast of evil—that's the only way I can describe it. Walking past Amsterdam Centraal (the city's largest railway station) to a meeting, I observed that the major intersection in front of the station was filled with taxis nose to nose and their drivers standing on their roofs shaking their fists toward the heavens. They looked crazed, angry, and completely detached from reality. I recalled the "major mischief in three days" comment. Something dark was being unleashed on the city, perhaps a sign of how God would trump the enemy's hand?

At a meeting that evening, the atmosphere was thick with anticipation. At five minutes before starting time, I asked where our speaker was. No one knew. I went to his room and knocked tentatively. I was greeted by one of our illustrious prophetic men of God, standing in his smalls, hair all askew. He asked, "Is that a violent wind outside?"

"Yes," I replied. "Taxi drivers are cursing heaven, and people are fighting the gusts—"

"I think we are in for a good night," he said, rubbing his hands together.

A good night, indeed! A violent wind had risen out of the North Sea and was wreaking havoc on the city and its citizenry. One of our staff sisters, who felt she should stay home with her boys, came to the meeting anyway, "not wanting to miss the presence of God." She told us she had been blown off her feet sideways as her helpless husband looked on. He reported that she had flown through the air directly toward the semi-frozen canal. Then, aided by the instantaneous emergency prayers of her husband, she made a miraculous left turn in midair (angels be thanked!) and crashed into a brick wall within inches of the icy waters. As a result, she lost hearing in one of her ears. I don't know if it ever came back.

It was a weird night, to say the least.

Despite the chaos in the city, all that can be said about that night is that "heaven came down" to our gathering of hungry hearts. With the presence of God thick in the room, the prophetic broke out.

In the ensuing days, godly dreams became commonplace in our children and staff, and the fear of the Lord fell on all of us. We were exposed! It was almost impossible to engage in any sinful activity due to our increased sensitivity to the slightest infractions and the desire to keep close accounts in our relationships. In the ensuing months, we gathered daily in God's presence. We were transformed. Normal ministry activities didn't resume for nearly six months.

During that windy night, the speaker singled out twelve of our leaders and said only one would be left in Amsterdam after a year: "Eleven of you are going to be sent as pioneers by the Lord to the nations."

I was the only one of those twelve living in Amsterdam a year later. My friends were scattered to England, Siberia, Prague, Budapest, and elsewhere by the word of the Lord during this "sending" season. We were changed and humbled. We felt dangerous for God!

This all taught me another valuable lesson: God will deconstruct or even stop our work when our relationships with Him and each other are out of order. This was a lesson that would play a large role in my call to reform the Church in the years to come, a call the Lord was leading me into on behalf of His global Family.

✦ ✦ ✦ ✦ ✦

Through a series of God coincidences and a common interest to push through Eastern Europe into Russia, we forged a friendship with Brent and Happy Rue, pastors of Desert Vineyard Church in Lancaster, California. We discovered that the Lord had been speaking to all of us independently about church planting in Siberia. None of us had ever been there, nor did we know much about the region—just the usual rumors about gulags, ice, and that it was a long way from anywhere.

David Pierce's band NLM ("No Longer Music") ended up being a key tool to spearhead the foray into Siberia. NLM seemed to carry a rare gift for reaching Europe's countercultural kids. We decided that Dave and the band would tour seven Siberian cities. Then church-plant teams would instruct the new disciples. Once that was going, NLM would move on to the next location.

Over the following months, YWAM Amsterdam, Desert Vineyard (Brent and Happy Rue's church), and Antioch Church of Waco, Texas (pastored by Jimmy Seibert) ventured into Siberia, with NLM leading the way. The results of the concerts were a deposit of new believers and a small church formed in each city (overseen by one of the partner ministries). This frigid trek produced many conversions and various forms of healing.

In the Siberian city of Barnaul, the Lord granted favor for our Amsterdam team, led by Derryck and Marie McLuhan, with a local pediatric oncology hospital. The facility's recovery rate for childhood cancer was only 5 percent. It had virtually no modern conveniences. The parents of children, often traveling from hundreds of miles away, had to sleep on the floor, next to their children's beds.

We brought pillowcases of candy, offering the children as much as they wanted. Completely unfamiliar with generosity, they would reach their little fingers into the pillowcase, pull out two candies, eat one, and put the other under their pillow for later. I couldn't imagine our Western kids taking just two candies. (Think of Halloween.)

One of the hospital administrators, an atheist, had decided that we were a bad influence on the children, due to our praying over every child. When he tried to bar our teams from coming in, the parents objected. They claimed, "Our children always improve when the Christians come to the hospital." In response, we were given a permanent invite by city officials. This led to our recruiting an oncological team from Atlanta, Georgia, who spent many months bringing new cancer protocols to the hospital. The health of many children improved, morale went up, and several doctors and nurses came to Christ and began attending our new church plant in Barnaul.

By 1994, American hospital administrators, Christian businessmen, and local city authorities were discussing plans for a pharmaceutical manufacturing plant in the area. It would produce pain medication for cancer patients. We had made divine inroads.

✦ ✦ ✦ ✦ ✦

In September 1993, as more opportunities opened for us in the Eastern Bloc, I thought, *I'm living the dream. This is what I hoped for when I thought about what I wanted to do with my life.* We were seeing all kinds of amazing things happen as the Gospel touched lives, cities, and nations. But my dream was about to get tested.

While in Oregon on a furlough that summer, we saw our family doctor for our annual checkups. My doctor was telling me how he had contracted thyroid cancer and was now checking all of his patients' thyroids. As he pressed his thumb on my throat, he exclaimed. "Oh, you have a little nodule on your thyroid!"

Five years, two surgeries, tons of prayer, and an overwhelming sense of peace later, I was cancer free. I remain so to this day. On the morning of my first surgery, still dopey from some "happy" medicine, I woke up with an overwhelming and tangible sense of the prayers of my friends and family shimmering in my small hospital room in Tahlequah, Oklahoma. I soon discovered that my community in Amsterdam had been interceding for me at that moment. God covered me in His "peace that passes understanding" from that point on. It has kept the irrational fear of the "c" word away from me all these years.

My dream was in for one more hit. Our kids were getting deeper into their teen years by this time: Amy was seventeen, Carrye fifteen, and Andy thirteen. The kids were doing well, except for Andy, who was struggling with school. We soon realized he wasn't connecting in class socially and was falling behind in his work. He's a super-creative, hyper kid, and he needed more flexibility than he was allowed in the Dutch system. He was not fitting in, nor keeping up with his studies. We needed a different strategy. In the States, we would have considered homeschooling him for a few years, but that wasn't allowed in the Netherlands. We weren't sure what to do.

Andy had just visited his grandparents, who were teaching in a Christian school in Germany. While there, he met several English-speaking kids his age and decided he might enjoy going to school there. He liked the kids there better than those in Amsterdam and felt like he could make some friends.

When Andy asked, "Can I go to the missionary school in Germany?" it pushed *all* my buttons. I'd sworn I'd never send my kids to missionary school, certainly not in a dormitory environment like where I grew up. But Andy really wanted to go. So Mindy and I traveled to the school to check it out. We prayed, and, feeling like it was the right thing to do, we enrolled him in the German school.

We were wrong.

Andy made it almost until Christmas before there was a major incident. After Thanksgiving, we received notification from the school. "He's very creative," they wrote, "but we're afraid he's just not fitting in with the structure of the school."

Andy had made some friends—but it sounded like the wrong kind.

Then there was "an incident" in the dormitory and Andy was blamed. The situation escalated quickly. When called in to be questioned about the incident, Andy was apparently disrespectful to the administrator in question. With his parents not there to help mediate the situation, things went from bad to worse. It appeared he was on the verge of being expelled.

Mindy and I decided to bring him home for a bit to see what we could do, so we drove to Germany and picked him up to be with us until after the Christmas break. We managed to smooth things over somewhat with the administration, but Andy was going to have to make some adjustments. We said we would talk with him about it.

We did, and Andy said he would do better. He told us he wanted to go back to the school and would turn over a new leaf. Out of other options, we thought we'd found a solution, so Andy returned to Germany in January.

Andy was fourteen, however, and the school was pretty much zero tolerance with respect to their discipline. The next call we got from the school was that he was being expelled.

It's hard to describe what something like this is like with a kid you know is good at heart but clinging to making some really bad decisions for a time. From our perspective and what we had been experiencing as missionaries, when people mess up, they need to be loved out of it. That was not the policy of the school, however. There was no tolerance there for belligerence. Being a parent, I sided with my son, of course, and having been a missionary school dorm kid, I had my own baggage about the discipline policies of private missionary schools. I have to admit, when I showed up to pick Andy up and bring him back to Amsterdam, I was pretty upset with everyone, which I'm sure didn't help matters much.

Before we left, Andy wanted to say goodbye to his friends, but the headmaster was the only person they would let him talk to. This didn't help my attitude any. There was no compassion there, I told myself.

With both of us mad at the world and more than a little upset with each other, you can imagine what the car ride back to the hotel was like for Andy and me.

Before we left for Amsterdam, one of the school counselors called us and offered to meet with Andy and me to explain what had happened. He wanted to give Andy a chance to tell his side of the story and express his feelings. He'd tried to champion Andy, but to no avail. He saw so much potential in Andy, but there had been no tolerance for him from the administration, and Andy was anything but repentant. He told us he was sorry things had turned out as they had and wished Andy the best. It was a small consolation, but it was something.

All the way home both Andy and I chewed on our attitudes and what had happened. It was a long, quiet ride. Neither of us dared speak a word.

Once back, Mindy and I had a long talk about what to do. Reenroll Andy in Dutch school? That wasn't really a great option. Find another boarding school in Europe or the States? No way. The longer we discussed it, the more we saw the best option was to homeschool him for a time until he was a little older and wiser and ready to deal with the world outside of our weird little missionary bubble. Since the Dutch didn't allow that, it meant returning to the States.

I was going to have to resign as director of YWAM Amsterdam.

Our time in Amsterdam had come to an abrupt and unexpected halt.

✦ ✦ ✦ ✦ ✦

Mindy, Amy, Carrye, and Andy flew back to California before the week ended.

Left alone, I stood in the apartment on the top floor of the Samaritan's Inn, thinking, *What the hell just happened?* I was somewhere between loving my son and wanting to throttle him. I resented that he couldn't get his act together. Then I thought, *Wait a minute! Remember the seventeen-year-old in Japan who threw his whiskey bottle collection at his mother's feet because he was so angry?* I heard the Spirit's counsel: "You must identify with this, certainly."

I did. I truly did.

I was in the middle of my ministry dream, but my family had to come first.

It was time for the Petersens to move on again.

UNVEILING YOUR FUTURE

Pushing into the Eastern Bloc after the wall fell would be the last part of my Ministry Maturing phase, and it would reveal another of my foibles. I knew I was getting better at this ministry stuff, and I wanted to do nothing else. It was becoming an addiction again. My accomplishments were defining my identity. As a result, my life was moving off its axis.

Time for another recalibration.

When a leader becomes addicted to ministry, everything suffers. At one point, the wife of a pastor friend I had worked with approached me and a friend, informing us, "My husband is having an affair . . ."

We blanched!

" . . . with the *ministry,*" she finished.

Families, friends, businesses, and churches all suffer when leaders are intoxicated by their own achievements. These successes become so central to how they see themselves that they are tempted to cling to them rather than to their families and other key relationships. Some even fall back on "that's the way we've always done it before, and it's worked fine" rather than putting a priority on the Father's leading. It's a subtle and deceptive bait and switch. We often fall for it if there isn't a jarring wake-up call.

In each phase of a leader's development, the Lord uses all manner of lessons and challenges to increase his or her influence. But influence for what? *For imparting Christ's image to other believers and those who don't yet believe.* The influence of character is far more potent than the influence that comes from a strong personality or a stunning gift or vision. The Father will go to any length to offend our puny thoughts and dreams in order to insert His superior vision for us and to bring forth the image of His Son.

Often there is abrupt change, or complete collapse. I felt like I had just experienced both. *Yet another failure.* It wouldn't take long, however, for me to discover we had done the right thing and that the failure was only in my eyes, not His.

We must realize that ministry and service are not about what we do for God. The focus should be on family—His Family and ours. Relationships come first—*always.* And if we don't learn how to balance ministry and family—how to take care of the most important relationships with which He's entrusted us—how can God trust us with His work? How can you demonstrate His love if you're more obsessed with what you are doing than the people you are doing it for and with?

During the Ministry Maturing phase, God is setting our lives on His weaver's loom to string the threads together—threads that will ultimately reveal the tapestry's pattern—the image of Christ. This is the Father's definition of success. When He brings us into the Life Maturing phase, He continues that work, but now the scope of what we do is broader. The larger pattern is becoming apparent. He is bringing all things into a coherent, interconnected whole.

For me, the last three years of my Ministry Maturing phase were "living the ministry dream." This was as far as I could go without experiencing an overhaul. The lessons learned in the catastrophe that was my 1990 strategic planning session (and the ensuing repentance) were historically significant for me. Our ministries and our lives are God's possession; He wants to be the one driving the ministry train, not the train driving us. He'd rather let the train derail than lose us to it. He wants our identities founded in Him alone.

When we get off course, He comes sweeping in with His magnificent Spirit to call us to repent, forgive, and reconcile. He never deconstructs anything He doesn't plan to reconstruct. (Identity deconstruction is never a pleasant experience—when we "die to self," something really does die.) And that's exactly what He did with me.

As I stood alone in our former apartment in the Samaritan's Inn, I was in pieces. I felt like I'd been weighed and found wanting—like God was firing me because I wasn't qualified to do His work. (Remember the accusations that had caused all the trouble back in Grants Pass? "Good Christians should have good, well-behaved kids." You don't think my inner doubts would forget to use that one against me, do you?)

Nothing could have been further from the truth, however. I was about to get a promotion, but I wasn't ready to handle what was coming next. It was time for metamorphosis. I was about to enter some cocoon time. It was time to do more growing up.

That January storm in Amsterdam, the release of the prophetic, and the dispersion of our staff throughout Eastern Europe and Africa was epic. God is so good to train us in His way, to do great works through us, and to implant lifelong lessons of dependency in our hearts. However, He never wants us to pitch our tent at the site of our victories. He is never done with us, and no dream is sacred and untouchable but His. There is no adventure like becoming a son or daughter of God, equipped to help fulfill His dreams. We should never forget that is first and foremost.

INTO AND OUT OF THE WILDERNESS

In April of 1994, just three weeks after bringing Andy back from Germany, I found myself in a small, run-down apartment complex in the high desert above Los Angeles, soaking in a murky hot tub listening to a Dodgers baseball game with my hurt and angry son. Dave Parker, the pastor of the Vineyard church in Lancaster, had invited us to live near the church while we figured out what we were going to do next. Our apartment was far from the standard of the penthouse atop the Samaritan's Inn, but we just needed a place to recuperate. Even if the water in the pool and the hot tub was a little cloudy for mysterious reasons, sitting there with Andy provided healing time we both needed.

Andy and I soothed our bruised egos and spirits in the bubbling water. For the moment, it was like none of the recent trauma had happened. We were just a father and son sitting in a hot tub listening to a baseball game. But it would take Andy another five years to fully heal. I just needed to be there with him though the process—and I would be. God was going to see both of us through.

As for me, I had lost my dream for ministry "magnificence," much of my confidence as a leader, and any faith I had in my ability as a father. I was torn between loving my kids and feeling stripped of the friends and the ministry the Lord had so clearly cultivated for us in Amsterdam. The greatest indignity might have been surrendering my ministry credit card (sigh) just before we left. That's when I realized the big ministry dreams were over. It was time to focus on my family.

At the same time, I had no job, no prospects, no ministry, and few connections in the United States. I was going to be a painter again.

In the short term, I returned to Holland to tie things up at the base and help appoint a new leadership team. Those two weeks were some of the hardest of my life. It was brutal. People felt abandoned. I still had a real love for this city. I had arranged meetings with pastors and civic leaders throughout Amsterdam; now I had to cancel them.

In the years after Floyd and Sally had left, we had engaged many of the local Islamic communities, and my former team was stepping up and making significant friendships with them. Drug rehab was happening, prostitutes were being re-socialized, and the team was constantly on the radio and television because of how lives were being changed. It was great to see them shine, but it was no longer my world. It was painful to watch. I was pleased about the legacy that Floyd and Sally and Mindy and I were leaving behind, but I was envious too. It felt like God had given my dreams to someone else.

When I returned to California, I had no plans beyond painting houses and helping my family find new footing in their somewhat-foreign homeland. This sixth "firing" felt final. Amy went off to attend nearby Biola. Carrye flew back to Amsterdam to finish high school and was living at De Poort. Mindy and I (mostly Mindy) began homeschooling Andy. Things slowly fell into a sense of routine.

I don't think I have ever experienced a longer six-month period in all of my life than in those bright desert days. I can still picture the airless sprayer blowing coiling clouds of paint onto new drywall. The rhythm of it can have a meditative effect, but my thoughts were anything but therapeutic. Peering over the parapet of heaven, the "cloud of witnesses" were getting a clinic on the gift of whining, from a champion. I moaned and yelled at God: *What did I do wrong? Why did You take all of that away from me?* As the paint settled into place, however, so did my heart. The simple rhythm of covering walls with layers of color gave me time to think. Once I got tired of my own bellyaching, I had time to reassess things.

I hurt, but as the days turned into months, I came to admit that God owed me nothing. It was His ministry, after all, not mine. No one knew me in the desert, and I had no bull's-eye to aim my ministry-addiction arrow at, so for the first time since leaving Japan, I got a chance to just be Jon again.

With the painting business becoming routine, being a father to my son and a son to my Father began to carry new weight. My world took a sharp inward turn. God's love was hunting me down again. In the wake of my latest—and at the time, I thought *final*—failure, I thought that love would wane, but it didn't. Despite His silence, God was right there with me blowing paint. He hadn't left. He wasn't going anywhere. He wasn't done with me yet.

God hadn't called me because I was useful to Him in doing His ministry. (I know we usually don't consciously think that, but it is an underlying supposition as we find success in anything we do.) Nothing I did could impress Him. I began to see that my ministry dream of doing big things for God was more for me. I was trying to be significant again. I wanted to matter to the world. What I really needed, though, was to matter to God. And I did.

Whether blowing paint in the desert or being His instrument to strengthen pastors in Eastern Europe, He loved me just the same. And He wanted me to know that so badly He was willing to pull the plug on my achievements, and then just stand by me and suffer my whining until I realized He was still there. That He still loved me. That I was still His son and that, more than anything else, I needed to base my identity in that and not in anything else.

It took six months in the desert for those realizations to start sinking in. As they did, I started to see that ministry wasn't a matter of exercising my gifts and getting better at the work in order to do more. God had been using ministry—my gifts and accomplishments included—to instead show me how to walk with Him and be His son. That was to be a foundation in my spirit; my place to stand, take hold of my purpose, and use it as a lever to move the world. It was the footing from which ministry was actually supposed to flow. On that ground, ministry or no ministry, I would better know who I was in Him, and that needed to be enough.

That revelation offered the chance of yet another new beginning.

✦ ✦ ✦ ✦ ✦

At the end of those six months, our friends John and Julie Dawson popped back into our lives. One phone call from them lifted our spirits. We met at the Santa Clarita Mall, and the women shopped while the men sat in the food court, pondering life. John told me, "I believe that within one week your next steps are gonna become clear."

I shook my head, unable to accept the idea.

Within a week, however, I got the call. An acquaintance named Joe Walsh phoned from Sacramento, asking if I might be interested in helping him bring prayer and unity to Sacramento's churches. Mindy's parents now lived there, so moving to Sacramento would be a blessing for our family, as well as a chance to develop our love for the body of Christ in a new city.

I met with Joe to see if this really was what I was supposed to do. Joe's a real go-getter, a do-it-all guy. And he really loves people. He carried a burden for Sacramento, and for the people of God there. We talked about his need for a friend to support him in his work. He didn't want bodies in an office doing stuff; he wanted a ministry partner confident enough in himself that he could trust him. After multiple conversations, I felt peace about accepting Joe's invitation, so I did, and Mindy, Andy, and I made plans to move to Sacramento.

The years in Grants Pass and Amsterdam had given Mindy and me a wealth of experiences, a vast chest full of ministry tools and hard-won wisdom (a lot of it about what *not* to do as well as how to do). Now, back in the States, the Lord would expose us to even more of what was in His heart, which was for His Church. I would be spending the next decade rediscovering His eternal plan for her. The focus was swinging from global mission to the unity of the Body—God's Family—something that would become a personal journey for us. And in this, the Lord had another major reconstruction job designed for my heart.

I've never felt very American, or anything else for that matter (a common challenge for third-culture kids), but now I thought I was hearing the Lord call me as a missionary to the land of my citizenship. He had baptized me with a love for His whole Church years earlier, but now He was upping the ante—I had to be purged of more biases. I needed to learn to love America and the American church.

God had shown me that I could not change what I did not love. It was time for me to learn to love a land where I'd never felt comfortable. (Help me, Jesus!)

✦ ✦ ✦ ✦ ✦

I was driving up Highway 50, hauling our stuff to Sacramento, when I passed a humongous church campus just off the freeway. There was a huge sign proclaiming "Capital Christian Center—an Assembly of God Church." It looked like a college campus. I immediately unleashed a barrage of righteous condemnation against the display of "opulent wealth" and "blatant arrogance." Having unleashed my self-righteous diatribe on the bricks, glass, and fountains along the freeway, I heard the Spirit's quiet and convicting voice: *"I dare you to visit there this Sunday."*

Right! Get thee behind me— Nope, wrong voice. It was so gentle and convicting. *It might even be the Lord,* I mused.

On a Sunday evening, I snuck into the back of the massive auditorium, surrounded by everything about the American church that nauseated me: pipe organs, hymnals, suits and ties, bouffant hairdos, and melodious baritone voices repetitively droning "Ga-loreh to God-uh" way too many times in a three-minute song—and, yeah, *hymnbooks.* Okay, this old hippie pastor and red-light district minister had a problem with this example of kitschy cultural American Pentecostalism. I was about to leave when the pastor stood up and said, "Let's throw out the agenda tonight and let the Lord move."

Okay, this is interesting, I thought.

"In fact," he said, "let's have all of you who have come to Jesus in the past six months come up front and tell us how you met Him."

Ah, testimony night! (Even we Baptists approve of this.)

I knew I was in trouble, as this was not confirming my biases. For the next two hours, I heard spectacular stories of salvation, spontaneous praise, and thunderous applause in gratitude for God's grace through genuine stories of healing and salvation. A brother and sister who had been adopted by separate families at birth found each other "accidentally" for the first time in thirty years—while sitting in a pew next to each other that night. The reunion was shared publicly, and the place went bonkers.

I left that opulent church building soundly rebuked. I returned with Mindy, and we adopted Capital Christian Center as our church family in Sacramento. As it turns out, the pastor, Glen Cole, announced his resignation a short time later. His son, Rick, moved to Sacramento from Nebraska to become lead pastor. (Rick would play a large role in my life and become an effective champion for city unity over the next five years.)

When we moved to Sacramento, I had one mandate from the Lord: "Seek the welfare of the city, for in its welfare you will find your welfare." (See Jeremiah 29:7.)

✦ ✦ ✦ ✦ ✦

Our little prayer ministry was primarily made up of Joe (who'd also been a missionary for years), another beautifully seasoned missionary brother, and me. We'd gather and talk about the prayer meetings in the capitol building, the politicians they'd pray with, and Joe's burden for the city. There was a pastoral network, but it was a network in name only. Nothing much was happening. Joe wanted to see it grow and become a vibrant catalyst for unity among the local churches. There were other ministerial organizations operating, but none seemed very passionate about the city. All were based on "approved" beliefs, rather than discovering Jesus's will. Most of these groups met infrequently, and none of them were friends with one another.

So, between painting jobs, I attended a variety of gatherings. I went incognito to prayer gatherings and to ministry or fellowship meetings. Every time, I'd meet someone who was a key to the next step in our efforts. I also got a feel for each group's passion for the city, and for what was troubling them. I began to see why it was hard for real unity to happen. Historically, Sacramento was the "gold city," a place where people had ventured to stake a claim—and then protect that claim from their neighbors. That mindset was still prevalent. Each group was trying to extract what gold they could from their little piece of the pie.

After about a year of my underground reconnaissance, I started feeling like nobody knew the city's heart. Everyone was so busy protecting their turf that few saw the big picture of what God was trying to do. So I thought, *Well, heck. Why not find out?*

With the encouragement of Joe and a couple of other beautiful brothers, I began researching Sacramento's spiritual history. This was in the days when "spiritual mapping" was becoming a big thing. People would research their cities for enemy strongholds to pray against. They saw areas of sin as targets for prayer. They wanted to "give the demons an eviction notice." Amazing things happened through such prayer, but it always seemed to be short-lived.

I have never seen any value in defining a city by its sins. Defining a city this way keeps its churches in warfare mode. It negates a church's ambassadorial calling to be redemptive. "Spiritual warfare," as many were defining it, was like a constant D-Day invasion—there was no recognition that the battle had already been won through the cross. That victory needed to be declared and ratified; there was no need to storm the beaches again and again—*and again*—if the victory was already won.

God is redemptive in all He does. He had tutored my heart in Amsterdam to define that city by its created purpose and covenantal promises, not by its sin or dysfunction. The Lord would never let our team define the city by what happened in the red-light district and the city's rampant drug culture. Sin was simply a sign that the city's covenant with God had been broken, within the Church or even the culture at large. Enemy strongholds often grow in the shadow of broken covenants. We needed to follow the shadow back to the broken covenant or discarded prayers. There, we could renew God's call for the city. I was sure there was a righteous root here to lay claim to and petition God to restore.

The first order of business was not warfare. Instead, we needed to discover the foundational prayers of previous generations. We needed to get back to the covenant root system. Only then could we gather to repent for forsaking those godly foundations and restore each region's redemptive roots. This was not a mandate for a few radical intercessors and pastors. It was the privilege of the whole priesthood of believers, unified and fervent in prayer as they pursued God's heart for the city.

So off I went, feeling a little like Nehemiah, sneaking around the wall of Jerusalem on his steed, not telling his friends "*what my God had put in my heart to do*" (Nehemiah 2:12). I spent most of the next year in church basements, looking through documents and newspaper articles on microfiche and interviewing local history buffs. At one point, I was led to the wife of a Methodist pastor in Fresno, who had researched the early days of the California church and church leaders in Sacramento during its "gold rush" origins. She had (pardon the pun) a gold mine of information.

I was shocked to find another gold mine of information in the belly of the Bancroft Library at the University of California, Berkeley campus. There, in dusty boxes, I found diaries, wallets, handkerchiefs, and other personal effects of Sacramento's spiritual founding fathers.*

A picture began to form.

Sacramento (from the Spanish for "sacrament") is an amazing city with a fantastic spiritual history. Four men founded churches in Sacramento's earliest days and walked in unbroken unity for nearly thirty years—through the turbulence of California's gold rush days and on through the Civil War era. They had a prominent voice in city affairs, and the newspapers devoted front-page coverage to their annual "state of the city" updates. Martin C. Briggs, one of the "Sacramento Four," rode his black horse all over the state, from Los Angeles to the Oregon border, preaching against the "evils of slavery."

Sacramento was bursting at its seams in 1849, because James Marshall had found gold at Sutter's Mill the year before. When the Sacramento River flooded, threatening many lives, the "Sacramento Four" mobilized the city to help those in danger. Martin Briggs, seeing the flood approaching his home, told his family to climb into the rafters of the church and wait out the floodwaters so he could continue rescuing other families. They did. He continued on in his little rowboat, rescuing many in his neighborhood. When he was done, he rowed back and rescued his family from off the church roof.

* The following paragraphs about what I found in these dusty archives is from memory. Unfortunately, sometime after I left Sacramento, the files and notes I kept documenting all of the research I had done were lost. If you do the same work in your city, I would suggest you follow the old adage, "Don't put all of your eggs in one basket." It's good to preserve these things for future generations. Lesson learned.

As more than 300,000 came to California in search of gold, Dr. Grove Deal would stand at the bottom of the gangplank as miners got off the ferries. He looked each one in the eyes and asked, "God or gold?" The few interested in God were led to a little stand of oak trees known as "The Grove," where they would worship the Lord while someone preached from a pulpit made from three whiskey boxes. (Those boxes eventually became a bone of contention for a rather religious lady who decried the "mixing of spirits." Thankfully, the Holy Spirit won out!)

These men and their congregations also saw an amazing vision, revealing that America's Manifest Destiny and westward expansion wouldn't end at the Pacific Coast. They prayed for the Gospel to penetrate Asia, Japan, and China. As Chinese labor came to California to build the transcontinental railroad and work in the mines, they found champions among these community leaders. Local believers investigated the mines and the railroad track system and demanded better standards of living for the workers, who were being treated horribly. These local church members spoke up for immigrants in the halls of government and in the community. And they prayed for them fervently.

I found hundreds of stories like this one of unified leaders, sacrificial families, and intense citywide prayer. Sacramento had a rich spiritual foundation. However, as I grew more excited about what I was learning, the Lord encouraged me to stay quietly in the shadows. I longed to tell my growing circle of pastoral friends about my discoveries, but God directed me to let them ask for the information first. I created a six-page summary of the best of what I had learned and started carrying it around in the sleeve of my jacket so that I would be ready when asked.

I carried those sheets around for months.

Finally, as I sat with a group of pastors one morning, one of the brothers turned to me abruptly and asked, "What do you know about Sacramento's spiritual heritage?"

I almost choked. I shot off a bullet prayer to the Lord: *Is this the time?*

It was.

"Well," I said, "I just happen to have a wee summary of the first twenty-five years of the city's spiritual foundations right here in the sleeve of my jacket."

"What?" he said. "In your jacket? Show me!"

After perusing the paper for a few minutes, he asked his secretary to make copies. We spent the rest of the morning rejoicing in our amazing spiritual family and the incredibly faithful men and women who had given their city such a rich and a righteous legacy.

For our little team in Sacramento, this discovery of our redemptive roots translated into public invitations to a variety of ethnic, denominational, and nondenominational churches—to come to public meetings and testify on our collective covenantal root system. This released much joy and prayer (and repentance for the infighting and our failure to demonstrate God's love to our city). Like the greedy people from gold rush days, Sacramento churches had adopted a "claim-staking" mindset. It was ugly, ungodly stuff. But when they realized their errors, many of Sacramento's pastors repented, and the joy that came from their newfound unity gave them new eyes to see their city from the Father's perspective.

We experienced the joy of friendship and unity with pastors from a variety of denominations and ethnicities. Out of the journey to know our collective spiritual history and pursue local church relationships through prayer and fellowship, leaders who were once suspicious of each other became friends.

Out of these relationships, we launched the Sacramento Pastors' Prayer Network. God was truly touching hearts and changing lives.

UNVEILING YOUR FUTURE

The brutal interruption of my life in Amsterdam because of family needs disturbed my equilibrium like never before. Sitting in the hot tub and listening to the baseball game that day, I was numb. I was sure my ministry days were over. I was in repair mode. There was something fundamental about serving God in this world that I hadn't figured out yet, and I deeply needed to.

I faintly identified with God's request of Abraham to sacrifice the channel of his promise and his dream: Isaac. Only after Abraham willingly left his home to sacrifice his son, with the arc of the knife at its zenith, did God intervene:

> ***"Do not do anything to him. Now I know that you fear God, because you have not withheld from me your son, your only son."***
>
> **—GENESIS 22:12**

God gave Abraham back his son, the seed of God's promised generations, but was He going to give me back my dream? It didn't take me long to find out.

I jokingly call this season my "male menopause," because God dried up my spiritual reproductive system as I knew it. After all of the focus on ministry gifts and activities, of living in various geographical locations and meeting many fascinating people, I needed to learn that true ministry wasn't about outward trappings. It needed to come from a stable base of knowing who I was in Christ.

Ministry was serving God as He directs. God doesn't count crowds; He counts individuals. He's always looking for hearts surrendered to Him. We're often attracted to the showiness of ministry, while God seems fascinated with the change of each human heart as it is given to Him and knit into His Family.

Often, He needs to remove us from the excitement, get us alone and quiet, to reach us. When He finally has us to Himself, He begins to unveil what's next. Then He can launch us into a ministry more central to His heart, even if it is less impressive to everyone around us.

The focus of this new season was to mature my character—thus I entered my Life Maturing phase. This period (late thirties to mid-forties) brings a shift in God's dealings with His leaders. It is a shift from developing the outer world to an intense focus on the inner life. It has to do with the security of our identity. This phase melds what was learned in previous years. This is the crucible season, an invitation from Jesus: *"If anyone would come after me, he must deny himself and take up his cross and follow me"* (Matthew 16:24).

It's a time to look at what we have built so far, appreciate it, and then (often) give it to someone else so that we can do something new—something more God and less us. When we gain more perspective on who we are, we are allowed to see and appreciate our destiny for what it is, flaws and all. Though it is part of us, it doesn't define us. The unconscious needs of identity formation no longer coerce us into actions without our realizing what's happening. Now we can see what ego is up to and decide whether we want to go with its inclinations or not. This is a blessed season when God grabs us by the ankles, flips us upside-down, and shakes out everything of personal value from our "pockets." This is jumping into the "deep end" of life.

During my season of reflection in the California desert (and of quiet meditation while spraying paint onto walls), I realized I had been subconsciously unwilling to sacrifice my dreams of "successful" ministry. Initially, I was mad at God for asking me to give up what He had given me. This was a revelation; I saw that I loved my calling and success more than I loved the Lord. At my core, despite the static in my head, I wanted the Lord to say to me, like He did to Abraham, that He knew I loved Him more than the promises and dreams He had given me, but I couldn't do it. It just wasn't true. It took a summer of blowing paint before the Lord finally won all of my heart.

Surrender is a strange thing, so hard to achieve, yet so freeing when you do it. By that season's end, I was free. I had become one of those guys whose ankles were grabbed. I'd been flipped and shaken to the point I could say, "*I consider everything a loss because of the surpassing worth of knowing Christ Jesus my Lord, for whose sake I have lost all things. I consider them garbage, that I may gain Christ*" (Philippians 3:8).

I wanted to echo Paul's words from my heart—without regret.

That experience began a journey into the assurance of my sonship in Christ. By the end of my Ministry Maturing season (moving to Sacramento), I had nothing more to protect, nothing worth achieving, and no concern for the future. Even my historic strongholds were being exposed and disarmed. I was forty-two, visionless, and more content in my Father's love than ever.

It was time to discover my new life as His son.

WHAT UNITY CAN LOOK LIKE

The next step in the journey was to tidy up my Sacramento spiritual history into something that could be presented as part of a forty-five-minute prayer meeting that could be repeated all over town. We would tell the story and then call people to repent if they'd fallen into disunity or into the claim-staking mentality—building their own kingdoms at the expense of working together to build God's Kingdom. Once this was done, we'd explain how to plug in to God's purposes for their city.

It all seemed simple and rudimentary, but the responses were unbelievable. People sincerely repented, but they always wanted to know "What do we do now?" After hearing that question a few times, we changed gears. "Let's make these prayer meetings about inviting the Lord back into the city," we decided.

Our core group meetings started to grow. Hispanic and African American pastors began to attend, and then we tapped in to the large and growing Russian population. Each of the two Russian churches in South Sac City served about 5,000 people. Sacramento was truly becoming a multiracial and multiethnic city.

We focused our core meetings on building relationships and becoming friends with each other, with the desire to seek more of Jesus as our foundation. Then we would hold similar meetings at churches throughout the area. Congregations repented of divisive mindsets and asked God to rekindle His covenants with our city. We'd stand in a row with the leaders of each church and tell them, "We're really glad that you're here and part of God's Family in Sacramento." Many of the groups had never been welcomed by any other church, so the results we saw were always beautiful.

Not long after these efforts began, an African American church was targeted by a racist group. It was burned to the ground. Our prayer network rallied immediately to raise money. Within three days of the fire, we had $92,000 to give to this congregation. The church's pastor shared that, shortly before the fire, he had dreamed that God wanted him to build a new home for his congregation. The congregation was bursting at the seams, and they needed room to expand. The pastor had asked the Lord, "How could such a building ever happen? We're broke." However, between the money donated by the various churches and the insurance settlement, they had enough to make that dream come true.

The congregation was overwhelmed with joy from the Lord, and with gratitude for the Sacramento church family. I vividly remember the church dedication celebration. It was unity in the Kingdom made manifest!

✦ ✦ ✦ ✦ ✦

We weren't the only ones working for reconciliation and unity in the Church.

In December 1992, a Solemn Assembly was held at Confluence Park in central Denver to commemorate the Sand Creek Massacre. In November of 1864, Southern Cheyenne and Arapahoe tribes, wanting peace (and being assured that they were under the protection of the State), were told to camp at Sand Creek, Colorado, on reservation land, in accordance with the Fort Laramie Treaty of 1851. While most of the men were gone to hunt for food for their families, two US Army Colorado Calvary units and the First New Mexico Volunteers, under the command of a former Methodist preacher named Colonel John Chivington, rushed the camp at dawn. The approximately 800 soldiers opened fire. Approximately 148 were slaughtered, more than half of them women and children.[11] The atrocities did not end there: The dead were mutilated in the worst ways. Survivors and body parts were displayed from town to town as trophies by many who took part in the raid.

Given the region's history, I found it significant that politicians, pastors, and representatives of the Native Americans from the Front Range attended the church's commemoration event. This gathering sparked another the following month.

At that evening (in January of 1993), Christians of all races gathered at the remote massacre site near the town of Chivington, Colorado. The events at Sand Creek and others that took place there in the 1860s were still a major cause for bitterness toward and a rejection of Christianity by many young Native Americans. Our friend John Dawson was one of the event's keynote speakers.

John pointed out that animosity and bitterness can fester unresolved for generations, particularly in the following categories: race to race, gender to gender, vocation to vocation, class to class, culture to culture, region to region, religion to religion, denomination to denomination, government to government, and institution to institution. He believed that the Church must promote reconciliation among people and "restore friendship" using four stages: confession, repentance, reconciliation, and restitution.

The Sand Creek Reconciliation events were just two of many gatherings that convened in the '90s—uniting fractured parties around the globe. In this spirit of humility, the International Reconciliation Coalition emerged. John Dawson, spokesman for the American chapter, stated that the purpose of the Reconciliation

Coalition was to heal America's wounds. He said, "Individuals can hurt each other through selfish and unjust behavior, but it's also possible for a wound to be sustained by a corporate entity within American national life." He'd written a book called *Taking Our Cities for God: How to Break Spiritual Strongholds*, which outlined how to use his four reconciliation stages to reconnect communities. John's book challenged the church to embrace citywide unity and recognize the "church of the city" over individual congregations and denominations. As pastors and congregations strived to walk in unity and intercession for their towns and regions across the world, "city reaching" began to capture the imagination of many believers. Church leaders began desiring to make their cities "prayed for," a phrase that soon became the clarion call to the worldwide Body of Christ. John's book became a handbook for movements around the world.

✦ ✦ ✦ ✦ ✦

At this same time, Bill McCartney, the coach of the University of Colorado's 1990 national-champion football team, got the inspiration for Promise Keepers. I attended one of their stadium gatherings in Oakland, California. Men had come from surrounding states in buses and caravans of cars: fathers, sons, and friends from all over the nation. Many were from formerly competing churches. You could feel the rustle of excitement as men and boys of all colors, ages, and vocations worshiped the Lord together. For many, it was the first time they had witnessed such a visual demonstration of unity from a cross-section of the Lord's people. It was a small reflection of "heaven on earth" to these men, a picture of God's norm for His Church. These men were challenged to keep their promises to their wives and families and to be "men of God." Promise Keepers was just one of the many flames that the Lord was fanning for unity in His family during the 1990s.

Around this same time, Dr. Joe Aldrich, president of Multnomah Bible College, wondered, "What would it take to initiate and sustain a significant work of God in a specific geographical community?" In other words, what would it take to see Jesus's prayer from John 17 lived out: *"Father, make them one as we are one."* Aldrich believed the answer to this question would come through a five-part process: holiness, humility, unity, community, and impact.

The goal of bringing together the critical mass of pastors from a specific geographical community for several days of seeking the Lord was realized in nearby Salem, Oregon. (Multnomah Bible College is in the Portland area.) At the request of pastors in Salem, Dr. Aldrich and Terri Dirks (another Multnomah leader) facilitated the first prayer summit in 1989. Since then, the movement (now referred to as International Renewal Ministries) has expanded to reach across the United States and into scores of other nations. Thousands of pastors have become involved in the movement, and local churches have been significantly impacted. Multiple communities have seen the benefits of a unified city-church walking through the process of confession, repentance, brokenness, reconciliation, and restoration. Walls that typically divided and fragmented were crumbling.*

I was invited to host many of these retreats with our Harvest Evangelism team in the late 1990s, in order to facilitate this growing affection among church leaders. It was like finding lost family. The fruit of this unity was the emergence of endeavors

* For more information, see www.Prayersummits.net.

such as "prayer-walking," "Lighthouses of Prayer," "Adopt-a-Cop," intercessory teams, "warfare prayer," "spiritual mapping," and "redemptive discovery." We made mistakes and fell into the trap of emphasizing the wrong things at times, but, overall, the churches were coming together to reach their communities, as the Lord refined our understanding of the churches' place in the city.

One of the most difficult lessons that the Church encountered—and is still wrestling with—was the difference between "functional" and "organic" unity. Much of the unity in the citywide prayer and fellowship movements was built upon "doing something together." Over time, many groups diminished or disappeared from the landscape because they hadn't built a deep affection for each other. Prayer gatherings, evangelistic efforts, and many genuine social actions in the city trumped the simplicity of pastoring each other's hearts and doing only what the Lord directed. This was a season when "doing" often supplanted "being" and doing what "seemed right" trumped waiting on the "word of the Lord" for how to act. Now, I'm speaking from hindsight, as there were some marvelous exceptions to this pattern. Nonetheless, after years of parsing the Church by denominational distinctives, we were celebrating Jesus as our unifier and ourselves as "one Church with many parts."

Looking back, I realize that we had learned valuable unity lessons in the Netherlands. After the move of God in Amsterdam, we saw increased unity in the church, the city, and the nation. But the church in the Netherlands was not yet one. Some churches made it bewilderingly easy to officially split from other groups:

"Yep, can't stand those guys across the street anymore. We're requesting a new identity for our church, please."

"Okay, Jaap, fill out these forms and the Council will vote on approving your disapproval."

What's that about?

Denominational disunity had become an art form, and the norm since the days of the Reformation. Rather than fight to be one in Christ, they decided to keep the peace by allowing for whatever theological distinctives and church polity made sense to them. While that ended the infighting, it also diminished the impact of the city church.

As noted earlier, in 1981 there were about ten Gospel-preaching churches in Amsterdam, none with a congregation of more than 250. Most in the city felt no need to increase the number of churches. The "small thinking" and disunity was palpable. God used Floyd McClung to gather leaders from various traditions in the Netherlands and mediate the love of God for them, many of whom had never crossed denominational lines to find the treasure in each other. His popular book *The Father Heart of God* was first printed in Dutch to access the hearts of this dis-unified nation, which had virtually no concept of God as a loving and merciful heavenly Father. That book has since gone global.

After Floyd returned to the States in 1991, our team continued the gathering of pastors and began prayer-walking our streets, proclaiming Jesus as Lord over the city.

As a result, the Satanic "church" got into some legal trouble and had to shut down, which meant the sex trade took a significant hit. Over time, the red-light district began shrinking. Several churches began engaging the area for the first time, witnessing daily to the inhabitants of this famous destination. An annual international conference of LGBT community leaders decided not to return to Amsterdam the following year, because the "atmosphere has changed."

The power of prayer as the engine of unity cannot be underestimated in the spiritual equilibrium of our cities. Today there are hundreds of churches in Amsterdam preaching the Gospel.

UNVEILING YOUR FUTURE

During this time, I began to see fundamental components of the church that we had gotten wrong over the years. So-called good ideas and cultural norms had slowly replaced what we were called to do as believers serving one another in a local body.

The Church at the beginning of the 1990s was constructed in such a way that pastors were so enmeshed in their own local churches that they had no time to deepen friendships with fellow pastors. Their schedules were too full of church board meetings, visitations, counseling sessions, administrative meetings, and the like. When citywide organizations sprang up, they joined enthusiastically, but they soon became exhausted from the multiple demands. Instead, simply showing up for functions and responsibilities trumped deepening friendships organically, let alone seeking the Lord's will for the city via time-consuming prayer meetings.

The current church wineskins simply couldn't contain the new wine God was pouring over the city. We needed a new paradigm. We would begin to see a slow change in this tension in the following two decades, as God began introducing us to new wineskins for organizing churches and ministries. One of these tenets came from John 5:19:

> ***"Very truly I tell you, the Son can do nothing by himself; he can do only what he sees his Father doing, because whatever the Father does the Son also does."***

I'm sure that Jesus's disciples had many good ideas about what He should do to build His ministry and mount a spiritual revolution. But Jesus had other priorities. The disciples weren't His "church board of elders." Instead, He fellowshipped with His Father and then did what His Father directed Him to do. That's how He set His agenda.

That distinction is easy to misunderstand. A pastor is not a free agent, accountable to no one but his own conscience (in relationship with God). The pastor is a head elder among elders, and all of them should seek God's direction together. While Jesus heard from His Father alone to direct His ministry, it's our calling today to hear the directions of the Father as a band of disciples *together,* not in a similar "leader-follower" paradigm. Each of us needs to get our piece of the puzzle from God the Father and then fit all of the pieces together with the other elders for the direction of our churches. It's easy to miss the "together" part, because there is so much to be done, and it can feel so inefficient. But that's what we're supposed to do "moving at the speed of relationship." We were discovering that the "together" part was fundamental to the facilitation of unity in city-churches. As we got that right in our multi-church meetings, it bled into individual congregations as well.

I can only summarize here what I covered in-depth in my book *Unravelled: Reform the Church, Transform the Culture,* but as the Industrial Age took over, the Church began to find success in that movement's methods and organizational charts rather than sticking to the guidelines of the New Testament. Pastors might seem like CEOs, but a church should not operate like a factory. In business, leaders often declare, "These are the things we need to do" rather than focusing on relationship and saying, "We need to lead from a place of deep connections with each other and God."

When we do the former, things get done. When we do the latter, communities of faith get formed and few things can stand against them. The first is about the success of the organization (in this case a local church); the second is about expanding the Kingdom of God throughout our cities. In a nutshell, these differences create two completely different approaches to what God has called us to do. Everything we do either centers on building our church in competition with everything else in our communities or infecting our cities by living His Kingdom everywhere we go. The dichotomies look something like this:

Church-centric Mindset*	Kingdom-expanding Mindset
TRANSACTIONAL People serve the ministry *"Do ministry together"*	**RELATIONAL** People are the ministry *"Do life together"*
CHURCH VISION MOTIVATES Leader-initiated, hierarchical	**"WORD OF THE LORD" MOTIVATES** Spirit-initiated, familial
CLERGY/LAITY SPLIT Education, knowledge-based *"Leadership is here to show you the way"*	**PLURAL LEADERSHIP/ PRIESTHOOD OF BELIEVERS** Equipping, character-based *"We are all here to equip you to be all God has destined you to be"*
SACRED/SECULAR SPLIT Church as a sacred organization to be maintained *"Go to church; serve the church"*	**SANCTITY OF ALL LIFE** Church as a people to be developed *"Be a family, multiply into all culture"*
EXCLUSIVE UNITY Conformative *"Be like us"*	**INCLUSIVE UNITY** Transformative *"Be like Jesus"*
NATIONAL CITIZENSHIP Temporal, tribal perspective	**HEAVENLY CITIZENSHIP** Eternal, global perspective

* This chart first appeared in my book *Unravelled: Reform the Church, Transform the Culture,* on page 104. I include it here for reference. For a deeper explanation, please read *Unravelled.*

When a church is centered on relationship and vision is determined by hearing God *together*, grace abounds when mistakes are made: "Oops, we got that one wrong. Let's pray and ask God where we got it wrong," rather than, "Ew, you messed up. Are you sure you should be an elder?" Hearing God together challenges people to know one another, to have grace for one another and not pull apart when mistakes are made. When people truly know and trust each other, they recognize and value one another's gifts and how important they are to the faith community overall. It's a lot messier, but when a church is more relational than transactional, it is a beautiful thing to behold. The body grows in depth and size organically, "moving at the speed of relationship."

In the mid-1990s, I didn't have the full picture of this yet, but the pieces were coming together. God used this season to hone our ecclesiology and our ministry philosophy. We began to put first things first. It was the on-ramp to the fruitful ministry waiting in the shadows of our futures. There was more I needed to learn before I would see the pattern come together.

In the next season, however, I learned how this kind of unity could transform entire regions.

CITY TRANSFORMATION

In 1997, while our family was still living in Sacramento, Ed Silvoso and I reconnected. Ed, his wife, Ruth, and their family and team at Harvest Evangelism were intimately involved in the revivals in Argentina. In the early '90s, as part of their desire to reach the nations, they'd taken great interest in our work in Amsterdam and had come to visit and minister with us occasionally. Ed was one of the most passionate lovers of people I'd ever met.

Harvest Evangelism was based in San Jose, California, at that time, and after a "chance meeting" with Ed at a conference in Northern California, he asked me to join the team in their endeavor to bring the city church together in prayer and unity.

Ed had recently written a book called *That None Should Perish: How to Reach Entire Cities for Christ Through Prayer Evangelism*. In it, he put city transformation into proper context: The goal should be helping people know Jesus. He focused on worldwide evangelism, revealing his passion for the lost. Up to that point, evangelism had been a smaller part of the overall goals of citywide prayer groups, but when Ed put it front and center, it changed the focus. This effort combined the missions emphasis we'd experienced in the 1980s and early '90s with the prayer and unity emphasis we were currently experiencing through our prayer networks and conferences.

Ed also had a passion for business. He was ahead of his time. Melding mission and business would really take off in the decade to come.

I loved everything he and Harvest were doing, so I told Ed I would join them.

It was a wild season! I lived in Sacramento, commuted to San Jose (six hours round-trip) three times a week, jetted off to scores of US cities for conferences, tagged along on Argentinian "revival trips," and led a ton of organizational endeavors aimed at initiating the Body of Christ into the amazing world of "city reaching/city transformation." (And only months before, I had thought I'd never be part of any kind of ministry again. Ha!) What I had learned about redemption via Sacramento's historical archives, I was now experiencing on the streets of San Nicolas (Ed's childhood home) in Argentina's Pampas region.

✦ ✦ ✦ ✦ ✦

Harvest had organized a diverse team of about 185 wild-eyed international disciples in a camp on the outskirts of San Nicolas. Through Ed's years of work, the local congregations demonstrated a level of unity among church traditions, cultures, generations, and genders—something I hadn't seen before. Witnessing a microcosm of the global Church supporting a local ministry, I realized how much our view of the Church had changed from the divisive days of the 1970s and '80s.

At our gathering, almost all of the churches in this city of 180,000 had come together through prayer and repentance. (Only one church declined to participate, for reasons unknown.)

When we arrived, we walked into a beautiful fraternity of new friends. We were determined to help them impact their city for the Lord.

Within three weeks, every home and every business was "prayer-walked" three times, and the home of every believer was sanctified and dedicated to the Lord. The Argentines, slightly unconventionally, didn't want to timidly anoint their doorposts with oil to dedicate their homes. Instead they splashed buckets of it on the outside walls. (Good for the Kingdom, not so good for painters like me—I knew that oil wasn't so great for the paint!) Intercessory "hit squads" were sent to direct prayer against a variety of witches' covens (which were popular in the region) while praying blessings on the witches themselves. (During that period of prayer, most of the witches' businesses were closed for lack of customers.) Other teams were sent to the "seven gates" of the city, where curses had been written by covens and embedded in the soil. Stakes with Scripture promises were driven into the ground to replace the curses. The Kingdom was advancing.

Throughout the week, several pastors sequestered themselves in a makeshift radio station, directing the prayer walks, sharing testimonies from the street, discussing the city's needs, and praying for them. Each morning, our whole team met with pastors, intercessors, and local believers to seek the Lord, worship, and deal with relational issues the Lord pointed out. In those beautiful gatherings, we cried, repented, and rejoiced. Faith rose to dangerous levels.

One morning, we noticed that the children who had been bussed in were unusually dour and distant. They wore mysterious little pins on their clothing. A quick investigation uncovered that a "nice lady" had stood outside their bus and given them small amulets, enabling a group of witches to "see" what transpired at our meetings. Think of them as "spiritual bugging devices." Once these pins were discovered and removed from the children, their moods improved and the joy of the Lord fell on them. Worship erupted. And those little "spiritual bugs" went dark. (I love it when the enemy's strategies are foiled!)

✦ ✦ ✦ ✦ ✦

Over the following week, we offered "free prayer" coupons through the local newspaper, and we ran radio ads inviting the city to a Saturday "Prayer Fair." As Saturday loomed nearer, so did a massive winter storm. In the morning, as the teams were prayer-walking the city again, a weatherman reported a severe storm headed for the edge of town. He urged people to take cover. Knowing that our Prayer Fair was to commence at 1:00 PM, the word went out to pray for a weather miracle.

I was driving in a car with Ed when he turned and said, "Do you believe the Lord can change the weather?" Being the man of faith that I am, I said, "Of course." But my mind was telling me, *No, you don't. You just don't want to own up to your embarrassment if this prayer thing doesn't work!* (So much for being a man of faith!)

Ed turned, picked up his phone, and called the pastors clustered in the tiny radio station. He told them, "Brothers, I am going to pray; please agree with me." With a lot of "Oh, amen, Brother Silvoso is coming over the airwaves," Ed launched into a bone-rattling prayer commanding the storm to stop at the city's border, for the weather to warm up thirty degrees, and for blue skies to reveal themselves by the start of the Prayer Fair. (Okay, *that* terrified me.) We were now on the record for either a miracle equal to Jesus's commanding the sea to still or looking like fools. We'd be heroes or get laughed out of town within the next four hours.

By the time the Prayer Fair began, however, the storm was nowhere in sight. It was thirty degrees warmer than when we had prayed in Ed's car, and the sky was crystal blue. Any who had heard this prayer on the radio, having their curiosity piqued, streamed to the city park, clutching their little "free prayer" coupons and eager to see what was going to happen next. (I guess no one had told them that prayer is always free.) We had prayer menus posted around the park, and seven stations devoted to specific prayer needs: job, family, depression, healing, etc. The seventh station was for "prayer for anything not on the menu."

I saw a witch get delivered of demonic struggles through the prayers of a sixteen-year-old girl from Chicago. The woman had been sent to disrupt the depression prayer line, but then this teenager spotted her. Her witch buddies were across the street, sending incantations and curses toward us. The sixteen-year-old realized that something was off about this woman, so she walked up to her, laid a hand on her shoulder, and asked, "Can I pray for you?"

"No!" the woman answered, shocked.

"Why are you lined up for prayer then?"

"Well, I just—I don't know. I was just feeling like standing here."

"What is that pendant on your neck?"

The woman's hand went to it quickly, and she dropped it into her blouse. It must have been a talisman of some kind.

Before she could escape, the Chicago girl, her hand still on the woman's shoulder, launched into prayer. She prayed that the Lord would reveal Himself to this lady and show her how much He loved her.

Moments later, the woman fell on the ground and started writhing like a snake. Our teenager was from an evangelical church and had never done anything like this before, but she didn't back down. The Lord graced her with discernment. She laid her hands on the woman and kept praying.

The woman was delivered from her oppression. The color in her face changed. She rose to her feet, rejoicing. It was amazing!

We prayed for thousands of people throughout the afternoon. Many healings were witnessed, new converts were received into the family, demons were cast out, and all who came were prayed for. Two more witches received deliverance and turned to Jesus before the day was over.

As the sun set that night, the Church of San Nicolas was worshiping God with their new disciples, and joy covered the city. There was also virtually no crime in the city for those three weeks, and automobile accidents decreased significantly. The chief of police was so blown away that he approached us, saying, "You have to let me in on the secret here. If we could have this kind of safety all the time, that would be a beautiful thing."

We left that church in great shape. There were only eighteen churches for 180,000 people when we came. They were packed full, and various church-plants were being considered when we left. It was incredible. We had never seen anything like it before, but as we knew, *"With God all things are possible"* (Matthew 19:26).

The mayor, the Catholic priest, the chief of police, various dignitaries and business leaders, and thousands throughout the city knew Jesus had come to town.

✦ ✦ ✦ ✦ ✦

In the days following the San Nicolas Prayer Fair, we received many invitations to citywide gatherings across the United States, as well as one to Haringey, a borough of London. There was often a lot of worship and spiritual warfare around our incursions into these various cities, making us alert to the Holy Spirit's prompting.

While in Haringey for a conference on city transformation, I was sleeping in my small hotel room, and I began to dream that a dark, malevolent force was trying to harm me. In my dream, I saw myself sleeping and someone trying to get through the window into my room, via the balcony.

I woke with a start. Curious about the dream, I cautiously walked to my window and peeked between the small slit in my curtains. There, to my amazement, were two large feet on the balcony. The bloke attached to those feet was slowly lifting the window. I stepped to the side, shot a prayer heavenward, said loudly, "I don't think so!"

Startled, the man fled.

No one else, including the hotel security, got a glimpse of him. I'm sure they thought some crazy American was hallucinating—but, no. I was being protected by my Father.

✦ ✦ ✦ ✦ ✦

Before it can transform a city, a church must transform itself. An untransformed church is powerless to transform its environment. The church needed transformation, and one of the best tools for making this happen is the gathering and unifying of a city's spiritual leaders.

At Harvest Evangelism, we received many invitations to host pastoral prayer retreats. One memorable retreat was held in Northern Florida. Our Harvest evangelism team hosted church leaders from a multitude of denominational and ethnic backgrounds. After a few days of prayer and worship, we decided to feature the perfunctory "hot seat" in the middle of the circle, a place where anyone could request prayer from the others. It was a gorgeous conflagration of saints: African Americans, Hispanics, and Caucasians, all taking turns asking for prayer, followed by a rush of laid-on hands—and words of prophecy, knowledge, or wisdom. There were many prayers, and lots of laughter.

About two hours into one meeting, an older, refined pastor sauntered over to the chair and plopped down. He sighed and said, "Okay, I have to get this out. I hate the Assemblies of God!"

Dead silence.

Then he began to weep, as he shared that his father and all his uncles had been Assembly of God pastors. His father had come under scrutiny by the denomination and was summarily removed. In a show of solidarity, his uncles followed him out the door. They all fled to the Methodists' camp, where they were received and restored to ministry. But they had never been reconciled to the Assembly of God leadership.

This man said that no matter how hard he had tried, he couldn't find the forgiveness that God expected of him.

A young man approached, knelt in front of the sobbing man, and put his arms around him. He said, "I am a young Assembly of God pastor. I wasn't alive when all this happened, but I wonder if you can find it in your heart to forgive our denomination for the heartless way we tried to bring correction to your father?" That young pastor broke down crying on the offended man's shoulder, and both men literally howled at the release of pain that God's Spirit provided. The older pastor voiced his forgiveness and began to laugh. The whole room erupted in the same backslapping and ridiculous outpourings of joy.

✦ ✦ ✦ ✦ ✦

Successes like this don't come without opposition and criticism. In the late 1990s, the Lord gave us a painful opportunity to avoid defending our reputation, to "respond in the opposite spirit." We had been demonstrating the beauty of "prayer-walking" along with medical missionary Steve Hawthorne (author of *Prayer-walking: Praying On Site with Insight* and many other books). An initiative called "Lighthouses of Prayer" was launched and adopted by a well-known national interdenominational organization. Harvest Evangelism had partnered with this team of leaders to train, equip, and release thousands of believers to walk their neighborhoods and consecrate their homes as "Lighthouses of Prayer."

A leader from one of our partner ministries sent a scathing letter to nearly a thousand American leaders, denigrating Ed Silvoso and Harvest Evangelism. The accusations were so counter to what we stood for, the letter was hard to read. After our team in San Jose had reviewed it, Ed simply said, "Let's pray and ask the Lord how to respond."

So our staff of about twelve began to pray. We asked the Lord how He wanted us to respond. One of our younger workers, with a twinkle in her eye, said, "Let's collect some money and send it to the three key leaders involved—and designate the money for a romantic getaway with their wives."

Perfect! A soft word might turn away wrath.

We had been learning that "when you are being accused, *bless!*" So we did. We raised nearly $3,000 from our impoverished little team of workers and sent the money, along with beautiful cards. Then we waited. The following Monday, we received three phone calls from the three leaders' secretaries, asking us to "stipulate the intention of the donation."

"For a romantic weekend," we said.

I'm not sure they ever believed it, or if they enjoyed a romantic weekend, but our intentions were dead-serious. We wanted them to be blessed.

Then the top leader of the ministry and his board heard the news of how we had responded to the letter. Soon, four of us from Harvest and a few of the ministry's leadership met in a hotel in Southern California. Our instructions: "Don't leave the room until there is reconciliation." We made headway. We held another meeting in a Midwestern city, which saw the man who had written the letter relieved of his duties. Ed immediately intervened and asked that the man be reinstated. Ed noted that he had repented, and that, at his core, he was "a good guy." The story spread, and the ministry drafted a letter of apology. Many were joyfully amazed.

That lesson stuck! "Bless those who accuse you and don't defend yourself." Check!

The church was learning the genetics of city transformation: "*keep*(ing) *the unity of the spirit through the bond of peace*" (Ephesians 4:3).

UNVEILING YOUR FUTURE

The assignment to serve Sacramento pastors and the invitation to work with Ed Silvoso and Harvest Evangelism constituted a "God job." God had called me into the Life Maturing stage. God doesn't stop assigning us just because we are going through the fire. He keeps expanding our influence, putting us alongside influential leaders, and filling our tool chests with helpful gifts and experiences. In this period of life, we often serve "in another man's vineyard," relinquishing the dream to work our own garden.

What I had learned in my painful early ministry years were tools in my tool belt, as were my leadership successes in

Amsterdam. Through all of the experiences, I built friendships and served the people I encountered.

At this time, Andy was coming into his own, and the girls were doing great, launching themselves into the marketplace. God was using everything I had learned before, delivering me into something bigger and deeper than the ministry dreams He had asked me to sacrifice.

Hindsight is 20/20, they say, and as I look back, I see a pattern in all that I have experienced. I have learned much that I can share with others, hopefully helping them avoid some of the pits I fell into.

Of course, I was still on a journey, still being transformed by my Father. There was still residual pain in my life, and I was still working hard for His approval—a great quest, but a foolish endeavor. How do you earn what you already have?

A major lesson during the Ministry Maturing season is how to love the source of your pain. For me, it was the Church and Christians. Through this season of seeing a vast array of churches, I made two conclusions: First, the Church is very wrinkly (imperfect). Second, if God loves her, wrinkles and all, why shouldn't I? I was offended that so many pastors and parishioners were fleeing their churches. I was angry that the Church was so stuck in her ways and irrelevant to the surrounding culture. I was in a fix.

Those years in Sacramento and traveling with Ed led me to a new conclusion: You have no authority to change what you do not love. *Ouch!* I am happy to report that the Father broke through my arrogant heart. Now, with eyes of faith and hope for the future, I can truly say, "Isn't she beautiful!"

At the same time, I was seeing the beauty of imperfect vessels working together to do God's work. God was in it all, bringing His children back to Himself.

CHURCH TRANSFORMATION

Sometime during this period, I was part of a team hosting a citywide gathering in Pittsburgh, where a large group of pastors, intercessors, and business leaders yearned to reach their city for God. There was always a lot of energy at these events, lots of hope, and a beautiful knitting together of believers from all sectors of the Church. As the swirl of activities and ideas accelerated, I became increasingly unsettled. I wasn't sure why.

Over the cacophony of the conference, the Lord surprised me with these words: "My Church, in the state she is in now, will never be able to reach the city, the way she dreams. So I'm bringing a reformation to the Church." I felt paralyzed, my framework and equilibrium shaken in one sentence. The Lord seemed to be saying that our large-scale church mobilization approach to reach cities was missing something. I could sense Him saying, "This won't work until she is transformed."

I left Pittsburgh realizing that the Church needed transformation before she could be successful in her cities. God was going to start digging into our collective root system to bring systemic change. I sensed that life was about to get more interesting.

✦ ✦ ✦ ✦ ✦

My experience in Pittsburgh would become a beacon to guide my direction in the years that followed. At first, it messed me up. The question, "What is church?" challenged pastors and other spiritual leaders. They became more determined to find real answers to the question. The next decade—the first ten years of the twenty-first century—would see the Church's thinking and practices being retooled. (I see this process continuing today, with local churches and the global Church.)

This was a pivotal time for me. I love the Church and have always felt that there was much to evaluate about the way we do church and the attitude of each congregation toward one another—and toward the culture at large. I was intrigued by the idea that the Lord wanted to change the way we *did* church by changing who each church was *being*. We'd experienced a major overhaul of church life in the '70s, and it appeared the Lord wasn't done weaving His image into His people at the dawn of the new millennium.

Standing near the end of the 1990s, I could look back and see that the Lord was systematically adding missing ingredients and strengthening existing ingredients, as He helped us build the Kingdom-centric Church. There was a steady embracing of "seek first His Kingdom" (see Matthew 6:33) through prayer and unity, a greater presence of the Holy Spirit, embracing the city-church rather than just the local congregation, and reconciling the nations to one another.

With a new generation emerging in the Church, I sensed a similar dissatisfaction in many of the rabid young disciples. My generation carried a residual anger at our fathers' generation, but this new crowd seemed more bored than angry. While churches were trying to retain their youth, the youth weren't interested in merely taking up space in the pews until they were old and experienced enough to be decision makers. They wanted to be part of the plan and the planning. They had dreams of their own. If they weren't listened to, and if they couldn't exercise their gifts, they would go someplace where they could.

Throughout the '90s, we saw great personal renewal through various movements of God in Kansas City, Brownsville, Toronto, and beyond. However, we didn't see much impact at the foundational, institutional level. Achieving that goal would require a greater revelation of God's plan for His Body.

You could feel the atmosphere changing. The Church had been central to many lives, through various activities and ministry endeavors, but now the Spirit was shifting the focus to the centrality of God's Kingdom. To many people, the idea of Church as a subset of God's Kingdom was new in both theology and practice. (Of course, this idea reflected older concepts, such as Martin Luther's "common grace," an environment where a city was so blessed that even nonbelievers could experience God's blessings through mere proximity. Ecclesiastes is right; there is nothing new under the sun.)

To impact our society and culture, God wanted to go deep with His individual disciples. These disciples wanted to be unleashed on their community's businesses, families, halls of government, media, schools, and arts and entertainment. Their goal was not to "take dominion" over culture, but to serve it in Jesus's name. Like the seeds of the sower in Mark 4, they would scatter and see what might take root.

As the year 2000 approached, you could feel the momentum shift. Leaders were becoming weary of serving in the popular church culture, which was not producing the results they had hoped for. Burnout rates were increasing, a trend that would soon hit home with me. Pastors' conferences began shifting from church-growth formulas to answering fundamental questions like, "Is this all there is? Can I keep doing this? What is the biblical framework for church? And how do we truly embrace God's Kingdom within this context? How do we reach our communities when we can't even keep our congregations engaged? What should we be doing differently?"

Many good-hearted pastors and disciples gave up on the current forms and became exiles from the institutional church. Things were getting dire as we entered the new millennium. Our understanding of God's Church structures needed an overhaul.

We began to focus on our need to have our preconceived notions deconstructed, then reconstructed by God's Spirit, so that we could become the transformed communities of faith God had wanted all along. Only then could our cities receive Jesus's transforming genetics.

Another change was coming too, each step designed by the Father to prepare us for His destiny.

✦ ✦ ✦ ✦ ✦

After leaving Amsterdam and YWAM in 1994, we remained in contact with Floyd and Sally. After they'd left Amsterdam, the McClungs took over the leadership of a YWAM training base they had helped start in Stonewall, Colorado. We were fortunate to visit them occasionally. Stonewall exemplifies everything one loves about Colorado: lots of sunshine, not too hot in the summer, trees everywhere, and crystal-cool creeks flowing by rustic cabins. Elk wandered through the yards, seemingly oblivious that humans were present.

In the late summer of 1999, Floyd called to say, "Something's up with me, and I don't know what it is. Can you come and hang out for a couple of weeks?" We had no commitments, and I was feeling some "mountaintop" time would be good for all of us. And, oh yes, Floyd and Sally were our dearest friends. So we went.

During our visit, a man flew up from Kansas City, uninvited. He rented a car, drove to the YWAM base, and knocked on Floyd's door. A staff member answered, and the man asked, "Are you Floyd McClung?"

"No," he answered. "Floyd's not here right now."

"Okay, I'll wait," the man responded.

Not knowing about the surprise visit, I returned to my cabin that night and found a note on my door. It was from Floyd: "As soon as you get home, day or night, could you come see me?"

Okay, I thought. It was late, probably about 11 PM, but I walked to Floyd and Sally's cabin.

Floyd answered the door almost before I knocked. I remember being surprised at how disheveled he looked. His hair was all askew. "Jon! Come in!" he said. "You gotta hear what this guy said."

"Okay, where is he?"

"Oh, he left. But we recorded it." (This fellow told Floyd to get a tape recorder, because he had a word from the Lord.) Then, mission accomplished, the man climbed in his car and headed toward home.

The upshot of his word to Floyd? A big change was coming. Floyd's world was about to become more pastoral—to the local church, rather than to the world at large. Floyd had already felt his gears shifting; this was confirmation.

Little did either of us know that we were both being retooled for a new season, the reformation of the Church and its mission.

Soon, Floyd received an invitation from Mike Bickle of Metro Christian Fellowship in Kansas City to meet with him for "fellowship" and to speak at a Sunday service. Mike was feeling the call to step down and start a ministry focused on praying around the clock, but he didn't discuss Floyd's role at the time.

In Kansas City, Floyd and Sally were attending a worship service at Metro when a young man stood up to give a prophecy for the church. He pointed at Floyd, declaring that the "man there in the front row" has been brought by God to be the new pastor of Metro Christian Fellowship. Mike was livid, Floyd was shocked, and the congregation fell dead silent.

Imagine trying to gather your wits to speak after a bombshell like that. The word was right; the timing was, well . . . *off.*

The post-service conversation between Mike and Floyd got straight to the point: "Would you, Floyd, consider being the new pastor of MCF?"

Floyd called me from Kansas City and asked if I'd join him there. "New developments are happening fast," he said.

"Of course!" I told him.

We spent a sensational few days with Floyd, Mike, and his team, talking about the possibilities and praying about what God wanted. Eventually, Mike asked if I would be "part of the deal."

"No way!" I choked out. In that season of my life, I was convinced God had called me to the city-church, not to pastor a local church. (Why was I always a step behind?)

After hearing a little of my journey with the Sacramento pastors, Mike arranged a beautiful luncheon with several pastoral leaders in Kansas City. At the meeting, they subtly pressured me to join them in Kansas City. I felt a little manipulated, but the idea began to take root in my heart.

After I returned to California, I received a letter from Bob Spradling and Howard Cordell, leaders of Kansas City's two main pastoral networks. They asked me to move to Kansas City and help with their city-transformation efforts. I felt the tug of the Lord, so I agreed to meet with them to explore the details. Suddenly the two things I loved most (leading prayer and unity endeavors and being near my good friends) were coming into alignment. I decided to reconsider the move.

That week I also received a phone call from one of the leaders of our Sacramento pastors' groups, offering to write a letter on behalf of forty Sacramento pastors, commending Mindy and me to the pastoral network in Kansas City. The Kansas City pastors had sent them a letter saying, "Jon has just been with us, and we would like to invite him to work with us, but not without your blessing." They felt it was God's plan as well, so, blessing granted.

I was grateful to the Lord for making our next step so clear, but I realized He was orchestrating my life in hyperdrive. He was opening doors to new things, and once again it was time to enter yet another phase.

Okay, that was quick—and very slick! I thought. *God wants us to move to Kansas City!*

So we were off again! New adventures awaited. Little did I realize that the move from Sacramento to Kansas City was a direct shift in focus for Mindy and me, from city transformation to church transformation. The word in Pittsburgh was still at play in my journey as the Lord began setting the stage for me to serve His Church to help her fulfill her dreams.

UNVEILING YOUR FUTURE

That word the Lord spoke to me in Pittsburgh ("The Church, the way she is, cannot change the city the way she dreams") was not only deconstructive and unsettling to me, it foretold a new direction as I moved toward the next phase of life in Kansas City.

For every leader, this process looks different, because it is uniquely tailored by the Father to address "un-surrendered" attitudes and paradigms of the heart. You can't see it coming. It isn't necessarily that we've been doing anything wrong; it is simply the Father's requiring a depth of allegiance to Him in areas we didn't know were broken or un-surrendered. Though the process is always different, the desired result is the same—a relinquishment of all demands, dreams, and personally devised plans. It's the season when the addiction to ministry is transformed by a kind and jealous Father.

One of the main indicators that God still has work to do in our hearts is the presence of fear: fear of failure, of being misunderstood, of being sidelined, fear of irrelevance, fear of the future, fear of lack of financial provision. And, of course, there is fear that the old defeats might be repeated.

One friend of mine, now on his second marriage, feared that his second wife would also be unfaithful. (He eventually got the victory.) I've seen other people so wounded by their past failures that they can't enjoy current successes. They often sabotage that success, doubting that the Father wants them to walk in the security of it. These people don't yet know who they are in Christ.

These fears are all in the crosshairs of the Father's redemptive plan for His children. His Spirit guarantees that He will transform us into Jesus's image, and that process solidifies our Gospel Identities. This process is our only hope for walking in victory. He will exert love's strongest prescriptions to ensure that the toxins of fear are removed from our spirits. God cleanses our hearts and teaches us to "live from the center."

Growth during the Life Maturing phase is critical, for two reasons. First, it changes the motivations for life, ministry, and work. Busyness turns to rest, ambition turns to surrender, and the need to be recognized goes out the window. God won't compete for attention!

Second, passing this test of sacrificing everything is a precursor to moving from a "doing to be" to a "doing from being"—not doing so that we can please God hoping He will love us, but doing because we know we please God and loving because we know we are loved. As Robert Clinton put it, "[God] wants to teach us that we minister out of what we are," and "Enduring fruitfulness flows out of being."[12] It's truly the complete opposite of the norm in the world around us—always trying to prove one's worth and never really discovering who one truly is.

By contrast, I lived through the rest of the 1990s discovering the depths of this truth: "I am a son of the Most High." I learned I could rest in Him, let Him guide, and let Him provide. I would never be disappointed.

However, in the year 2000, I had no idea that God still wasn't done with me. A few years later, I would experience a pipe-cleaning process that would eliminate even more detritus from my past and help me be more confident of God's love. I had no idea how much more lay ahead.

When we were transferred to Kansas City in 1999, God opened every door. I didn't feel the angst, the sweat, or the "push" to make something happen. I was just along for the ride.

After all, dead guys can't negotiate.

PART FIVE:

...OF THE LOVING FATHER

MEETING *THE* FATHER

So we moved to Kansas City, found another marvelous home in incredible time, and stepped expectantly into a circle of new friends in the pastoral prayer movement and the wild tradition that was Metro Christian Fellowship. Kansas City was famous already for the prophetic move of God that had taken place there during the 1980s—and for a disagreement between two pastors that had received national attention. We were about to be part of two major prayer movements God would birth in the twilight of the twentieth century. We would also learn much about city transformation as we uncovered Kansas City's amazing spiritual history.

There was just one problem: I was bored. I'd been going hard for a long time, and though I loved it, I found myself tired of it. Something was wrong. Something was missing. I was exhausted, and a big part of my identity seemed incomplete. My soul was restless. I was burnt out, but it was also more than that.

God was dropping another roadblock in my path so He could give me another overhaul before I moved on. I was still out of alignment!

You see, I thought I knew the Father, but in the early months of the year 2000, I began to realize how shallow that knowledge was. Although I was increasingly secure in my standing in Christ,

I didn't really know the Father. I was still working hard to please Him, without having any idea if I was succeeding. By the end of 2000, I ran out of juice and didn't know why. I couldn't get the neural synapses in my fuzzy brain to fire. My motivation for ministry was sluggish, and I was thinking about getting out of ministry and making "real money for once in my life." But I didn't feel right about that either; I was drifting without real direction.

I remember telling Floyd, "I can hardly get up in the morning. I'm not depressed. It's not depression. I know depression; I've struggled with it for forty years. This is different. Maybe I'm just burned out? Something's not right."

Floyd counseled me, "You know, we had a couple visit us in Stonewall, Colorado, when we were with YWAM there. They were gorgeous people. She was a music therapist, and he was an Episcopalian priest. They had just started a counseling ministry in Marietta, Georgia. You should go there for a week to talk through your past and hear what God wants to say to you. They call it 'Healing for the Nations.' You should check it out." (Dear friend Floyd made a career out of picking up my pieces.)

So I called the couple, Steve and Rujon Morrison. Their retreats were often full, so I wasn't sure what to do. After I spoke with them, they found me a place right away. (Probably because they loved Floyd so much!)

So off I went to Georgia's mountains.

There were about sixteen of us in our group. All were in some form of ministry or business, all senior-level leaders, both male and female. We'd attend a little teaching/worship session in the morning. Steve had a real shepherd's heart, and Rujon was a go-getter: a teacher, a trained counselor, and very prophetic. Every afternoon we would gather in threes, do some exercises together, and talk through the events of our lives.

The Morrisons created an environment of safety that allowed us to talk about our pasts—*all* of our pasts—and then we would give each other feedback, allowing the Father to minister to us through one another. It was like filing through fifty years of my life, looking at the moments when God stepped in or the devil tried to take me out. I began to process my childhood dreams, including my kidnapping by the Shinto priest during the *Oshogatsu* parade, the episode with the young sailor, and the chance encounter I'd had with the strange man who gave us the pornographic picture. Then there was my teen rebellion against my parents, along with the feelings of isolation and abandonment I felt in the school dormitory. All this had fostered a tenacious depression exacerbated by many years of struggle to prove myself worthy of God's love as a pastor and missionary. In the safe environment the Morrisons created, I was able to bring up stuff I'd all but forgotten—as well as the memories that had felt too raw to mention for years and years.

Just like compacted garbage, I hadn't realized how many unresolved questions, how much pain and disappointment, still remained in my spirit. A "dirty bomb" had been lurking in my soul. It left me angry at God. It was like being on Balaam's ass and being mad at the animal for not moving me in the direction I wanted to go. Meanwhile, that donkey was only trying to keep me from falling into a pit. I was angry at what was saving me.

That week I was able to examine each part of my past in the light of Jesus's perspective, and on who I had become. Where was I in my journey? What did it teach me about myself? How had I allowed lies to become entrenched in my mind and my identity? Recognizing those lies now, how do I replace them with the truth about who I am in Christ?

By the week's end, I was like a linguini noodle limp from overcooking. All of the failures, all of the messages that I was a failure, all of the attacks on my character, all of my self-doubts and my doubts about who God was and how much He loved me—all of that was brought to the fore. Even though God had dealt with those things incrementally over the years, it was like He wanted to deal with them all at once and once and for all. I'd come to know Jesus well. I'd come to know the Holy Spirit well, and I'd become acquainted with the Father. But I didn't *know* Him.

By day, I processed these things. By night, God affirmed them in my dreams. He did the same during my contemplative walks, during times of meditation, and as I prayed. He told me, "You're never gonna have to wonder if you're loved again. I'm your Father. You're a son to Me. I love you with an everlasting love. With arms of love, I will always embrace you."

It wiped my slate clean and shook me to the center of my being. I cried more during that week than I ever had before. That week became a line in the sand for me, a boundary staked in the ground, a monument constructed in my heart. It would carry me, unshaken, through some rough years ahead. It would allow me to be solidly there for others when they were tested and accused. It would help me stand through difficult days. I never again doubted that God was always with me. I was His son, and He was my Father! It was a revelation seared into my heart.

Not only that, but it relieved me of needing to accomplish anything to prove my worth. My Father was with me, and I didn't need to do anything to gain His validation. I didn't need to be busy going to events to establish my *bona fides*. Again, new freedom.

Sometime after that, God asked me, "If I called you to the Zaragoza Desert in Spain to live in a cave, would you be satisfied?"

"Yep, as long as You're there."

"Although I've given you family and friends, I want to be your only source."

Never again would I doubt that God was enough. (And that was nineteen years ago!)

✦ ✦ ✦ ✦ ✦

I left Georgia with a profound revelation of my Father's love and presence throughout all the years of pain, sin, and frustration I'd accumulated since I was a small boy. Love broke through! God's years of drilling through the dark strata of my unredeemed heart now resulted in reaching the artesian waters of His redemptive mercy. I could finally say, "What the enemy meant for evil, God has turned for good." He came to me and surrounded me with perspective, forgiveness, and hope. He launched me back into the fray in Kansas City.

My Father loved me, and I knew that nothing would separate me from that love. I could do nothing to *earn* that love—nor anything to lose it. My need to prove my worth to Him—a symptom of the isolating orphan spirit I had been fighting for years—dissipated. I was a beloved son!

In my newfound sonship, I began to walk in a new level of His peace, clarity of focus, and affection for those around me—people who had often driven me nuts before. I was no longer a slave to Christian productivity, nor addicted to ministry for the notoriety it brought me. I could settle back and do "what I saw the Father doing." (And now I understood what that meant.)

It was powerfully freeing and gave a different slant to everything I did. No longer was I going to do things to try to please God or show off my gifts. I would operate from a place of *already* being pleasing to God and not needing to impress anyone else.

The Father had just set the table for what lay ahead in my calling.

✦ ✦ ✦ ✦ ✦

I returned to my spiritual foundations research with a new sense of purpose and a renewed confidence in following the Spirit. Much like my time in Sacramento, I knew discovering Kansas City's spiritual history was crucial to ministering there. This time, though, I had the backing and partnership of the pastoral groups I was fellowshipping with, and a wonderful team of eight people to help pillage the archives. They were my "propeller heads." They were the type of people who are wired by God to love detail and data, research and digging through archives of crumbly old books, letters, and papers. I laid hands on my team and asked the Lord to give them eyes to see the covenants and the prayers of the area's early founders. Then I sent them off to Kansas City's basements, back closets, and cobwebby archives.

For the next two years we dug, prayed, discussed, and collated our findings. The more we researched, the more God's redemptive pattern emerged from the dust of history. We found some fascinating notes from a meeting where God moved in incredible ways.

At one meeting, Caucasians, African Americans, and Native Americans all came under God's power simultaneously. Preachers reported how God's glory became so great that they couldn't speak. One preacher and his Native American interpreter, Mr. Blue Jacket, went through the crowd scattering "holy fire."

The African American community itself had a series of revivals near Brush Creek, the current site of Kansas City's famed Country Club Plaza area.

As we looked at these events, and considered the covenants that lay in the shadow of the city's strongholds, all of the pieces came together. They could be summed up in five redemptive roots that coursed through the church's history in Kansas City:

- It was to be a place of visionary leadership and entrepreneurship (innovation and new start-ups).
- It had always been a launching pad—a staging area and equipping center—especially for those going west to Oregon and California in the days of Manifest Destiny.
- It had a reputation for advocacy and championing outsiders.
- It had a heart of mercy and mission.
- It was a place of strategic partnerships between the marketplace and the local church community.

After uncovering these roots, things got fun! In the coming months we took nearly 500 leaders and intercessors on bus tours of three spiritually significant locations, where we rehearsed these five redemptive roots, rejoiced, repented, and asked the Lord's Spirit to reconnect the church in Kansas City with the covenants of her spiritual forebearers. We took children to these sites so that they could hear a different perspective on their city than the one they were taught in school. What a joy to watch kids kneel or raise their hands in blessing at Kessler Park, on the bluffs overlooking the Missouri River. What a way to give these children redemptive eyes for their communities.

It's amazing to me how revelation becomes fuel for prayer. We saw prayer break loose throughout the Kansas City area.

The influence of prayer has been with the Church since Jerusalem. In the past five decades, however, we have seen it increase in breadth and strength in the global Church. Prayer is essential for Kingdom people. It would be insane to neglect prayer, or to relegate it to weekly or monthly gatherings. I have not witnessed a time in my life when prayer was given such a predominant role in the lives of God's people. At the turn of the millennium, we witnessed a surge of global prayer that mobilized intercessors and the priesthood of all believers.

I find it fascinating that both the International House of Prayer (IHOP) and 24-7 Prayer International were birthed, independent of each other, in the same month in the fall of 1999. By the early 2000s, they were both thriving and still continue strong today roughly two decades later. I remember the meeting at Metro Christian Fellowship where we laid hands on Mike Bickle and his team, launching this highly energized group of "Levites" into the ministry of "day and night prayer." Mike and the IHOP team envisioned a "house of prayer for the nations," where God's people could pray every hour of every day. Mike referred to it as the "Harp and Bowl," referring to the Old Testament pattern of temple priests worshiping and "praying in their courses"* day and night before the Lord. It was to be a place for believers to come for unified prayer and worship.

The most remarkable characteristic of that first prayer room was the Lord's constant presence. What was initially a dream was catching fire, as it became a national and then a global movement. People from around the world began to come, catch the virus, and export it home. Prayer was being re-seeded into the psyche and practice of God's global family—a living thread that was continually being woven into the tapestry of past generations.

UNVEILING YOUR FUTURE

After moving to Kansas City, I learned that the Father wasn't done with getting to the core of my inner motivations, or with

* Shifts taken in prayer to cover the twenty-four hours in a day.

loving me into my sonship. That sonship would soon lead me into the journey of becoming a spiritual father myself.

My 1994 encounter with the death of my dreams and ambitions when leaving Amsterdam continued into the 2000s. The journey of an exchanged life, mine for His, is ongoing. It takes time, patience, and long-suffering. Only the Father knows if we've truly absorbed His lessons, lessons that continue as long as our obedience and trust mature.

My journey of the heart wasn't over. At a "Healing for the Nations" event in 2000, I basked in the light of God's love as I discovered yet more about my foundational years, about the lies in my spirit, and the orphan patterns deep in my soul. On the retreat's final night, I had an encounter with the Father that put the final nail in my coffin of unbelief. (It's those pesky lies that keep laying poisonous eggs in our heads.) A wave of love came over me, and I knew that I was a beloved son and God was my Father. It was a tangible encounter with the Father that hasn't left me to this day.

This assurance is the well I draw from as I strive to be all that God has called me to be. I'm His son and He's my Father. I am free to do "only what I see Him doing." This love frees us from the prison of fear, from feeling pressure to please people at the expense of our own souls.

I don't believe there is a point of arrival on this journey with Jesus. Leaders can think, "I'm over that now, learned my lesson." Then—*Bam!*—that issue rears its ugly head again. There are levels of God's redemptive love, levels that we experience as we grow in Him.

I'd thought that the revelation of my sonship in the '90s meant I knew the Father. So, when I had a deeper encounter with Him in 2001, I was surprised: *I thought I learned this already.* Pride is a nasty thing; it thinks having a modicum of knowledge and experience on a topic makes you an expert. We can note it on our "on the way to perfection" checklist. This is a behavioral measure based on "good" and "bad" actions and attitudes, not a relational mindset that chooses to *"be found in him, not having mine own righteousness"* (Philippians 3:9 KJV).

Our hearts don't understand why revelation must trump our head knowledge—a revelation of the Triune God that is part of an eternal journey, not just a step in the temporal pilgrimage. The lessons we learn in this life are never over. They prepare us for the forever-life with Jesus. In this season of life, we are meant to learn that there is no refuge in ministry success, but only in friendship and favor with the Father. It is one of the most important lessons of the Life Maturing phase.

THE CALL TO "FATHER" LIKE HIM

In 2004, Pete and Samie Greig (pronounced "Greg") and their two boys, Hudson and Daniel, entered our lives. It was a divine assignment. Pete, while a staff pastor of Revelation Church in Chichester, England, confessed his disability in the area of prayer to the Lord. He and a few faithful friends asked the Lord to teach them to pray. Out of that journey, the first 24-7 Prayer room was launched. It was wobbly but genuine. It soon caught fire!

At first, the founders wondered if they could sustain continuous prayer for a week. Then the week became a month, and months turned into years of unbroken prayer.

Many people came to Christ. Believers from various churches visited to see what was happening, and almost all of them caught the prayer virus.

Soon, prayer rooms began to multiply across the United Kingdom, before leaping over to the Continent. These prayer rooms provided a "sacred space" that suited the culture of many churches and denominations.

Today, more than 120 nations provide such prayer rooms.

As 24-7 Prayer was growing beyond anyone's imagination in England, doctors discovered a tumor in Samie's brain. Life instantly changed for the Greigs. Seeking to keep the new prayer movement in motion, work toward Samie's recovery, and manage a household, the couple quickly realized they needed time and space. They came to Kansas City, at Floyd's invitation, for a year of rest and refueling. Mindy and I were invited to be their hosts.

During a meal at the revolving Skies Restaurant & Lounge, Pete and I became fast friends. We talked about family, pain, prayer, and the move of God in the nations. We enjoyed adult beverages and scrumptious appetizers, not knowing that the Lord was forging a lifelong partnership between us.

During that year in Kansas City, Pete was instrumental in influencing a Covenant Church pastor named Gary Schmitz to start a prayer room in his church. Gary had been "ruined" by reading Pete's book *Red Moon Rising,* which chronicles the author's journey with the Lord in prayer, and describes how prayer can transform communities and nations. Gary, after experiencing the power of prayer in his church family, became a self-appointed distributor of *Red Moon Rising* to churches in Kansas City. He loaded boxes of the book in his car and dispensed them to every pastor or leader who seemed remotely interested. Gary was so enamored by God's presence and the call for the Church to be "the house of prayer for the nations" that he eventually resigned his pastorate to become a primary influence for "effective, fervent prayer" in Kansas City.

Pete also fueled the founding of 24-7 Prayer USA while in Kansas City, appointing David Blackwell as the first US national leader in 2005.

✦ ✦ ✦ ✦ ✦

On the global scene, prayer was spreading like wildfire. In July 2000, God captured the heart of South African Christian businessman Graham Power with a vision based on 2 Chronicles 7:14:

> ***"If my people, who are called by my name, will humble themselves and pray and seek my face and turn from their wicked ways, then I will hear from heaven, and I will forgive their sin and will heal their land."***

Power challenged Christians across South Africa to unite in a "Day of Repentance and Prayer." This quickly grew from 45,000 Christians in South Africa to the whole of Africa. On May 2, 2004, history was made when Christians from all fifty-six African nations participated in the first continental "Day of Repentance and Prayer for Africa."

On Pentecost Sunday, May 15, 2005, Christians from 156 of the 220 nations of the world united across denominational and cultural borders for the first Global Day of Prayer. Mass prayer events continue today as the Church is realizing that without unified prayer, the Spirit of the Lord would not come to our nations in His fullness.*

IHOP and 24-7 Prayer were two of the many ministries that came into the fore along with 24-7 Burn and many local, citywide, and national endeavors in Asia, Africa, Latin America, and Europe. Adding to His intercessory corps of "Generals of Prayer" in the '80s and '90s, the Lord was now raising up foot soldiers. In the 2000s, we saw believers from all walks of life begin to display a lifestyle of prayer, offering their prayers to the Lord on behalf of their home and work environments. Paul's injunction that *"petitions, prayers, intercession and thanksgiving be made for all people. . . . This is good, and pleases God our Savior, who wants all people to be saved and to come to a knowledge of the truth"* (1 Timothy 2:1, 3–4) began to take root in the spiritual formation of many of God's people.

---

* For further reading, see http://www.globaldayofprayer.com/wp-content/uploads/1.-History-20141.pdf.

Churches in Nigeria saw tens of thousands of believers bringing their petitions to God through daily ongoing prayer. In England, Phil Togwell started "Prayer in Schools," and thousands of young children were invited to enter God's presence through prayer.* Prayer-walking in neighborhoods and inner cities became increasingly commonplace.

✦ ✦ ✦ ✦ ✦

In 2005, as Pete and Samie were preparing to return to England, Mindy and I were sensing that our time in Kansas City was coming to a close. We had been working with the city-church for five years, and I had stepped into a pastoral role at Metro for the final two years of Floyd's tenure there.

As Mindy and I pondered our future, a poignant Scripture kept rattling around in my heart:

> **Even if you had ten thousand guardians in Christ, you do not have many fathers, for in Christ Jesus I became your father through the gospel.**
>
> **—1 CORINTHIANS 4:15**

I asked the Lord to teach me the difference between the roles of brother and son, as well as a father and instructor (which I had been much of my life). I wanted to know what it was to "birth sons and daughters through the Gospel." In response, the Lord initiated my journey into my next life assignment.

We knew that we had accomplished what the Lord had called us to do in Kansas City, but we had no clear guidance for our next steps. We loved our time in Kansas City and at Metro Christian

---

* Check out the 24-7 Prayer website for details: 24-7prayer.com.

Fellowship. The church had an amazing legacy: welcoming the Lord's presence, sparking the prophetic movement, and training people to move in the Holy Spirit. Although the church had experienced a turbulent transition from Mike's leadership to Floyd's, Mindy and I left with a deep gratitude for the many lessons learned and the many new friends added to our large basket of treasured relationships. Mike had launched the International House of Prayer, which had gone global, and Floyd had birthed the All Nations church plant movement that thrives today from its base in Cape Town, South Africa. The city-church in Kansas City, inspired by the emphasis on prayer, launched a "Year of Prayer," drawing churches from many denominations and ethnicities. I left Kansas City satisfied and grateful.

Sometimes the Lord transitions leaders into new seasons while giving no noticeable guidance—just a desire in the heart and a sense of overwhelming peace. This modus operandi was new to me. Shortly before I started contemplating our next steps, our daughters, now married, both moved to Colorado. The Lord gave my offspring life-mates that we could not have orchestrated for them. All three of our kids got married in one thirteen-month period. (I almost went bankrupt!)

I began thinking my ministry life might be over and that the Lord was putting me "out to pasture." Despite this short bout with insecurity, this "amazing, experienced man of God" received several offers. However, I had no sense of peace about accepting any of them. I wasn't looking for the next great opportunity; I wanted to go where I knew I would be pleasing God. I was a son by spiritual birth, not a church leader by hierarchical appointment.

Thus, I got caught completely by surprise. Knowing that we were unsure of our next steps, both of my daughters called me, and we had almost-identical conversations:

"What's the problem? Why don't you just move to Colorado?"

"I'm not going to move somewhere just because you're there, as much as I might like to."

"Why not? Your grandkids are here. We want you to move and be near your grandkids, to help us raise them."

"Well, that sounds good, but I'm a man of God. I've got to hear from the Lord." *Whatever.*

After that, Mindy cut in: "Wait a minute. Why is a calling to your kids and your grandkids any different from a call from some big hongo-bongo international ministry guy? God's calling is about whom we should be with more than what we are doing. It's about legacy, and what's more important than *family* legacy?"

"Okay," I acknowledged. "Let's drive out there and check it out."

So we drove to Colorado, spent a month with one daughter's family, and then switched basements to be with the other daughter and her tribe. We toggled back and forth like this for nine months.

Finally, Mindy and I realized that Colorado was *it.* (Mindy had already figured this out, as usual, and was quietly waiting for me to get the picture.) I love Colorado. I love mountains and snow, and I *loved* being close to my kids and grandbabies. Plus, Mindy had just been hired as a Southwest Airlines flight attendant, and Denver International is a "focus airport" for Southwest. It was meant to be.

We bought a town house in the tiny mountain town of Georgetown, nestled along beautiful Clear Creek, elevation 8,600 feet, just twenty minutes east of the Continental Divide and about an hour and fifteen minutes west of Denver International Airport. It would be home from 2006 to 2011. It was the first time in my adult life that I had no local ministry team, no office, no meetings, and no schedule. It was almost painfully blissful, and we didn't lack for things to do.

I was under the Father's instructions to avoid making phone calls or sending e-mails to initiate ministry. But people reached out to me instead. My life as "the wandering friar" had begun.

I was moving into "father mode" in my relationships with people God brought my way. I began "coaching" a church in Tulsa, Oklahoma, called Believers Church, showing them how to transition from the traditional megachurch wineskin to the new wineskin of "friends, together, praying and dreaming, stumbling and growing" God gave us as a biblical framework for how to do church, and we were putting it into action.

I was also playing spiritual father to the infant Kansas City Boiler Room—led by Adam Cox, Dave Blackwell, and Nathan Chud.

I'd also met this guy named Ken Janke, who was doing some interesting things by planting a "friary" in a town and then opening up a coworking space to minister to the community. (I'm still walking with this same circle of friends today, as well as a growing number of others.)

As these things were happening (and I played with my grandbabies), I realized there was no greater calling than to bring spiritual fathering to my kids and grandkids. That would be hard to do if I couldn't drive to their homes whenever invited or just drop by "because we were in the neighborhood." Our kids and spouses had invited Mindy and me to help shape their destiny in the Kingdom. I had little idea that this calling to my biological progeny was just a foreshadowing of the fathering I would be called to in the coming years, with an emerging generation of young leaders.

During that "wilderness" season of simply taking the next step and trusting God to do His thing, Pete Greig asked me to form a task force in Europe to help craft an organizational framework that would enable 24-7 Prayer to handle the international growth they were experiencing. I came as a consultant of sorts, and a year later I signed up full-time. Because I struggled to feel like I really belonged to this rabble of Brits, Pete cheekily suggested that I needed an induction ceremony. So there I stood one night in 24-7 Prayer's parking lot in Guildford, England, one pants leg rolled up to my knee, as I toasted my new compatriots with a very fine single malt. I was in.

With the prayer movement and the Boiler Room church plant newly birthed, I found that the years of preparation to be a father to the new generation was coming to fruition. This fairly young movement was loaded with inexperienced, wild-eyed leaders with their hair on fire for Jesus. I was the oldest wolf in the pack. I now understood why the Lord had opened no "ministry doors" to me in the years since Kansas City. He was calling me to this emerging generation, not to a ministry that showcased my "incredible stuff." Neither was I being called to a vision, but to people, to build them up and prepare them for doing mischief for the Kingdom of God. I was being called to be a spiritual father to this rabble, without any of the weird excesses and control battles that others had stumbled through.

In those days, I found myself serving on 24-7 Prayer's international team with a conspiracy of spectacular Brits. I oversaw the development of global prayer through 24-7 Prayer and the emergence of several church plants and neo-monastic prayer communities. We were friends, seeking to have fun and follow the Lord as He opened doors in Europe, Africa, Asia, and North America.

During my journey into the Father's heart, I became gripped again by the centrality of prayer and unity as two primary tools in the Kingdom tool chest. Receiving the Lord in my heart and accepting my sonship in Him elevated my need to communicate with Him (prayer) and love His family (unity). Prayer as a discipline is important; prayer as a lifestyle of speaking and listening to the Father is a necessity. Giving this season of my life to partnering with my friends in 24-7 Prayer to infect the Church with a passion to communicate with God as a lifestyle has been one of my greatest joys.

UNVEILING YOUR FUTURE

God's preparation for spiritual fathering goes beyond finding our identity in the work we do. It leads us to surrender personal ambition, and it creates a longing to see the family legacy extended to spiritual (and natural) sons and daughters. All we have learned starts coming together in powerful ways, and Robert Clinton's fifth stage—the Convergence phase—of our development begins.

The Convergence phase is marked by little to no trust in human intellect alone, but instead a reliance on and confidence in the gracious impartation of the Father's love through revelation. Resting in His love ignites the intellect surrendered to the Spirit. It is a gift to be treasured and dispensed liberally.

As a leader moves toward Convergence, he or she exchanges the fear of man for the fear of the Lord. (That concept has always sounded a little harsh, but when all you fear is the Lord, what else is there to worry about? Is there any better place to love from? It is the "*perfect love* [that] *drives out fear*" [1 John 4:18].) Honesty in love becomes a greater commodity than unsanctified loyalty and the fear of offending God's people. The Father supplies the wisdom and boldness we need.

The influence of spiritual fathers increases during this phase, replacing the satisfaction of "blessing" with the necessity of building foundations in the hearts of Christ's disciples.

Wineskins, like foundations, hold and preserve the blessing. Eventually we "outgrow" the wine of Christian activity and turn our energies to discover appropriate wineskins to contain, preserve, and build up Christ's people *"until we all reach unity in the faith and in the knowledge of the Son of God and become mature, attaining to the whole measure of the fullness of Christ"* (Ephesians 4:13).

As I entered the Convergence phase of life and leadership (leaving Kansas City for my place in the Rockies), I realized it was not a goal to attain to "but something that manifests itself as a leader keeps on responding to God."[13] In this season, all the lessons, all the relationships, all the experiences, and all the gifts come into synergistic alignment. You find yourself saying, "I was made for this."

During Convergence, we realize that the journey is all about the Gospel and our identity in it. The Father sent His Son to get a family. What does that make us? Sons and daughters. How do we live our new identity? By loving one another from the heart. When Jesus came as the Servant King, what did that make us? Servants of an inverted Kingdom, where power comes from death and weakness. What does that make us? Servants, not authoritarians, perhaps unacknowledged by the world, but definitely seen by the Son. What do we do as His servants? Walk in His footsteps, putting others before ourselves and blessing our enemies. When the Spirit was sent to manifest God's Kingdom on earth, we were identified as ambassadors of a new Kingdom. As ambassadors, we spread God's heart, His plans, and His commands to every corner of the earth. That's our Gospel Identity, which blossoms through the years. This identity validates our ministries and sows the Trinity's DNA into the soil wherever our feet go.

OUR GOSPEL IDENTITY*

Who God Is	What He Has Done	Who We Are	What We Do
FATHER	Sent His Son to adopt us into His family.	Sons and daughters in the Father's family.	Love one another as a holy family under the authority of the Father. (A heart issue.)
SON	Established His Kingdom on earth as a Servant King.	Servant-heir subjects of the King—princes and princesses (the younger siblings of the King).	Serve the least among us and one another in the name of the King. (A matter of practice.)
HOLY SPIRIT	Sent to manifest the Kingdom on earth and fill it with the presence of God.	Spirit-equipped and empowered ambassadors/ missionaries/ emissaries of the Kingdom.	Proclaim and demonstrate the Kingdom for all to see.

When I was thirty-eight and engaging in Intercultural Leadership Development studies at the Fuller School of World Mission, I learned a fascinating fact about the leadership stage of Convergence. Leadership studies show that only 20 percent of global leaders ever truly get to this fifth stage of Clinton's leadership development. Many people in the professional, church, mission agency, and business worlds often get promoted to the level of their incompetence and away from their destiny and passion (the old "Peter Principle"). Seniority often makes way for more corporate responsibilities, which causes leaders to drift away from their primary dreams and passions. Instead of becoming fathers and mentors to disciple the incoming generations, they are often relegated to their executive offices and tasked with keeping the

* I am deeply indebted to Jeff Vanderstelt, leader of Doxa Church in Bellevue, Washington, for his scholarship and practice of what is shown in this chart (any alterations are mine).

"machine" well-oiled. Many retire unfulfilled and hope they can do something more rewarding in their retirement years.

Not wanting to be in the 80 percent who would never reach Convergence, I asked the Lord to help me reach my full, created potential. God has faithfully fulfilled that prayer, through decades of divine relationships strung together. I have made many exquisite friends, many of whom remain in my and Mindy's lives, despite physical distance. The Kingdom is less about accomplishments and more about the deep, soul-exposing friendships, the people who won't let go of your life, the ones who see the best in you, even when you are a wreck.

Our friends have steadfastly stood beside Mindy and me and cheered us on so that we could reach *"the prize for which God has called me heavenward in Christ Jesus"* (Philippians 3:14). To my many slightly strange but wonderful global friends: thank you!

BECOMING THE FAMILY OF GOD

One morning in 2010, I heard the Lord when I woke up. He instructed me, "Move down the hill and engage the Church. It's time." Thus we moved to Castle Rock, Colorado, early the following year.

I was still in my wilderness mode shortly after that move—still not able to "make anything happen"—when I was divinely introduced to Dave Powers by a mutual friend at a Famous Dave's restaurant north of Denver. Dave was a twenty-nine-year-old musician with a strong entrepreneurial chip, and he had formed what he called a "team of missionaries" under the moniker "Worship and the Word." They started by going to churches and leading worship via Word-centric lyrics. Dave and his wife, Tara, had cranked out many recordings, traveled extensively, and founded a one-day extravaganza called HeavenFest, hosted in locations near Denver. They launched this "Jesus festival" when Dave was just twenty-seven. It had grown to nearly 33,000 attendees and featured more than seventy Christian bands on seven stages. HeavenFest was a celebration of Jesus combined with a prayer focus, replete with a prayer tent and myriad volunteers. It was an organizational marvel.

However, after three successful years, the festival had hit a wall. Dave, who has an intense love for the poor, had committed large amounts of money to various organizations and churches along Colorado's Front Range. These groups ministered to a rainbow of needs, especially among the disenfranchised. When the numbers, income, and donations declined in 2012, Worship and the Word was unable to cover the costs of HeavenFest—or to make good on their dreams of funding those who minister to the poor. In debt, dejected, and heading toward depression, Dave and his board decided to investigate what was going wrong.

Sometimes "divine disasters" yield answers to problems. Failure forces us to examine the motives of the human heart, which is God's primary concern. Such was the case for Dave, Tara, and the Worship and the Word team. Dave invited me to their next board meeting to help them explore the question, "Did the Lord instruct us to run HeavenFest again this year? Or are we missing it somewhere?"

Answers varied, but Dave's answer was clearly in the affirmative. As we talked, however, it became evident that Worship and the Word had pressed forward with the festival, even though the team had been unsure about it.

Uh-oh.

Some had felt they should move forward only because Dave seemed so sure. Others had doubts, but lacked the confidence to register their concern. These people couldn't agree on what "the word of the Lord" was for them as festival season approached.

This led Dave, the team, and me on a journey of discovering the difference between building on one man's vision and becoming a *team* that heard the Lord before moving forward. Despite the pain of learning to hear God together, the Lord began to unveil what He had designed for this beautiful group of millennials. After an extended time of dealing with the shame of "failure," the ensuing depression, and some uncertainty about delegating the festival to another ministry, the Lord began to settle the team's hearts. Hope snuck back into the equation.

I noticed that these people carried a beautiful love for each other. They were passionate about prayer, about gathering as friends, and about being in the Word. They came from various church backgrounds, and some were dealing with lingering pain as a result. I noticed a reluctance to establish themselves as a "community of faith." I knew they might balk at the suggestion to "plant a church," so I suggested that they add food to their existing gatherings. This would fit the pattern of Acts 2:42: "*They devoted themselves to* the apostles' teaching *and to* fellowship*, to the* breaking of bread *and to* prayer" (emphasis added). They were already enjoying the apostles' teaching, fellowship, and prayer, but they were missing "*the breaking of bread*" (food) part of the "program." Food is a major ingredient in a family-based culture. (Never underestimate the centrality of food in Kingdom work. It is the equalizer, the common denominator of all God's creation!)

Just the thought of slowing down their crazy travel schedules to begin "planting" an intentional local community provoked Dave and Tara's first response: a visceral "*No!*" I smiled to myself. I knew what was coming.

Sure enough, after more prayer and debating the question, "Should we add a meal to our gatherings and gather as a more intentional community?" they reached complete unity on a new direction. They didn't realize it, but they had just moved from being a "mission organization" to an "organization (family) on mission"—something I'd been working out with the leadership teams at Believers Church and the Kansas City Boiler Room (now renamed Navah Church). They were taking the first step in transformation:

from being led by the vision of one to listening for the will of heaven and following the consensus of a knit-together *team.*

Sometimes we have to go backward to move forward, or experience subtraction before multiplication. In this case, the team adopted a deliberate, multigenerational expression of family, replacing the previous "hair on fire," mono-generational tribe mode. For the past eight years, I have had the joy of walking with Dave, Tara, and the Worship and the Word community as they've added other generations and their own spiritual fathers and mothers to their gatherings. They have grown spiritually and numerically as they've moved from house to house and engaged in intentional study of the Word. They share life, celebrate the Lord's meal, and cultivate a culture of love and care for one another—and those they encounter in their surrounding community. They are now composed of young and older, are led by males and females, and represent numerous walks of life. They have fought their own personal demons, their own historic strongholds, and their fears of "church" together, and they have become a healthy "bouncing baby" church.

✦ ✦ ✦ ✦ ✦

Since the turn of the millennium, I believe God has painted a new portrait of what constitutes "a church." There are now fewer big names, big ministries, and big church organizations. (We've seen how "the power of big" has affected the egos and moral character of some prominent church leaders, and it hasn't always been good.)

"Small" has become a "big" thing. "Come and experience our great programs!" has been replaced by movements that are centered on relationships. A focus on the centrality of the Father—and being His Family—can now be seen (and felt) in churches worldwide.

As He had done in the '90s, God was highlighting His people as the Church, and her alignment with His heart. We began to see Jesus's disciples as members of His Family. We realized that while many thought of each individual congregation as a church, God saw all of the Christians in a city as that city's true church. (He's never been much interested in our divisions and categories.) With these new paradigms gaining inroads into our current structures, Christian leaders are asking questions. I attended several pastoral gatherings in the 1990s and early 2000s and the questions were basic, such as:

- » "What is church?"
- » "What should we do at our gatherings?"
- » "How should we organize ourselves? What should our leadership structure look like?"
- » "Is what we have today a result of tradition or biblical pattern?"

Some went as far as to say, "I don't think I can do this anymore" and walked away from their callings. They became like a *ronin* (a transient Japanese samurai, removed and often disgraced from service to his shogun, wandering the countryside and looking for causes to champion), doing ministry where they could, but not knowing what it meant to be part of a family or to have a "home church."

We had seen a massive exodus of pastors from the 1980s through the 2000s. (That exodus continues today.) Some who decided to keep at it were so disgusted with "church as we know it" that they began to deconstruct everything they had known or done in their ministry careers. A friend of mine was so convinced that the church was something that he had built on the "traditions of men" (not the Bible) that he let it deconstruct. He lost nearly all of his people and was left with a small, bewildered remnant looking at each other as they gathered in a living room, not sure what they were about.

Many believers have disconnected themselves, not from God, but from the traditional church culture, for a host of reasons. The depersonalization of church has left many people hurt, disenfranchised, and searching for a genuine community of faith, where the individual is not sacrificed for the sake of church growth. The industrial business model our culture has endorsed as the way to successful organizations is not the biblical pattern for planting churches. It doesn't help coordinate God's Family or build His Kingdom.

Many of us who lived through this exodus have realized that only God can deconstruct our churches, and He does so to move His people into the church pattern He established in the New Testament through the apostles and prophets. Where we've built on human traditions and wisdom, He will, when we invite Him, lead us into "holy demolition" mode. He will restore us to the biblical pattern and shape us into His image. He will bring us home and make us beautiful. He is the Redeemer determined to transform us so that we can transform the world. And such change is best done in the safe context of family.

We saw many new churches form in the 2000s. Some churches are destined by God to be hub or resource churches. Saddleback Church, with Pastor Rick Warren, and Bethel Church, led by Bill Johnson, are prime example of churches with trans-local influence. They have become training, teaching, and sending centers whose ministries impact people around the world. They have learned to do "big" very well. Other churches meet in homes and have adopted a "missional community" construct, focusing on reaching out to their neighbors and communities as a grassroots expression of God's love.

In the midst of this process, I realized I was being invited into the joy of fathering the young leaders who were beginning to emerge in Kansas City. David Blackwell, Nathan Chud, and Adam Cox, young twentysomethings who'd met at Metro, had begun to forge a lifelong bond. I was invited into their circle as a friend and mentor. The Lord surprised them with a dream to plant a community in Kansas City's Westport neighborhood. In time, these three young musketeers planted 24-7 Prayer's first "Boiler Room" church in the United States, and the "Boiler Room Network" of churches and communities was born.

In our Boiler Room Network, we began the discussion of planting "hub churches" back in 2005. We envisioned theses hubs to be similar to the New Testament church in Antioch, whose modus operandi was training and sending church plant teams into other areas. As of this writing, we now have two viable hub churches (and one more coming online this year) in the United States and two more in process in the UK. We have established these hubs to build the foundations of the church locally and replicate the DNA the Lord has given them into new church plants and house churches.

This trend brought a renewed interest in small groups and house churches. Small became popular, with "life groups," "house churches," "monastic communities," "simple churches," "organic churches," and "missional communities" all focusing on life at the cellular level.

However, replicating this model proved to be very difficult for those without a biblical framework and an accompanying relational journey. Some, seeking to stamp a new model or program over an old framework, soon suffered the disappointment of unrealized hopes. The new wine demanded a new wineskin.

Some, like Navah Church, considered the current conversations in the light of Scripture and the Holy Spirit. Navah embarked on a relational journey with the Lord, each other, and a few father figures as they sought to allow Jesus to build His Church, His way.

These groups are now multiplying "missional communities" in Kansas City and are dipping their toes into church planting in Asia and Africa.

The 2000s were experimental in many ways as new, biblical, and relevant forms of church were being engaged. Some felt called to build big churches, while others became enamored by small-church constraints. Others sought to find a happy medium between large and small. Believers Church in Tulsa, Oklahoma, moved slowly from a typical congregational megachurch to embrace a glacial move toward becoming a hub church: a big church that spawned and supported new, smaller church expressions across the city. Glacial is good when morphing from old to new. It is the only way to respect relationship as a core value ("moving at the speed of relationship"). That which grows too quickly in the Kingdom also tends to disappear equally fast. Building fast seldom allows sufficient time for laying firm relational foundations.

Overall, the 2000s saw a move away from the church as an organizational construct to embracing it as a family-based cooperation. The idea of the church being a "family on mission," introduced by people like Mike and Sally Breen, has fueled many churches seeking to engage their neighborhoods and cities with the Gospel—a reversal of the "doing everything in the four walls of the church" paradigm. This emphasis made every home a sanctuary, every believer a minister and missionary, and the world around them their "field." The Breens and the 3D Movement (the outreach they are a part of) have been helping God's people embrace a missional lifestyle for several years.

✦ ✦ ✦ ✦ ✦

After five years of serving on the Boiler Room Network's international team, shaping the organization, and overseeing several church plants, I was starting to feel a new shift in my spirit. I found it increasingly difficult to give my energies to organizational matters, because my heart longed to spend time with the emerging leaders within and beyond our movement, not by fulfilling a role, but as a by-product of who I was in God. I felt I was in danger of becoming obligated to organizational demands, rather than the personal and developmental needs of the leaders and their churches.

In 2013, I told my international team that it was time for me to step away from the organizational responsibilities of Boiler Room church plants and devote myself to go where the Lord was sending me—within and beyond our network. I was quick to explain that I wasn't leaving them relationally, just asking to be released from my role so I could be a "wandering father."

These leaders are my friends, and God has connected our hearts for a lifetime. So they trusted my calling to lay church foundations. After some deliberation, I was "blessed off" of the leaders' team and released to serve them by strategically shepherding the Boiler Room Network of churches in which God was leading me to invest. The wandering "Friar Jon" had just been catapulted into his new global parish.

By this time, the Boiler Room Network had clear leadership in Europe and North America, allowing me to flow into any field by invitation and support the leadership there. I was stepping out of all organizational responsibilities so that I could roam according to the Spirit's leading, continuing to partner with my boatload of friends and see what new doors God would open. The millennials and the Gen-Xers were most on my heart. I wanted to honor, accept, and champion them. I'm a father after all, and a father's primary function is to love his kids.

UNVEILING YOUR FUTURE

City-Reaching (née City Transformation) was the vehicle God used to increase my love for the Church, engage more with church leaders, and experiment with researching the spiritual roots of Sacramento and Kansas City. Now, however, Convergence dictated that I be less involved in "my ministry" and more engaged in serving lives and the ministries of pastors, leaders, and church elders. The Convergence phase is a time of increased influence and confidence in God's gifts and His calling. Destiny takes hold and begins to manifest. It is a season of leverage, when a little energy now lifts weights that once took much grunting and groaning.

Though the shift from Kansas City to Colorado was abrupt and we were in limbo for a full year, Mindy and I experienced little fear or worry. I occasionally wondered if I was being put out to pasture, but I never doubted that God would call me again. (And it didn't matter anymore if He didn't. I was content in His hands. I had Him and didn't need anything else to satisfy me or validate my calling.) I felt like one of the priests of Old Testament Israel. When every tribe was getting their inheritance, the priests got nothing—but the Lord! He was their portion, and that portion was enough for me.

As we settled in Colorado and the doors to 24-7 Prayer's Boiler Room church-planting movement opened to us, I realized I had no business left in the "church," other than to invest my life in the stunning young leaders who were emerging. I was now a full-fledged father, and these were my "kids" (sorry guys; I do feel a little paternal at times).

When the Lord instructed me to "move down the hill and engage the church" that day in Georgetown, I didn't know what that assignment would look like. I soon found out. I was to have no plan, no personal ambition but displaying Him. I was not to call anyone, open any doors, extol my fabulous qualities in dazzling résumés, or worry about provision. God had promised to go before me, and He has never failed me. I was becoming content to be *"God's handiwork, created in Christ Jesus to do good works, which God prepared in advance for us to do"* (Ephesians 2:10).

As I launched into my new vocation as a spiritual father, I realized I was initially operating as a consultant rather than a father, as someone who "shows up and blows up," downloading information and insight, then moving to the next assignment. I *needed* to be a father instead, one who raises up sons and daughters and lays biblical foundations for God's Family. I was getting too spread out around the globe and wasn't able to maintain the depth of friendship I strived for. Neither was there ample time on international trips to lay proper biblical foundations in my young charges. Fortunately, the Lord raised up regional leadership for our churches, enabling me to stay closer to home to have the time and relational depth locally to create the "engine" for establishing churches in the Gospel and raising leaders out of them.

PART SIX:

PULLING IT ALL TOGETHER

24 THE UNVEILING

Four years ago, I was invited to give a five-minute report on church planting to foreign missionaries and Japanese church leaders in Tokyo. Later, while having lunch with the attendees, I noticed a gentleman lurking nearby and looking at me. I angled toward him slowly and realized he was looking around to see if anyone was watching us. I felt like a CIA operative.

"I like your ecclesiology," he whispered.

"Oh." I didn't know what else to say.

He went on in hushed tones, "I'm the president of the organization, and I wonder if you would be willing to be our keynote speaker next year?"

He was the president of the same organization my father and mother had served fifty years earlier. I felt permission in my heart to accept the invitation immediately.

Without so much as an "I'll contact you," he slunk off.

Wow, I thought, *I wonder if I'll ever hear from him again?*

I did.

The following year I spent three days with these beloved missionaries and pastors. I was standing in front of the same missions organization I had been so bitter toward in my formative years. Heart healed and relationships reconciled, I was now pontificating to them on the finer points of biblical ecclesiology on my chosen topic: "Church as Family."

We ended the event with a rousing three-hour prayer meeting as we walked, prayed, and reconciled over a masking-tape map of Japan laid out on the floor. Every attendee stood on the area of Japan he or she was from, as we prayed over each other, sent blessings to various cities, and invited God's Spirit to move in the nation.

On the train back to my hotel, I marveled at the irony of what I had just experienced. My parents were still alive at the time, and you would have thought that Jesus had come back in full regalia. I'm glad Dad could see the beauty of God's redemption in my life before he passed on in November 2016.

✦ ✦ ✦ ✦ ✦

Looking back, I can see how the Lord has woven my life together by laying the threads of the Kingdom into every season or decade of my adult life, pulling out the rebellious and errant strands and rethreading them into a tapestry to reveal the pattern He had designed as me. I can see the beauty and design of my life, and how it has been connected to the Spirit, Jesus, the nations, the Church, and a loving Father. I think of the strong teaching and pastoral gifts birthed in the '70s and the emphasis on doing *"the work of an evangelist"* (2 Timothy 4:5) that thrived in Amsterdam in the '80s. In the '90s, I was tutored in the prophetic and how it encourages God's people. I had come full circle!

After five decades of God reemphasizing the five threads of His Kingdom—the Holy Spirit, the centrality of Jesus, engaging the nations, the Church as His Family, and truly knowing God as our Father—the pattern is still not complete. In this second decade of the new millennium, we are still discerning the Master Weaver's full pattern: His image of Christ in the Church *and* in culture—the greater implementation of His Kingdom.

The 1960s' emphasis on the Holy Spirit has blossomed into a global maturation of the Body of Christ—His gifts, convicting power, and throne-room directives. In this decade, the Lord's Spirit obliterated many of the barriers churches had erected against His character. Historic animosities within God's family began to be slowly dismantled by the Spirit's ministry in the Church and in culture.

In the 1970s, with Jesus's name on the lips of a new generation, we saw this thread woven into the Church in a more intimate and central way. Jesus, true to form, began confronting the pharisaical and "religious" spirits and traditions in the Church and softened our hearts to say, "Whosoever will may come." The Gospel of Jesus Christ was beginning to go beyond evangelism crusades and evangelistic campaigns. It was becoming the currency of the Lord's redeemed people.

The 1980s put the realm of His rule front stage and expanded our global focus to unreached people, nations, and societal domains. Prayer movements and evangelistic enterprises were raised up by an army of well-honed warriors and "average Joes." No other decade birthed more strategic approaches to global evangelization and church planting.

In the 1990s, the wine was flowing, but the wineskins needed replacing. This decade illuminated the inadequate nature of the Church's current constructs, as well as the opportunity to see her more unified and more engaged in her own backyard. Though this process would continue into the next two decades, questions were raised about the Church's theological underpinnings and modus operandi, and these questions fomented a revolutionary journey into the hearts of spiritual leaders, who worked to return churches and other ministries to a more biblical foundation.

The third millennium since Jesus's coming opened with a new focus on the Father's nature and His presence over His Church, and over the plethora of sons and daughters who were pursuing the high calling of fathers and mothers in God's Family. As many were trading in their identity as "workers" for "sons and daughters," they could be seen exchanging their executive roles in church hierarchy for the humble clothes of spiritual parents to an emerging generation.

Now we can see the loom, with its five threads firmly in place, awaiting the shuttle's journey across the threads, intersecting and revealing Christ's image. This decade, and those that follow, will see the Lord's Spirit equip the Church to become all that the Father dreamed: *"For God did not send his Son into the world to condemn the world, but to save the world through him"* (John 3:17).

When God sees errant or misplaced threads, He will remove and reweave them. When we are blind and deaf, He will heal us. Just as the Jews couldn't recognize God's Son among them, today's church is exhibiting the same blindness. *Anything* that we have built as "blind men" that is not according to God's pattern will be deconstructed and removed from the loom.

However, while deconstruction is sometimes necessary, it's never God's goal. He wants to build. If we allow Him, He will carefully reconstruct us personally and collectively until we embrace the pattern of His Word, through the Holy Spirit's power. His loving commitment to "tearing down" and "building up" is for the sole purpose of transforming us, His Church, and all of earth's institutions so that we conform to the pattern of Jesus Christ. God is replacing our allegiance to human philosophies and political systems with a dedication to King Jesus, in all of life.

Sometimes we resist God's discipline and "tear-down" strategy because we don't realize how far we have strayed from His plan and purposes. When we embrace ideas that conflict with His, He will return us to our first-century biblical roots. When we elevate leaders to hero status, He will send His Spirit to ensure that they live like the selfless servants they are called to be. He will not allow anyone to drift and wander forever.

Like Moses, God has sent us "in" to bring His people and creation "out" onto the Weaver's loom and to see Christ's image emerge on the landscape of human hearts and endeavors. As God examines this emerging tapestry, He is committed to completing the image of the Son in His creation.

As I have watched God work beautifully in the Church (and the world) over the past five decades, one word comes to mind: *redemption!* God has redeemed the Church's inadequacies and sins, and this flood of redemptive energy has shown the world that nothing is outside the scope of His redemptive power: not souls, not human institutions, not demonic oppression, and not the worst offenses humanity has concocted against its Creator.

> **His intent was that now, through the church, the manifold wisdom of God should be made known to the rulers and authorities in the heavenly realms.**
>
> —**EPHESIANS 3:10**

We have been set up for victory!

As I reflect on my myriad friendships, the many new church plants, and the efforts to bring transformation to hungry churches, I see God's faithfulness. He has opened every door; He has brought me to rest. He has exceeded my expectations, and I'd be a fool to change the equation now. There can be no Convergence without a brutal incursion of the cross—into our character, motives, and mindsets. The years of "dying daily" are worth it all. God is worth it all. He imparts "the life of Christ . . . made manifest in us." It doesn't get better than that!

Spiritual fathers never have to take initiative to create space for themselves. God goes before them to orchestrate the relationships that will impact the Church's future. After experiencing decades of His faithfulness, I can truly say, "*We always carry around in our body the death of Jesus, so that the life of Jesus may also be revealed in our body*" (2 Corinthians 4:10).

In the 2010s, I realized how the various emphases of each decade culminated into my call to be a father to the household of faith: a father to lay foundations in the home and champion beautiful sons and daughters in their callings. It's about the King and His Kingdom.

It's a never-ending story. I've put a lot of miles on my shoes. I'm slightly stooped, and I move a bit slower than I used to. But there's still a mischievous grin on my face, and I'm still on the road preaching and teaching His Kingdom come.

NOTES

1. From the "Japanese declaration of war on the United States and the British Empire," *Wikipedia* (last edited January 10, 2019), https://en.wikipedia.org/wiki/Japanese_declaration_of_war_on_the_United_States_and_the_British_Empire.

2. Sam Storms, "History of the Pentecostal-Charismatic Movements," *Enjoying God* website, http://www.samstorms.com/all-articles/post/history-of-the-pentecostal-charismatic-movements (accessed: December 30, 2017).

3. Richard A. Bustraan, *The Jesus People Movement: A Story of Spiritual Revolution among the Hippies* (Eugene, OR: Pickwick Publications, 2014), eBook: location 924.

4. Bustraan, location 951.

5. ____________, "What is the Calvary Chapel Global Network?" (Retrieved February 13, 2019), https://web.archive.org/web/20161222165055/https:/calvarychapel.com/resources/article/view/calvary-chapel-global-network/.

6. Hugh McLeod, *The Religious Crisis of the 1960s* (Oxford, GB: Oxford University Press, 2007), 1.

7. William C. Martin, *A Prophet with Honor: The Billy Graham Story* (Grand Rapids, MI: Zondervan, 2018), 447.

8. "The Legacy of the Lausanne Movement," Lausanne Movement website (accessed: December 19, 2018), https://www.lausanne.org/our-legacy.

9. Stuart Robinson, "Paying the Price of Revival (Part Two)," Christian International School of Theology website (2015), http://www.cistonline.org/7articles/prayer-101-praying-the-price-of-revival-2.htm.

10. Greg O'Connor, "Miracles in Cuba," *New Day*, May 1990, 7–9, in Stuart Robinson, *The Prayer of Obedience: Causing Supernatural Growth* (Upper Mount Gravatt, Australia: Chi Books, 2005).

11. History.com editors, "Sand Creek Massacre," History.com (updated December 13, 2018), https://www.history.com/this-day-in-history/sand-creek-massacre.

12. J. Robert Clinton, *The Making of a Leader: Recognizing the Lessons and Stages of Leadership Development* (Colorado Springs, CO: Navpress, 2012), 39, 45.

13. J. Robert Clinton, "Leadership Emergence Patterns" (Syllabus, Fuller School of World Missions, 1990).

JON PETERSEN is the founder and CEO of CityForce, an organization aimed at revitalizing churches and businesses with the hope of transforming their cities and nations to be more effective in dealing with social justice, neighborhood empowerment, and multicultural collaboration. In many ways, he's a wandering father to younger leaders and an engaging friar in reaching out to communities. Jon's journey of being pastor, missionary, citywide prayer organizer, and advisor started in the late '60s spanning from the Jesus Movement to being part of seeing 24-7 Prayer rooms sprout up around the globe and being a "resident father" to the Boiler Room Network of churches.

Today Jon makes his home just south of Denver, Colorado, where he has access to his nine grandchildren and from which he continues to train and be engaged in raising up the next generation of church, business, and "culture shapers" for the work of the Kingdom of God in cities around the globe.

Made in the USA
Middletown, DE
17 July 2022